Nightmares in the Saudi Arabian Desert

By Alexandra Symeonidou

This is a true story, my memoirs of my time as an air hostess for Saudia (Saudi Arabian Airlines) and then as the wife of a prominent Saudi in Saudi Arabia.

In loving memory of my Mother,
to whom I owe my life in more than one ways...

© 2016 English Version V14 cs

Alexandra Symeonidou was born and raised in Athens, Greece. She studied in France (French and English Literature at the University of Aix-en-Provence, and at the Institute of Political Sciences – IEP). She worked for the Greek National Tourist Board at its Paris offices, in the Public Relations department. Later, she was employed by the Official Journal of the European Union, a position she left to work as an air hostess with Saudia (Saudi Arabian Airlines). She lives with her son in Athens. Currently, she divides her time between writing and public affairs.

Other works by Alexandra Symeonidou:

Autobiographical Nonfiction - Tetralogy:
Nightmares in the Saudi Arabian Desert (also available in French)
Merciless Struggle (available now on Amazon.com)
The Saudi's Son
The Kidnap (available now on Amazon.com)

Fiction:
Secrets in Heaven
Coffee in the Savanna
From Sandals to High Heels

Translation Works:
Andromaque: Racine's play, written in 1667, from French to Greek
Iphigeneia: Racine's play, written in 1673, from French to Greek
Alexander the Great: Racine's play, written in 1664, from French to Greek

All books and translations are available in Greek. In addition, *Nightmares in the Saudi Arabian Desert* is also available in English and French, while *Merciless Struggle* and *The Kidnap* are also available in English on Amazom.com. Part three of the *Nightmares* Tetralogy, *The Saudi's Son* will also be available in English on Amazon.com soon.

A Personal Note to the Reader by Author Alexandra Symeonidou

This is a true story, the story of my life, which I wrote in Greek, my native language, and then translated into English, so that it can reach out to a wider audience. First published in Greece in 2004, the book has been a tremendous success, becoming a best seller and receiving plenty of TV, magazine, internet and newspaper coverage as well as personal interviews, which continue to this day.

The current events in the Middle East and the atrocious, inhuman behavior in the region have led me to revisit my life experience and realize that what I went through as a Muslim's "wife" in Saudi Arabia was hardly a random or unique case.

My personal experience is yet another manifestation of a warped way of thinking and understanding of life and the world on the part of a group of religious fundamentalists who are sunk in a darkness of rigid, callous, relentless ideas and notions. I am in a position to fully comprehend the "emotional" motivations of these people who are blindly striving to preserve a counter-evolutionary social system, obediently and submissively defending their often misguided reading of a religion, and showing to the outside world the hardest and most repugnant face of humanity.

This book describes the excruciating adventure I went through during my years as a young adult, a time that should have been the best years of my life. I felt an inner need to reveal my story to the public, to communicate and share the human agony I experienced while I was skating on thin ice between life and death in a foreign, hostile environment.

And why did you go through this ordeal? one might ask. What did I do wrong that I had to pay for my sin with my own blood? What was that sin for which I had to go through such unspeakable torments and nearly pay with my own life? The answer is simple: I married the man that I had loved with all the innocence and passion of my youth, but he repaid my love with the most unheard of behavior and cruelty. I committed the supreme foolishness of marrying the man whom I believed to be an ideal husband, but I failed to take into solemn consideration the fact that he was a Muslim of Saudi Arabia. Ignorant of certain facts and deprived of an unbridled imagination, I could not fathom that there existed other worlds that were so different from mine, so I fell victim to a man whose hands and actions were guided by a harsh religion—or interpretation thereof—which often subdues and manipulates its followers to extremes.

I witnessed the brutality of an irrational cruelty exactly as it is currently described by the mass media that shed light on some of the most ardent religious fanatics. I felt I was required to tell my story and thus protest against such atrocious acts that are still being committed in our day and age. I felt I had to speak out about the bitter cup of suffering I had been forced to drink myself, about the inexplicable hatred I had experienced, a hatred cultivated through religious interpretations serving to blindly fanaticize people and turn them from "children of God" into persecutors of humans.

Alexandra Symeonidou

Nightmares in the Saudi Arabian Desert

Table of Contents

Chapter One: Page 8
THE BEGINNING - THE FIRST ENCOUNTER

Chapter Two: Page 40
SAMI

Chapter Three: Page 51
THE RETURN TO ATHENS, THE WEDDING, AND MOVING TO SAUDI ARABIA

Chapter Four: Page 77
INTRIGUES – SINISTER CONSPIRACIES

Chapter Five: Page 130
THE INFERNO OF KNUZ AL ELM STREET

Chapter Six: Page 228
MOTHER'S ARRIVAL

Chapter Seven: Page 255
SAMI IN MADRID – BACKSTAGE IN JEDDAH

Chapter Eight: 326
THE GETAWAY

Nightmares in the Saudi Arabian Desert

CHAPTER ONE

THE BEGINNING - THE FIRST ENCOUNTER

It was a day in Athens unlike any other. It had snowed heavily! I was already of two minds about whether to pick up my suitcases and head out to the airport, destination Luxembourg, or to listen to my ever-increasing inner misgivings and say that I would not go. My doubts became all the more profound as I watched the snowflakes falling outside my window. I could never imagine how my decision on that snowy day in Athens would bear such a dire effect on my life to this very day…

Unbeknownst to me, I was headed towards a point of no return. After my college graduation in France, I had found myself returning to the Athens I knew as a child, seeking a career with prospects of stability that would enable me to fulfill my dreams for the future. I stayed jobless for quite a few months in a vain attempt to find a job that would live up to my expectations. My alternating bouts of disappointment and reminiscence of France were making it even more difficult for me to decide what I really wanted.

Then, one day, as I was casually flipping through the classified ads, I came upon a vacancy for secretaries at the European Parliament. The position had appealed to me, especially because I would be given the opportunity to be near France, which I had come to love so much. I applied for the job and was surprised to find out a short while later that I was the only one selected for the position out of some forty applicants. The overenthusiastic person in charge had even sent me the details of my employment by formal envoy from Luxembourg. And yet, at the moment when I was all packed and ready to go, a strong sense of foreboding made me change my mind. For reasons I cannot explain to this day, I decided against it. Perhaps because, as they say, "one cannot escape one's destiny"…

Having turned down the Luxembourg job offer, I resumed my quest to achieve my goal. Paris had enchanted me so much that I could not wait to be there again; but I would have to have secured a decent job there first. There were several notable job options available to me at the time, but one of them really stood out: air hostess for Saudi Arabian Airlines. It was an option which I had never considered before but now looked quite appealing: I could explore new worlds without pinning myself down to any one location.

The Orient, and especially Saudi Arabia, was a faraway unknown world, which had nothing in common with the one in which I was brought up and had gotten to know: my world, the world of Greece, the Western world.

I tried to avoid dragging myself through the same emotional turmoil and indecision that I had recently experienced in relation to the Luxembourg dilemma and, pulling up my forceful state of mind, I persuaded myself that I simply "had to" go ahead and do it. A career as an air hostess would open wide my horizons to the four corners of the earth.

So, on a beautiful May day in Athens, I took the pertinent examination to soon find out that I had passed it. I was overcome with happiness and excitement about my newly gained prospect in the world of the Orient. The die had been cast. Everything was ready for my departure.

It all begun on a warm July afternoon, when I found myself taking off on a Saudia flight from the Eastern Terminal of the old Athens Airport to Jeddah, Saudi Arabia. I was not worried the least bit. Inside my head, I kept telling myself: *You've got nothing to lose. At the very least, you will get to see a country that is very difficult to visit under any other circumstances.* I was feeling at ease, laid back, unwilling to torment my mind with doubts or fear of the unknown I was about to encounter. Besides, I was not alone; there were ten of us boarding that plane on our journey to new jobs with Saudia; and the mystery of this new, uncharted life absolutely enthralled us!

As the airplane was making its final approach, an abundance of lights, countless lights, suddenly emerged through the absolute darkness.

"It's Jeddah!" all of us shouted out in excited unison. "We're here!"

Vast, thick darkness and then—Jeddah. To be honest, when thinking of Saudi Arabia while still in Athens and packing my suitcases, I could have never imagined I'd need to pack any other type of clothes except the usual outdoors staples: a few pairs of jeans, some t-shirts and some light casual dresses for the really hot days.

But the bright lights I now saw left me wondering whether I had perhaps miscalculated. My apprehension became even stronger as soon as I entered the King Abdulaziz airport terminal. The place was characterized by an incongruous luxury, a flashy display of wealth, as if straight out of a storybook about Aladdin. A sea of swarthy faces over snow-white *thobes*—the typical Saudi Arabian outfit—dotted with a few scattered women covered in black from head to toe composed the unfamiliar image unfolding before my eyes. That picture gave me an eerie feeling and I couldn't help but wonder how these people could possibly believe themselves to be part of the twentieth century. Alas, I was forgetting—travelling to Saudi Arabia was much like travelling back in time. In the Hijri calendar, it was the early 1400s...

Before I had the chance to sort out my thoughts and first impressions, a petty misunderstanding with Kate, an English girl, over her luggage brought me firmly back to the present. A voice suddenly informed us that the Saudia minibus had arrived to pick us up. I can still feel the stifling hot desert heat I felt on my face the moment we stepped out of the terminal in order to board the bus. I felt as if the oxygen was being drained off my body; it was that humid heat that I had heard about.

The Arabic music playing on the bus radio and the driver, who was surely "imported" from some third-world country, were in perfect harmony with our surroundings.

My mind was working nonstop, taking in everything I saw around us all the way to the "compound," the place where all the air hostesses would lodge. We had been told during a pre-departure cocktail party in Athens that all female flight crew would be staying together in a segregated compound, seeing as social mores in that country, Saudi Arabia, were largely dictated by Islam.

It was eleven at night. There was no traffic; the streets appeared rather deserted. I started to feel the difference between that and the traffic-jammed streets of cities in the West. Everything here appeared so peaceful beneath an inconceivably clear starry sky! In my imagination, this Jeddah night sky transported me to *"One Thousand and One Nights"*. Once again, I was mystified!

As we reached the entrance of the compound, a large bar was pulled up, allowing us to enter the gated community. I remember seeing several foreign air hostesses dressed in the Arabic *abaya*—a black robe covering the clothes they wore underneath—lined up at the entrance of the compound. *What are they doing here dressed like that at this time of night?* I thought to myself. For a brief moment, this inner question was coupled with the feeling that we had somehow arrived at the wrong place. I felt scared for my safety, fearing that we might have been taken prisoners by some slave trader. Puzzled, I turned to look at the woman sitting next to me and my gaze was met with a similar look of bewilderment on her part.

The minibus passed the barred gate and proceeded to drop us off in front of a kiosk. That was the reception area. It was the checkpoint monitoring all comings and goings of the air hostesses based in Jeddah. So, we too had to sign ourselves in (and out) with Nina, our Lebanese chief. Her heavily made-up face with its coarse features made her look like an over-the-hill, retired prostitute, to whom time had been all but kind, trying to assert her authority over new recruits by putting on a stern scowl. I did not like her at all, neither her looks nor her demeanor, and decided to keep my distance and exercise my diplomacy so as to go as unnoticed as possible.

"Your name please," she said hoarsely rolling the "r" as she filled out the necessary paperwork and issued me the building and apartment number where I'd be staying. At the end of this process, she informed us that we should be up at eight o'clock the next morning to begin our training.

As I began to find my bearings in these new surroundings, I started to view the compound in a different light. I started to like it more and more. Perhaps it was the multiethnic environment that gave me a sense of familiarity, as if Europe was all around me. The compound was outfitted with a tennis court, a swimming pool, a hair salon and a restaurant, all of which I got to see on my way to my new residence, the place that would be the roof over my head during my stay in Saudi Arabia.

"Here we are, Madam," said the Filipino porter as he set my suitcase down on the second-floor apartment that I was meant to share with another woman. A look around the sparkling clean, fully furnished, spacious apartment attested to my belief that coming here was the right decision. By that time I was so tired from the long trip that even the deafening racket produced by the air-conditioning units sounded like a lullaby to my ears. Amidst what sounded like a massive factory at work, I was soon lulled to sleep by that strange, sustained air-conditioning tune.

Saturday, July 5th. That day I woke up farther to the east than I had ever been before… I don't know why exactly, but deep inside I was feeling a furtive delight. Perhaps it was the flood of bright sunlight that made me feel so hopeful, in spite of the heat.

It was seven thirty in the morning and all the new recruits were gathered together in the reception area. After we signed in, as stipulated by company rules, we boarded the designated Saudia vehicles that would take us to the training center, somewhere in downtown Jeddah.

How interesting! I thought to myself. This trip would satisfy my curiosity, allowing me to get a first glimpse of this mysterious land under the light of day.

We drove along vast highways cross the Arabian Desert until we suddenly saw several buildings bobbing up left and right and realized that we were nearing the city. We were now driving down Medina Avenue, which was lined with luxurious buildings, some beautiful and others not so much, dotted with interspersed remnants of a Bedouin town dating from before the golden age of oil.

After we drove by two or three plain public squares, adorned with monuments featuring hands and fists—as I later found out, Islam prohibits statues and representations of humans—we arrived at the training center that we were to attend for the next six weeks.

My contact with the Saudi Arabian instructors was very satisfactory. They were pleasant and courteous and did their best to make a good impression. I was starting to change my mind—seeing as at first I was a little worried about their different mentality and about how I would be treated as a woman—and wrapping my head around the idea that they might in fact be open-minded, accommodating and helpful people. Nevertheless, the American woman that was teaching us a part of our theoretical courses, kept warning us of the assorted risks, what we shouldn't do and where to pay attention. "Don't forget, this is Saudi Arabia." I was confused because the warning was incongruent with what I was experiencing thus far.

The first few weeks went by slowly: training center and studying during the day and nothing to do in the evenings. My only relaxation was at the swimming pool or a jog around the compound through the July nights. There was no stress at all. It felt like vacation! Absolutely no worries; just studying and doing sports. Naturally, this healthy lifestyle appealed to me, but after the first couple of weeks I began to get curious about what lies beyond the walls of the compound. So, a couple of friends and roommates of mine and I made plans to go out and walk around the most significant sights of the city.

There was a shuttle service connecting the compound with Jeddah, so we got on one of those buses and took off. It was Ramadan and life for the Saudis began after nine or ten at night. We had been told that we had to wear abayas to go out, and so we did—the fear of the unknown compelled us to abide by the rules.

The shuttle bus dropped us off at the Souk, the traditional market. The overpowering stench from the sewage network that covered the whole area, all the way down to the port of Jeddah, made me feel uncomfortable and negatively biased. Still, we kept walking uphill towards the King Abdulaziz mall, all the while being scrutinized by dozens of dark prying eyes of swarthy Arab men. As I later found out, foreign women were quite the rarity and spectacle.

The short stroll around the Souk had enchanted me; there was a never- ending line of shops selling gold and jewelry and people bustled around buying jewels as if they shopping the basics at a supermarket. One gram of gold sold for less than a liter of bottled water! Gold jewelry was an everyday accessory for the local women.

Our little escapade came to an end when it was time to go back to our drop-off point in order to be picked up by the shuttle and driven back to the compound. As we hurried there, the call of the muezzin resounded, beckoning the faithful Muslims to pray in the streets and in the squares.

The first days of training went by in the same uneventful pace: attending classes, studying and talking with the other colleagues now and then. The only event worth mentioning from that period is my getting to know two French women who had arrived there before me. It was the first time I heard French since I had arrived at the compound and, naturally, I rushed to join this small group that lived and breathed France. The working language among the women and instructors coming from all around the world was English. There were women from many different countries in our multinational and multicultural compound, but none from Saudi Arabia. Saudi women were not allowed to work—let alone become an air hostess.

Together with my new French friends, we developed our social life; we made new acquaintances and started going out more in order to gain a better understanding of the country we were staying in and alleviate the monotony of life at the compound. We no longer had to use the company shuttle; we now knew several Saudis, one of which was always available to pick us up from the compound gate and escort us to the Souk or show us around the city. Whatever the outing, we had to be back at the compound by midnight. And every night around twelve o'clock, there was a regular parade of cars in front of the compound gate. "Bye, Mohammed. I'll see you," "Bye, bye, I'll call you," "I'm not off tomorrow," were some of the last words typically exchanged during the last few seconds before the gate. And then we would all head towards the reception area to sign in that we had returned to the compound.

The last few days of my training were absolutely fascinating. I was still attending classes in the morning, but every evening we would gather at the apartment of one or another colleague and on Friday—a day off—we would go to the beach at Corniche, where a few friends had access to houses. My life was beginning to be truly magical, my senses were overflowing with an amazing feeling of euphoria. There was no problem at all; everything was going like clockwork.

It was finally graduation day and we would be awarded our diplomas! During our training, we had been given strict instructions as to how we were to present ourselves both on the airplane and in this ceremony. Our hair, particularly long hair, had to be pulled back so as not to draw the attention of the passengers. On domestic flights, we had to wear trousers in order to avoid showing our legs; but on VIP flights, we were allowed to wear our hair and make-up in a "seductive" manner and were supposed to wear skirts in order to show off our well-shaped calves to the demanding passengers. What a blatant contradiction and ridicule of the status quo!

Having successfully completed my training, living in Jeddah had become an interesting proposition. My carefree, stress-free life was about to become even better now that I was an active member of the company's cabin crew, with a flight attendant ID and payroll number 3002557, licensed to fly aboard B747, B707, B737, Tri Star and Airbus planes.

My first test flight was to—where else?—Paris! I had to put to the test all the theory that I had learned in the meantime and get graded for it. On August 17th, a colleague and I reported for duty at 10 o'clock at night in the flight crew scheduling room, in order to sign in as members of the cabin crew. After the preparatory briefing, we were ready to go and followed the rest of the crew to the plane. Meanwhile, the excitement and stress of the day were taking their toll on me and, by around five in the morning I dozed off on my seat only to awake when an Asian colleague's hand alerted me.

"Wake up before the chief purser sees you," I heard an Asian fellow flight attendant warn me as she patted me on the shoulder. But I could think of nothing other than that extremely pleasant morning snooze...

The thirty-two-hour layover in France was a godsend. This was *my* Paris, the place I loved so much and was thrilled to once again lay foot on. Looking out the window of my twelfth-floor room at Hotel Nikko, I enjoyed a magnificent view to the Seine and the Eiffel Tower. Nothing could hold me back: the Paris air had awakened all my senses in the sweetest way... I had to hurry. I had so much to do: visit my favorite *quartiers* of the city, meet up with people I knew, do some shopping—I always loved shopping in Paris—and then cap the day with a get-together with my Greek friend Nontas at the Champs-Élysées for a drink and a chat...

The thirty-two hours went by too quickly. Everything was ready for our departure from the Charles De Gaulle Airport. As I was leaving Paris, I felt like I had come full circle and renewed a vow I had made to myself when graduating from college there: Paris is where I wanted to live and I would make sure it would be my new base of operations after Jeddah. I couldn't wait to make this dream come true and relocate to my beloved City of Light! Living in Paris and flying out to Saudi Arabia from there: it would be the perfect combination! I had come a long way!

As we arrived to Jeddah after a seven-hour flight, my colleague and I realized that we had left our suitcases back at the hotel in Paris. What a shame! After such a wonderful trip, this was such a disappointment! We immediately took all necessary steps to recover our luggage, feeling quite anxious about the outcome of our quest… Thankfully, our luggage was indeed located—and, in the process, we had been taught a valuable lesson in view of our future trips.

The entire month of August I was on stand-by. My commencement would take place mid-August and, in the meantime, I sat around and waited, in case I was called in to fill in any unexpected vacancy. My day-to-day life in Jeddah was quite pleasant, in fact unexpectedly so, contrary to various stories and theories that I had heard thus far. It was a period of never-ending dolce vita, a time so fulfilling that twenty-four hours were not enough to do everything I wanted to do in a day. Invitations were flowing in and the telephone rang nonstop. My days were filled with activities: larking about in the crystal clear waters of the Red Sea, meeting up with friends at the compound, visiting others at houses where we were always welcome. You see, air hostesses enjoy high prestige in that country, so much so that they are sometimes worshipped and praised like goddesses on earth.

Indeed, as strict as our way of life might have seemed to both locals and foreigners, the very existence of the cabin crew compound gave a group of especially privileged Saudis based in Jeddah the opportunity to experience their heaven on earth. Every night there were parties and celebrations at the houses of the various sheikhs, to which air hostesses of all nationalities, creeds and colors were invited, in order to cater to the diverse tastes of the assorted hosts. These noblemen had plenty of houses and plenty of women, but their greed for more and more harems was insatiable.

So, on one of my early days at the compound, I too found myself invited to one of those parties. Still a stranger among strangers, I decided to accept the invitation extended to me by one of my colleagues. My curiosity was urging me to experience the unthinkable. Steve, our driver from the Philippines, was constantly driving to and from the compound, picking up young women and dropping them off at the mansion of one or the other congenial sheikh.

The mansion I was driven to was filled with people; the music playing was nothing short of the latest hits from the most exclusive European dance clubs; the food was fantastic, carefully prepared by resident chefs. All this made for the perfect setting for some delightful times—however short-lived the delights. The sheikh's guests and friends, all men in high positions, officials or moguls, were happy to succumb to temptation and satisfy their desires. Under the influence of the general ambience, they would let the masks of sternness and decorum fall off to the point where they would be reduced to slimy, foolish, doting and vulnerable men at the feet of a beautiful air hostess, whom they would treat like a queen for that brief interval of the dalliance. There were large sums of money and very expensive gifts flowing, all in the name of beauty. And the air hostesses were even allowed to abstain from their work duties for as many days or even months the love affair would last. This way, the sheikh secured his prize in his harem for as long as he wanted and when his "love" for her gave way to his affection for another woman, the air hostess would return, wings clipped and feathers ruffled, to her days of working for a living.

These Saudi men went to great lengths to get what they wanted and frothed at the mouth if someone or something was refused to them. They were accustomed to no barriers, thanks to the power vested on them by their wealth. The places they lived in were genuine palaces and oases in an exclusive part of Jeddah, comparable to the most upscale lush suburbs of Europe, called Al Hamra. That area hardly felt like Saudi Arabia. The only telltale feature that clearly differentiated the locals' luxurious villas from their western counterparts was that, for all their extravagance, these houses were completely devoid of any works of art. Other than that, everything was over-the-top in quality and size. The sitting rooms were lined with multiple sofas and armchairs to accommodate the numerous guests, some of which were magnates who had come all the way from Riyadh to make sure they didn't miss out on a shindig. The rivalry between the Saudis for these social gatherings was fierce and there were parties being held at different houses every evening.

One high-profile Saudi, had turned the upper floor of his luxuriously decorated mansion into a state-of-the-art modern dance club, comparable to the most famous clubs of Europe capitals or even New York. There was an abundance of drinks to be had and a walk-in cellar containing the most exclusive labels of rare vintage aged wines. They most certainly knew how to enjoy life! They knew no limitations; they could afford every pleasure and had created their own heaven on earth right there, in Saudi Arabia—but would also carry it along with them on their travels, seeing as they were always escorted by their servants and even their concubines, in order to be sure that they had everything they wished for at all times. Their respective families were kept in another dimension, still in luxury, but far from these excesses. To this day, I still wonder how these people found the time to lead all these different kinds of lives. Their cornucopia of money led them on a constant search for material pleasures: private yachts moored at Obhur Creek at the Red Sea, private airplanes, limousines and super-expensive sports cars, were all at their disposal for their daily joyrides. Being around them, a woman couldn't help but join into this feeling of owning the whole world. And, of course, some women couldn't help falling in love with one or the other super-rich Saudi, infatuated more by the comforts that his wealth provided and less by his swarthy, masculine charms. These women would lose their mind and float on cloud nine, all the way to the bitter end—and bitter it was, every single time, both the end to full-blown love affairs and the end to casual flirtations. There was a ceremonial search, on both sides, a recycling through time until the final extinction. Even the purser of our VIP flights, who did not possess any noteworthy charm, was quite successful with the women, thanks to the amounts of money he could spend for his pleasures. And after trying the merchandise for himself, he would pass on his 'conquests' to the highest bidder when and if he pleased. I was not surprised to find out that he also possessed a series of houses in the most sought-after high-end resort towns—a level of possessions that was completely unjustified by his job and salary.

They had it all figured out: they could buy anything and anyone in exchange for some money and a little fun. And they knew all too well how vulnerable these particular young women were: they had come there to work for a living and suddenly found themselves amidst all these riches! It took a great deal of strength, character and will power to resist the temptation and come out unscathed. I had heard so many accounts that had left me speechless. One day, shortly before we landed at Riyadh, a colleague of mine from Tunisia approached me and said:

"Would you like to come with me once we are in Riyadh? Three or four of us will go to a Saudi's place, he'll take his pick and the rest of us will be paid half price."

"Not on my life," I told her, turning my back on her.

One had to have a rock solid moral foundation to face up to and resist all sorts of alluring propositions. Some women gave in, so the Saudis had drawn the conclusion that this type of bartering was okay. Both parties were responsible in that situation; and both parties were involved in a clash of civilizations.

Although closely tied to the biblical world of Moses, the Red Sea was an enormous source of energy and joy for me and I would spend most of my free time at its beaches— mind you, only foreigners were entitled to the joys of the sea. This type of recreation was totally prohibited to local women, due to the predominant mores, which were directly related to religious grounds. We and they were two different worlds living in the same place, each with their own set of rules and prohibitions.

As the summer passed, the weather became better and better and the temperature more moderate and more easily accepted by our bodies. I will never forget those sunsets with their violet hue… If I were an artist, they would be my endless source of inspiration; but I was a canvas, and their beauty has been brush-stroked onto my memory and essence forever.

September and October were very busy months; my flight schedules increased and my career took off—a career, nevertheless, that was to be quite short-lived. You see, this particular company strives to make the best of the present, without any regard for our future. Thus, we too had to run our own parallel race against time and accumulate as much as we could, in terms of income and material possessions, as fast as possible. The punch line among us was: "We've got to beat them to the punch."

It was one flight after another, according the schedules issued by Saudia. So, for me, September was a month of the unexpected, a blur of time, constantly changing between regular and VIP flights. I had been promoted to the class of privileged air hostesses serving at VIP flights. These flights were set aside for the high-standing Saudis: the mega-rich and officials. As far as I knew, all attendants were hoping to get into the VIP flights, but very few had the privilege to be selected. I can still recall some of the relevant remarks at the scheduling room, where we all gathered: "See that Tunisian girl? She's flying VIP with Prince so-and-so. And that English girl too; she is at the permanent service of that other Prince…" As for me, before I even realized what these VIP flights were all about, I had been selected to serve on them.

My first VIP flight was to Kuala Lumpur with a stopover in Bangkok. The trip there was dreamlike; an empty airplane with only the crew as passengers, travelling to the Far East to pick up our exclusive travelers. I had never imagined how much I would enjoy that flight. We even celebrated the birthday of a colleague mid-air with an enormous birthday cake.

Once in Bangkok, we had to change into a MAS plane. As we reached Kuala Lumpur, we were struck by the lush tropical vegetation. It was monsoon season there and that afternoon there was a sudden torrential downpour of rain. The hotel we stayed at was a miniature world of leisure and pleasure, the best one available for the time being. I spent the following day doing some shopping, buying some local souvenirs and taking the usual tour of the city and photos of the sights. Then back to the airport again to leave the country of the orchids. "Oh, how I'd love to bring back with me a massive bouquet of orchids to give to my mother—she loves orchids!" I thought to myself. Wherever I went, I always passionately bought presents to bring back to my loved ones at home, namely my mother and my three brothers in Athens. Yet, the destination of that return trip was quite far from home.

After the Kuala Lumpur trip, I worked on a flight for cabinet members from the Saudi resort Taïf to London. The trip back on the following day was quite unpleasantly eventful, bearing some negative repercussions for a colleague and myself. Seeing as neither one of us had given into the Saudi pilot's advances, he took it upon himself to make our lives miserable over the next forty-eight hours. As soon as we reached Paris, the two of us were placed in confinement, under the premise that we had to be on standby. And when we boarded the plane the next day for our flight to Geneva and Jeddah, it became immediately clear that the entire Arab cabin crew were conspiring against us because things hadn't transpired as smoothly and painlessly as they had planned. I had great difficulty understanding how they believed that women should have no initiative or mind of their own and simply give in to the men's whims.

Early the next morning, the phone rang in my room. I recognized the colorless voice of Ellen Debs, the chief hostess from the VIP headquarters, commanding us—to our great surprise—to report swiftly at her office. Taken aback, we hastened to the company's VIP department. That was the first time I would get to meet these people up close. When Ellen informed us that the pilot had accused us of improper conduct throughout the flight, we were dumbfounded at how underhanded and sly the Saudi pilot's behavior was. Being foreigners, we were easy targets and any accusations against us were taken at face value. Fortunately for us though, the truth triumphed and the defamatory remarks against us were dismissed. I earnestly looked my superiors in the eye and explained in all honesty what had happened and they were convinced by my account of the events. That first experience did not break me; instead, it firmly established me as part of the VIP flights team. But that particular episode had also taught me one thing: that the easiest accusation to fabricate against a Christian in Saudi Arabia was to accuse him or her of having insulted Islam.

It was back to normal the following month, as I worked domestic flights and got to visit several towns around Saudi Arabia. Our passengers on these flights were local people, including many quaintly attired Bedouins, who came into stark contrast with the surroundings of a modern-day mode of transportation. They would often board the plane barefoot, their only carry-on luggage being a canvas bag, the men with their beards dyed with orange henna and the women proudly displaying their manicure of black henna covering both their nails and skin—only their hands were visible, seeing as they were covered head to toe, as is customary in those places. They would squat on their seat, signal us to approach and make various gestures signifying that they wanted "asir" (fruit juice) or "moya" (water)—some of the Arabic words we were required to know in our job. Quite often the women would breastfeed on the plane, and this was something that had struck me as particularly odd: on the one hand, they were covered head to toe and, on the other, they would simply flash out their breasts to feed their children in the presence of all those passengers! It made no sense! It was the point where coyness met provocation! And after their disembarkation, they would leave behind a pile of tossed out paper towels and boxes scattered all around the airplane cabin. In spite of all this, the Bedouins were quite likable in their simplicity and nescience. No one could criticize them for their lack of luster and they simply had to use the plane as a means of transportation—flying is a must in Saudi Arabia; the vast expanse of the Arab desert is not amenable to other means of transportation.

All big cities in Saudi Arabia have been constructed in pretty much the same style: extravagantly designed modern buildings which combine the contemporary Arabic style with traditional elements. The presence of the nouveaux rich was evident all around. Immaculately polished luxury cars—Buick, Mercedes, Rolls—were crossing the desert featuring a Filipino chauffeur driving shrouded women or some Saudi man boasting in his snow-white thobe. This is undoubtedly the land of great contradictions, where the age-old traditional Islamic folklore collides with the ultra-modern.

My string of experiences was interrupted by some time off work to take a trip back home to see my family. It was my first time back in Athens in four months. Full of excitement, I conveyed to my family how good I felt and how surprisingly satisfied I was with my job. I had even started depositing my first paychecks with the bank, in spite of all the great temptations to spend money, especially on gold, the price of which was tantalizing enough for one to want to spend his every last penny on it. Truth be told, this particular job in Saudi Arabia was seen by most of my colleagues, coming from all four corners of the earth, to make lots of money in no time, rising from rags to riches at the blink of an eye. But that presupposed a series of humiliating concessions on the part of the woman, to the point where her shattered personality was looked down upon by the Saudis. Still, easy money was like an avalanche, sweeping along many of the women working for Saudia. As a result, any woman who wished to differentiate herself from that path and preserve her dignity had a fight of her own to give, as odd as this might sound. She had to make it clear to advancing men that a woman is not supposed to be treated as an object of lust. The Rolex watch had become a trademark for flight attendants with Saudia. In fact, it was the first paycheck, or rather the first gift, which, although readily accepted, would quite soon lose its prestige. So, one had to come up with something else to make oneself stand out and avoid the reputation that went along with that watch. Holding one's ground and preserving one's dignity at that Tower of Babel featuring all creeds and nationalities was hard, but certainly not impossible to achieve.

As time went by, I fully adapted to my working environment and completely familiarized myself with my job. At the same time, my trips were becoming more and more exciting. Working on VIP flights definitely offered many perks and opportunities; "routine" was totally a word of the past. At the drop of a hat, you could discover yourself preparing to fly to the most unbelievable destination in order to accommodate a VIP's whim to go on holiday or travel for whichever other reason. One such case was when I was called upon to work on a Royal Aircraft—the royal fleet of aircrafts comprised super-deluxe Boeing 747 planes, a number of Boeing 737's and Lear Jets. I felt extremely privileged when Hindi—another VIP flights manager—summoned me to include me in the crew at a VIP flight from Jeddah to Khartoum (Sudan) to Washington DC. We had to go to Africa to pick up the Sudanese President and accompany him to Washington DC for several days.

Every moment we spent in Khartoum after our landing there was unforgettable! Four gleaming white Mercedes limos where waiting for us, the crew, at the runway. Apparently, the members of the crew working on VIP flights were treated like VIPs themselves. We were formal guests of the country's President.

At one o'clock in the afternoon of the next day everything was ready for our departure from Khartoum. The VIPs boarded the plane and we all took off on a short flight to the Cairo Airport, where a long red carpet had been laid out for us. The VIP we were escorting was due for a brief meeting with the President of Egypt. Seeing the reception of country officials up close was such an unforgettable image, it has been impressed firmly on my memory.

After Cairo, we embarked on our long-haul journey to the New World. I had never been to America before and, at last, that wonderland of our childhood stories was about to appear before my very eyes. After twenty-three hours of travel from the time we left Khartoum, and after flying through three continents thanks to the stopovers in Cairo and Paris, we arrived in America and back to the present absolutely exhausted.

It was daybreak on a Saturday in Washington, DC. We had been through different countries, continents and climate zones in a very short period of time, now experiencing the chilly fall weather of Washington after the African tropical heat.

"Passports, please," said the voice of an American official who had boarded the plane to check our passports and, after going through this mandatory procedure, they drove us for what seemed like quite a few miles, to the old aristocratic Shoreham Hotel, where we were to stay for one week.

I was still extremely tired after such a long flight, but absolutely nothing could hold me back. I had a good breakfast to regain my strength and made plans of where to go and what to see. Camera in hand to capture images of all the sights, I sought to visit as many as I possibly could. As a welcome surprise, two enormous black limousines had been commissioned to tour us around the city. As if we were some distinguished officials, we had a Spanish-speaking chauffeur, who also served as our guide, although my Greek colleague and I had already looked up quite a bit of information ourselves. When the rest of the crew rested, we had made the best of our time.

Thus, we covered every nook and cranny of Washington during our touring escapades, visiting places like the White House and several museums of the Smithsonian, as well as the famous Arlington Cemetery. When I set eyes on the grave of the Kennedys, my emotion was overflowing. The vast shopping centers made quite an impression on me, because such establishments were relatively unheard of in Greece at that time, although quite common in Americanized Saudi Arabia. Some shopping surely could do no harm. And some "USA by night" would certainly help this tour come full circle. And even though the clocks were still ticking, my time seemed as if it had magically stopped: just by doing my job I was having the time of my life and getting paid for it.

When the itinerary for our return journey to the Asiatic continent was in place, I began, for the first time, to feel a strange sense of fatigue. I guess this is the price of flying around the world.

By the time we returned to Jeddah, I was already into my days of leave from work. Faced with the fact that two of my valuable vacation days had already been used up, I was left with not enough time to take a trip back to Athens. So, I informed the scheduling department that I would not be taking the rest of my leave at that time.

And, yet again, I was pleasantly surprised.

"Alexandra, tomorrow at eleven in the morning you are to report for duty on H.M.1." This was the Royal Jumbo Jet, used exclusively by the royal family. Our destination was Morocco, so I packed my suitcase once again, mostly with spring and summer clothing.

I felt especially flattered and eager to serve on this special flight: our passengers would be King Fahd and his Councilors and the aircraft an immaculate Boeing 747, specifically built and configured like a flying palace. All the top VIP personnel were called to arms, headed by purser Abdullah, who only served on the royal flights, the so-called VVVIP flights. Seeing as the passenger was the highest-ranking official of the state, these flights were particularly demanding in terms of etiquette and form.

The time came for us to embark. Once again, the red carpets were laid out and lined with high-ranking company personnel, dressed in their ceremonial thobes, to welcome the distinguished passenger. To my eyes, all these happenings were donned in an air of magic, laced with mystery and enchantment; a world of fairy tales coming alive and true for all your senses to experience.

The King was an affable, down-to-earth, kind-hearted man, with an enjoyable sense of humor, which I immediately picked up on despite my limited knowledge of Arabic. The eight members of the cabin crew had divided the tasks among us and I had the honor of seeing to the requirements of King Fahd himself.

"What is your name?" he asked me, feigning a dry cough.

"Alexandra, Your Majesty," I replied.

"Where are you from?"

"I'm Greek," I said with a smile.

After seven hours of flying amidst a wonderful cooperative atmosphere, overflowing with satisfaction and good will, we arrived in Morocco and the city of Fez. The VIPs disembarked and we continued on to Casablanca, as the hotels in Fez were all fully booked.

We were approaching the end of November, but the weather was still pleasantly warm on the coast of Mohammedia. A bit of jogging along the Meridien Hotel's beachfront would be just right, I decided. After all, this "working holiday" of mine seemed to know no end. I toured around the picturesque Casablanca and had a close-up look at the Arabs of North Africa, of whom my experience in France had left me with not exactly the best of impressions.

Four days later, our supervisor Abdullah made us extremely happy when he gathered us to announce that we would be flying the King to Marbella, Spain, the following day. There, we would be put up and treated as special guests of the great sovereign. I had heard lots about the celebrated Costa del Sol, haunt of the international jet set. Until then, I had privately only visited the Balearic Islands and Barcelona.

Still, the luxurious, easy-going, carefree VIP lifestyle did not make me lose touch with reality. Firmly keeping my feet on the ground, I was constantly striving to make the best of that experience, knowing full well that it would be over soon and, once back in Jeddah, I would not be—or treated like—"royalty" anymore. Nevertheless, I at least had the opportunity to escort numerous princes and kings on their travels and be awarded, along with the rest of the crew, with some generous tips for it.

When we landed, Abdullah started to hand out wads of dollars to all of us on the King's behalf. This was one of the great perks of these flights! And once in Marbella, we had some unforgettably good times dining together amicably with the unmistakably rich and powerful.

The unparalleled journey that allowed me to live, even for only a short while, like the Saudi Arabian royals, had come to an end. All is well that ends well; but as we were chatting about our memories of the trip on the Saudia minibus that was taking us back to the compound, something happened that nearly spoiled everything. When we got off the bus, I heard an English colleague in a state of panic mumble something about her "vanity case" and realized that I had inadvertently picked it up thinking it was mine (they were all identical and kept in the same place together). "So where is mine then?" I asked now panicking myself. As it turned out, it had been left behind on the minibus, which had already taken off. The driver was swiftly informed and returned to bring it back to me, thus putting an end to this crisis. You see, that vanity case did not only contain my make-up; it also contained, as it happened, my generous cut of the royal tip.

For quite some time, I continued to work on the VIP flights, travelling between capital cities or towns around Europe and some of the easternmost destinations and, thusly, between seasons. In addition, I served on plenty of domestic flights, escorting VIPs and their families in their travels within the kingdom.

On one such trip, we were in Medina, one of the two holy cities of Islam, waiting for our distinguished passengers, all members of the royal family. When it was boarding time, all I could see was a group of women, including King's wife. She was rather old; her black hair was parted down the middle of her head and pulled back, covered by a chador. She was dressed in the traditional Saudi attire and was laden with precious gold and jewels. But what really caught my eye was her footwear: she was wearing slippers!

Male passengers were usually congenial and sociable, but female passengers were rather distant, dismissive even, and did not engage in conversation with the members of the crew. Through these travels, I had become acquainted with the whole array of behaviors and had come to the conclusion that it was only the women who, by my standards, enjoyed a special type of status that was closely tied to their existential profile as women of Saudi Arabia.

After a long flight back from a trip to London and before even putting down my suitcase, I received a call from the VIP flight manager telling me to report for duty in a few hours in order to work on the next flight departing to some country in the Middle East. For security reasons, they never disclosed to the crew exactly whom we would be taking on board with us. Also, an unpleasant aspect of VIP flights was that there was never any strict adherence to the time plan of the flight itinerary. Thus, although very tired, I was obliged to report for duty at four o'clock in the morning. I was to be the only cabin crew, apart from a Saudi cabin supervisor in a super-deluxe G3 or Lear Jet, an aircraft that can carry up to fifteen people. Once up in the air, it seemed to me as though we had been flying for endless hours in the Middle Eastern airspace without any prospect of landing.

"For goodness sake, where are we going?" I asked the supervisor.

"I don't know it myself," was his response.

At two o'clock in the afternoon we finally landed in Amman, where we had to wait inside the plane for three hours. It was the first time that I felt like I wanted to give it all up and leave. It wasn't until much later that we found out why we had to wait for so long: The passenger we were supposed to pick up from Amman was none other than Yasser Arafat, who was on his way there from Syria by car. Nevertheless, he never made it—for reasons we never found out— and we ended up lodging in Damascus for the night, utterly exhausted.

Such were some examples of the unexpected elements associated with those flights. They had their charms, but they also entailed some risks due to the international political background.

In addition, not all of the VIP flight destinations were so pleasant to visit. One such place, for instance, was Quetta in Pakistan. Situated only thirty kilometers in from the border with Afghanistan, it was a rather small village plagued by great poverty and despair. Under such difficult and miserable conditions, we were forced to spend the night at a ramshackle hotel—which, mind you, was regarded as the best one around. It had broken windowpanes and four camp beds in each one of the rooms that opened directly onto the street outside. It was December and freezing cold and there was a woodstove burning all night to keep us warm. The bed covers were scant and filthy and the night seemed endless. I had excruciating cramps in my stomach; I wasn't sure why, but perhaps it was the food that I had consumed at a garish stall earlier or maybe the fumes that I was inhaling from the stove that had me doubled up.

We left early in the morning, because the Prince and the Minister were in a hurry to return to the comforts of their home after they had finished their falconry session. Both of them were extremely fond of this particular sporting activity. On another such flight of ours from Tunisia, the falcons were boarded on our plane, seeing as they couldn't be locally sourced in that area of Pakistan!

As for myself, I had collapsed even before the princely jet took off. Upon our arrival in Jeddah, I was rushed straight to the medical center, where I was fortunately diagnosed with a case of food poisoning, which passed without escalating into anything more serious.

My next flight after my full recovery from the recent episode in Quetta was on a Lear Jet again. This time the dignitary we would serve was one of the King's advisors, who boarded the plane in Jeddah. He was an elderly man, refined and dignified, a countenance which commanded the appropriate level of respect on our part. His conduct was irreproachable throughout the journey to London. The next day we took him to Fez, Morocco. Nothing gave away that a storm was brewing.

In Fez we stayed in a luxury hotel, comprised of two separate wings: one for royalty and one for the super-rich! When I opened the door to my room, I was literally dazzled by the extravagance and luxury. Of course, at the time I had no idea that I was enjoying some sort of special treatment in the allotment of rooms. A short while later, I met up with my supervisor to go out for a stroll around the city and asked him what he thought of his room.

"It's nothing special," he replied.

"What do you mean?" I insisted and proceeded to describe my room, without really thinking twice about it.

When we got back to our hotel, I went up to my room to leave my stuff and was puzzled to notice that there was another door in the room, one that connected my room to the adjacent luxurious suite and was now open. Flabbergasted, I began to put two and two together. I let my bags drop on the floor and dashed out of the room. I called up both my supervisor and the American captain of our plane and told them what I had just seen. Their reaction was quite passive, as if there was nothing they could do to help me out. My next stop was the reception desk, where I requested a change of rooms. But that request too was met with silence. My heated protests were falling on deaf ears. No one dared alter the plans of the mighty passenger. But where others faltered, I, alone, a woman, went against all odds and protected myself. Unperturbed, I asked my supervisor if he would please let me sleep over on the sofa in his room. He very graciously agreed in order to put an end to my plight. Very early the next morning, the supervisor's phone rang. It was the dignitary, furiously demanding explanations as to the whereabouts of the air hostess.

"She's here sir," said the supervisor and the dignitary slammed the phone on him.

Less than two hours later, the phone rang again. It was hardly ten in the morning.

"I want to talk to the air hostess!" the dignitary commanded.

"Just a moment, Sir," my colleague responded, signaling me to come to the phone.

"Have you no shame?" his voice thundered.

"Why would you say that, Sir?" I nonchalantly answer his question with a question of my own.

"You should be ashamed of yourself for having slept with the supervisor," he said.

"On the contrary, I am thankful to him for his hospitality. Seeing as there was no way that I could sleep in a room with the door wide open!"

Temporarily at a loss for words, he ordered me to present myself in his suite to apologize. I didn't go and chose to calmly expect the worst, i.e. to get fired. But neither Saudia nor the VIP department fired me. I was there to do my job, that of the flight attendant, and I had no intention to entangle myself in any other businesses and transactions, although I knew that there was plenty of easy money to be made on them.

I guess every flight held potentially a secret or some unexpected turn of events. To say the least, experience taught me how VIP flights were sometimes about combining business with pleasure. In any case, it was up to the respective woman and her set of values to deal with the matter in the manner that she deemed appropriate. As a rule, there were usually few scruples or objections and money trumped any moral principle or inhibition. Everything was sacrificed on the altar of money, both dignity and ethics. But what good was it to make so much money while having lost your dignity and being pegged with the corresponding label?

So, one day I was approached by the director of the VIP flights, who proposed that we go on an outing and have a drink at the palace of some prince in Geneva.

"I will take you there and leave you to it!" he said.

"I am flattered to be offered the opportunity for this acquaintance, but I'm afraid I cannot accept," said I.

He glared at me and asked, "Do you understand what you're saying?"

"Absolutely!" I responded, with steadfast resolve.

Word got around soon; it seems I was "bad for business." To get back at me, on the return journey, they obliged me to walk into one of the lounges of the royal plane to offer my company to the dignitary that was in there. I blushed and duly apologized as I walked in on a group of them talking, explaining that I really did not mean to disturb them but my supervisor had insisted. They just gave me an inquisitive look and I quickly left the room. Luckily, the rest of the flight was smooth and we landed safely in Jeddah.

Such were the mishaps of the otherwise enchanting VIP flights. Everything comes at a price, I guess...

A dream I had around that time upset me so much that, the more I tried to put it out of my mind, the more it kept coming back and haunting me. In that dream I had seen a black cat angrily barging into my room, glaring at me and then knocking down and smashing everything in sight. That image affected me deeply. I didn't want to pay any attention to it, but deep inside me I felt the unnerving premonition that something momentous was about to happen in my life.

CHAPTER TWO

SAMI

In January, I took a few days off and vacationed in Athens. I had assigned Maro, a Greek colleague, to sort out my options for the new work schedule and convey my request for flights to New York as my first choice. I had decided to try my luck on standard flights, which would give me a break from the standby VIP routine.

This change of schedule would prove fateful. That first month of the new year was to decide my future. The wonderful times I had had up until then were about to give way to a very different route ahead.

One of these new trips was Flight 125 from Riyadh to London. Upon our arrival there, my colleagues and I happened to meet up with another cabin crew that had arrived before us. Sami was the copilot at that flight. And that was how we first met.

That night, the whole crew and I were enjoying a drink at the Skyline Sheraton bar. Sami was also there, together with his flight engineer and copilot, and he wouldn't take his eyes off me even for one minute, all the while feigning to participate in the conversation that was transpiring within his party. He was a dark-skinned Saudi with extraordinarily expressive eyes, both charming and devilish at the same time. I don't know why this was, but I had found on numerous occasions that the people of that particular ethnic group had extremely radiant eyes. You could feel them drawing you in and you felt powerless to escape. It was as if their white-and-bloodshot eyeballs with the jet-black pupils in the middle possessed magical magnetic powers.

After the members of both crews had gone through all the formal introductions our evening ended on a happy note. We had to turn in rather early as we had an early departure the next morning for Jeddah. The next morning at breakfast, I was surprised to notice Sami sitting at the table next to mine. Seeing as he didn't have the chance the night before, that was his only chance to get to see me before we left and make sure he got my contact information. And so he did.

Exactly two days after he, too, had returned to Jeddah, my phone rang—and I simply knew it would be him. Coming from the other end of the line, I heard a gentle, warm voice.

"Hi. How are you?"

And so, one phone call in-between flights led to another. Before long, he also proposed that we meet. And so we did, one early afternoon, at the scheduling center, where Sami very politely invited me over to his place for a cup of tea. You see, people don't really "go out" in Saudi Arabia. It is a country of privacy and most activities take place behind private walls.

En route to Sami's place, I tried to picture what it would be like. I imagined it very original, decorated with objects that he would have picked out himself on his various travels around the world—at least this was what other people in his line of work had done, as far as I knew.

With a sudden slam on the brakes, the car stopped on a dirt road in front of a three-story building. I tried to hide my nervousness. As we stepped into his apartment on the second floor, I was astonished to see a vast empty space, half its floor covered by a carpet. The space began to look more like a home as we proceeded further inside. It was rather unkempt for a pilot's abode and perhaps my facial expression unwittingly gave away my disappointment. Immediately reading my expression with his sparkling glance, he supplied a swift explanation.

"You know, I live alone and I'm expecting my mother and the servants to come in from Riyadh and tidy up the place." Then he added, "Our main house is in Riyadh. We are a big family, quite well known."

He was attempting to impress me, but it wasn't really working. After getting the cold shoulder, he served me a cup of hot tea despite the hot weather.

"I love living in big places," he said in an effort to elicit my opinion.

We both talked about ourselves and I told him about my hitherto life in Jeddah. Feigning nonchalance, he asked me questions to extract information about my personal life. At that point, the progressive spirit of France in me was instantly set into motion and it was only natural that I would not take his chauvinistic comments regarding women at all lightly.

Unconsciously, I had just probed into the inner sanctum of the Arabic world. He was trying to get me to accept the ethos of the Arab mentality, but I would not sway. It was getting late so I asked him to escort me back to the compound, as I had to get ready for a dinner party I had been invited to attend together with my girlfriends.

Apparently, I had made quite an impression on Sami, who kept calling in from wherever around the world he happened to be. Always courteous, patient and persistent, always with a warm smile on his face, he'd constantly remind me how interested he was in me.

At that time I had resumed my VIP flights, from which he strove to avert me by exerting his own degree of brainwashing. It took me quite some time to realize that his ulterior motive in wanting me to give up working on these privileged and lucrative flights was his own jealousy and envy. He had quite the swelled head, garnished with a massive dose of egocentrism.

Eventually, after serving on several more Lear Jet flights that month, I gave in and parted ways with the fantastic world of the VIP flights. I was proud to have soared through the skies and over the continents next to distinguished passengers under the best possible conditions.

Sami's frequent calls were starting to become tiresome. I felt stifled and troubled. Wherever he was, he would phone in. I really did not want to go forward with him. Free of any emotional loads or ties, I wanted to by free to move about wherever I wanted, in whichever way I wanted, without reporting to anyone at all. Getting into a relationship or marrying was completely out of the question for the foreseeable future. My career was not cut out for such restrictions and, anyway, I was expecting a base transfer from Jeddah to Paris. It was a matter of time before I was due to move. But, instead, time had some very unpleasant surprises up its sleeve. I was never to return to my beloved Paris...

Devastated at the prospect of my leaving Jeddah, Sami mustered all the emotional power he possessed and put it to work with such intensity, that I not only stayed in Jeddah, but was astounded to see what had started as nothing more than a frivolous flirtation with an expiration date turn into something quite more serious. Never before had I encountered such a persistent and inexhaustible display of interest, which came into stark contrast with the cool, tepid European style. I had acceded. His persistence had won me over, in spite of all my attempts to discourage him by saying that he should not expect anything from me. The more firmly I would stand my ground, the more he'd get hooked on me. He would show up on each and every one of my flights, either as a pilot or copilot, or as an ordinary passenger. He'd always find a way to be around me.

The deal was sealed during a week-long vacation I took in Rome. Around that time, Sami claimed that he had to take a trip to Athens, but in fact he ended up travelling with me to Rome. We had some great moments together; I introduced him to genuine Italian *ristorante* pasta dishes, showed him around the Roman monuments and even took him to the Uffizi museum in Florence. He was fascinated by that unprecedented induction into Western culture and that alternative way of life, but he made a point of concealing his emotions, attesting to the beginnings of his deep passion for me, a passion which culminated in the vacation we took together the following month, when we spent an unbelievably romantic, love-filled week in Bangkok. What had started so inconspicuously in London was made abundantly clear in the Far East. We had become two souls in one body. My life had been identified with his.

He began to make the relevant moves to prepare the ground with his family back in Riyadh, so as to warm them up to the idea of our relationship. In doing so, he came into frequent contact with his mother Enaam, the only woman in a family of seven men. The long-distance calls between them were nonstop.

"I love my Mama very much," he told me one day when I happened to be at his place during one of their phone calls, in the course of which he would give her a full report on absolutely every aspect of his life. I was able to grasp a word here and there, although I did not really know the language.

Before long, the day came when I was to meet his beloved "Mama" of whom I had heard so much.

"Today I'm going to introduce you to my Mama," he said to me one afternoon in his car, on our way to his home.

I was very nervous as to what I would come up against. I was wary of these mysteriously shrouded women. The mere sight of their attire had made me keep my distance from them in my flights. I understood absolutely nothing about them and even less about their opinion of foreign women. One thing was for sure: they looked at us in a different way, probably one of jealousy and resentment because they were not allowed to do the things that we did.

I bit my lip and said nothing, bracing myself to face this trial calm and composed. When we got to his place, I saw an extremely plump and short woman with massively wide hips. Her smiling expression gave off a vibe as though she reckoned herself a goddess of beauty on earth. Her Lebanese ancestry became her, her Mediterranean complexion making her stand out among the Saudi women.

"*Marhaba*," she greeted me and I could feel myself blush as if I had done something wrong.

I used to think Islam was a very prohibitive religion as it allowed no freedom to women even in the simplest of things, seeing as they were not allowed to eat or even sit around men. But something else appeared to be the case here. They were either an exception, happily straying from the established order, or they were trying to feign a more Western-type lifestyle.

After "Mama" I met one of his brothers (or rather a minion of his, since Sami was the first-born and wielded his power over his five younger brothers), his grandmother and the Filipino woman who accompanied the old lady in her trip. They were on a pilgrimage journey to Mecca.

Before my visit ended, "Mama" Enaam had invited me to go to her house in Riyadh at the first available opportunity; only I would have to show up in an ankle-length dress, allegedly on account of her Islamist husband, Abu Sami. At the time, I did not take the invitation seriously because I didn't want to go or meet the rest of Sami's family. Unfortunately, what I was hoping to avoid was exactly what happened...

I was on a flight assignment with an overnight stay in Riyadh. And when I got there I found out that—what a coincidence!—Sami was already there. I was to spend the night with the rest of the crew at an outlying Marriott hotel, so Sami drove by to pick me up. For some reason, I had always felt apprehensive at the prospect of meeting his father and that day was no different.

Sami pulled up in front of a huge gate surrounded by high walls.

"Here we are," he said.

The buildings inside were like fortresses because, as I found out later, they were meant to protect the chastity of the women, who were not supposed to be seen by outsiders under any circumstances. Past the gate sprawled a vast courtyard at the end of which I saw a large two-story house, perfectly suitable to accommodate his multi-member family.

Hair loose and perfectly preened, "Mama" welcomed me and simultaneously introduced me to everyone present. Sami's father only appeared for an instant, as brief as lightning. I rolled up my sleeves and swallowed hard, but he was gone again in no time—and I couldn't wait to be out of there myself.

A huge tablecloth had been set up on the floor and I was expected to partake of the Arab-style dinner. Unaccustomed to sitting on the floor, I tried as best I could to get into a comfortable position. Fortunately they had made provisions to have silverware—eating with one's bare hands is no easy matter. Dinner was followed by a guided tour of the drawing rooms on the ground floor, as if I were in the Palace of Versailles. At the end of this "lovely" affair, I thanked them all and Sami drove me back to the hotel.

There were many more trips and flights, always with Sami, who had become a permanent fixture in my life; whether working or vacationing, we seemed to always be together. Easter time found us working on a flight to Bangladesh and experiencing first-hand the unpleasant situations of an ever so poverty-stricken third-world country. But the next milestone in our relationship was our trip to Greece. In Athens, Sami got to meet my mother and one of my brothers. Sami's reaction was composed and his comments scarce—although I cannot say the same about my brother, whose comments ranged from negative to dismissive.

Undeterred, Sami kept on his wooing routine with unabated interest. That is, until the first signs of his mother's influence on him began to show their ugly heads. We were in Paris when I first noticed his behavior had changed, but Sami played the whole thing down, chalking it all up to love and cajoling me into thinking everything was just fine. While in Paris, we also met up with Olga, a friend of my brother's. It was raining cats and dogs on that May day in Paris, but she did everything in her power to come find us. She had met Sami at my home in Athens and had been captivated by his charms; so much so, in fact, that she wouldn't leave! She had stayed at our place from lunchtime until the wee hours of the next morning, probably in the hopes of getting to spend some time alone with Sami. Oh, how I wish he had run off with her instead of me! I would have been spared of so many woes to come! But, as they say, "one cannot escape one's destiny."

As time went by, everything pointed to Sami being completely enthralled by me. Besides, we had spent all our summer holidays together, touring the United States, all the way to Puerto Rico, a precursor-trip to our future honeymoon.

We went back to Athens and spent a fortnight with my mother. We also went to Mykonos where Sami met my other two brothers. When June was almost over, it was getting time for us to get back to our work. And then, Sami hit me with this:

"Don't go back," he said. "Stay here in Athens."

"Why would I do that?" I asked him.

"Because you have to stay here. I don't want you coming back to work for Saudia."

"Don't even think about it!" I replied firmly.

He had spoken to me of marriage while we were in America, but I had no idea that this entailed my giving up my work. Without paying much more attention to the matter, I promptly took the next plane out to Jeddah.

"Mama" had infiltrated our life, stretching out her venomous tentacles to get to me. She conveyed her orders via her weak-willed son who blindly executed her commands for fear of "committing a cardinal sin"—according to a relevant verse in the Koran, Mother holds a place next to none in the eyes of the Almighty and he didn't want to displease his in any way.

The first few flights during the first ten days of July were truly a nightmare. We had an increased workload because it was the month of Ramadan, a religious holiday during which people in that country tended to travel extensively. At the same time, the immense pressure I was getting from Sami was unbearable. His only concern was to persuade me to give up my job and leave. He kept playing the marriage card, saying that was the reason why I ought not to work. "To work as an air hostess is regarded as degrading and looked down upon in my country," he would say convincingly. His relatives were not to know that I was a flight attendant, as if it were a crime. I was unable to fully grasp his mother's plot of intrigue. At one point I had told her, "I can stop seeing your son, but why should I destroy my career?" But I was 'the voice of one crying in the wilderness.' Everything had been cunningly predetermined for me. I had to leave…

I had made it absolutely clear to Sami that I had no intention of ending a career that I loved, but he forced his will upon me using the method of persuasion. He pledged his love to me and comforted me that he would soon come to Athens to marry me. That promise of his left me unsatisfied and wondering about what was really going on. Perhaps my leaving my job and Jeddah was "Mama" Enaam's way to get rid of my presence there once and for all. Perhaps she had gotten concerned that I was becoming too much a part of her gullible son's life. Yet, the truth was a long way off…

I tried to find a solution, soliciting the advice of my supervisor. But, unfortunately, time was counting down for me. No help was visible anywhere in the horizon; circumstances, people and facts were all advocating my 'termination' with a velvet glove. To make things worse, Sami was keeping my entire personal belongings (clothes, electronic devices, etc.) "hostage" at his house. You see, I trusted him so I had asked him, during one of my moments of weakness, if he could keep my belongings safe while I was working, seeing as there were some trainee air hostesses from Pakistan who were regularly "raiding" my room at the compound whenever I was away.

CHAPTER THREE

THE RETURN TO ATHENS, THE WEDDING, AND MOVING TO SAUDI ARABIA

Even though at the time I wasn't marching to the beat of Sami's drum yet, my future had been pretty much mapped out for me. As a last resort, I requested a few days leave from work for family reasons. Still, I found neither support nor assistance to my problem, which had started to take root and intensify in relation to my existence. It was uncanny how every avenue lead to a dead end.

So, on the morning of the 11th of July, with only my handbag in hand and an eerie feeling in my gut, I found myself leaving the compound, that fascinating place that had so generously been offered to me and where I had managed to create my own wonderland of sorts. My only hope at the time being the prospect of my return to the compound after a short stay in Athens, I steeled my heart and left in accordance with my partner's instructions. With mixed feelings of sadness and rage against Sami, I was abandoning my second home, which gave me several cherished indelible memories and would always have a special place in my heart.

Bright-eyed and bushy-tailed, Sami met me at the gate to take me to the airport. His eyes and face were gleaming of joy, as he had even taken care of my ticket without my having to rely on the company's bonus for services rendered. Everything had been arranged in the utmost secrecy. At that moment, I hated him so much; I could feel the world vanishing around me. He was cutting off my wings, which I had once spread open and soared so high above the earth that the world seemed too small for me. His decisions knocked me down, brought me to the ground and felt I could hardly ever get up again.

Misty-eyed, I reached the departure lounge at King Abdulaziz airport. His shouts drew upon us the prying eyes of everyone present, even of the Bedouins. It was another one of his usual misunderstandings. One piece of my luggage, all of which he had been keeping at his house, was already there to accompany me on my journey. He had packed it himself…

Smile wiped off my face and hope off my heart, I embarked the plane to Athens. It was a tragic day; that man had started to take full control of my life.

We landed in Athens at dusk and my feeling of gloom was intensified by the event that ensued: An Egyptian air hostess had picked up my suitcase instead of hers and disappeared. *When it rains, it pours*, I thought to myself. It took quite some time and energy that I didn't have to sort out that mishap, and it was already very late when I finally got home to be greeted by my surprise-stricken mother—she had no idea I was coming. Before I even had a chance to explain to her the true reasons of my return, the phone rang.

It was Sami calling from Saudi Arabia. He was trying to sound calm and composed in his inquiry to make sure everything had proceeded according to his plan, but the tone of his voice gave away his feeling of triumph.

From that day foreword he would besiege me with multiple daily phone calls, completely unconcerned about their cost or duration. All he wanted was to convince me of how much he loved me and cared for me.

Four days into my trip back to Athens, I had already made up my mind to return to my work after my leave and abandon that relationship, which was setting unbearable, suffocating and restrictive terms on my life. But before I had the chance to put my plan into action, Sami beat me to the punch. He suddenly appeared in Athens to reinforce his position and counter a thundering "No" to my return to Saudia. The way he enforced his authority made me yield. His aura mesmerized me. I so wanted to react, to resist, but it was all in vain. Something held me back; I surrendered to some sort of inertia. And so I fatefully gave my consent, although deep down I did not embrace his viewpoint. He had a strange power of persuasion and some bizarre opinions at that. But he had a knack for making things seem right by straying off the point and, in the end, always arriving at the conclusion that he was right and justified.

"You are going to be my wife and I don't want you to work!"

The law had been laid down! With an air of unimaginable charm to him, he would analyze how wonderful our life together would be, filled with comforts and travels and anything else it takes to see things in a different light through rose-colored glasses. These pipedreams made me give in momentarily; nevertheless, my having abandoned my work had affected me in a very negative way.

What I was going through was completely unprecedented. He essentially had me thrown out of the company, causing me to reshuffle my entire emotional world. And he had an answer to every question that could possibly spring to my mind.

Everything inside me was in a state of utter confusion. Life had hitherto shown me her smiling face, but was now radically reconsidering her stance. I once was a carefree girl whose every dream came true; then came along he, a reincarnated Circe, to sweep me off my feet and ensnare me in my own irrational emotions. Trapped in a prison of my own making, I was torn between my thoughts and feelings for Sami and those about the loss of my professional career. The idea that I was giving up a fulfilling and emancipating career just because he wanted me to was wearing me down. Still, my heart was beating for him…

He, on the other hand, was dutifully abiding by his country's traditions on "women and work"; you see, in Saudi Arabia, as in the rest of the Arab world, the general attitude towards women and their role in society is quite different than that prevailing in the rest of the world. Religion is deeply ingrained in them, guiding all aspects of their lives.

We spent the entire month of August together in Greece. Sami had become the bearer of good news: we were to formally announce our relationship in front of our respective families and close friends. He arrived to Athens a week before everyone else to prepare the ground for the arrival of his mother, who would come alone as the only representative of his clan.

The day and time was approaching when the airplane carrying "Mama" was due to touch down on Greek soil. A strange anxiety was casting a shadow over Sami's as he was becoming more and more nervous and irritable, for reasons that were unknown to me at the time. As it became clear later, his odd behavior was stemming from his wavering between his emotions for me, on one hand, and the pressures exerted by his mother, on the other.

Finally, the "Great Lady of Riyadh" arrived. Stubby and voluptuous, all covered in black (she hadn't changed one iota from the way she used to dress in Saudi Arabia), she did not pass unnoticed.

She greeted me coldly, feigning no effort to disguise her dislike of me and everything about me, making it patently clear that she had been coerced into accepting this relationship, without really accepting it at all in actuality.

"Where are we going to stay?" she asked in Arabic and in an arrogant tone, clearly insinuating that she was distancing herself.

"At a hotel!" Sami responded all but spontaneously.

He had reserved two rooms at the Meridien, in order to ensure a comfortable and luxurious holiday for the "Princess of Riyadh."

I stayed there myself most of the time, which was apparently putting a serious damper on their plans, whatever they were; and Sami, who was supposedly fervently committed to me and a paragon of loyalty, began to give me a hard time in an attempt to destroy my morale. I was being trained in obedience and in the proper way to behave according to the status quo of his fatherland, seeing as, in his mind, everything I had been taught thus far was wrong and did not correspond to his understanding of a woman's nature and to what was expected from a woman in Saudi Arabia. Little by little, I was being taught to stifle my thoughts and not to take almost any initiative at all. My "training" was performed on a daily basis and with various methods of instruction, and usually his mother was pointed out to me as the perfect example for me to imitate.

The Western paradigm was the most abhorrent of all to them as to the standing of women. Nevertheless, this did not stop them from going out to numerous upscale Athens restaurants to entertain "Mama," who was happy to take a short break from her confined lifestyle in Saudi Arabia and briefly becoming more Western than the Westerners themselves in some ways.

The day of our engagement provided a wonderful opportunity for Sami to give the performance of his life so as not to disappoint Enaam. The "poor" woman had gone to great lengths to break us up. Never could she have imagined after my dismissal from the company—her doing, too—that she would have to one day follow her son all the way to Greece for our engagement. The deal was sealed with a jewelry box filled with jewels; and "Mama" Enaam simply let her little boy play a little longer—for now...

Besides, what was it to them to squander a few more dollars in order to spend a lovely night under the moon of

Greece? Things are so easy and simple when it comes to a foreign woman, and one with a different faith at that. Everything is over and done in the blink of an eye.

After an enchanting evening of dining at the Asteras Hotel and Club on the beachfront of Vouliagmeni—a renowned resort town on the west coast of Athens—we continued our vacation on the island of Mykonos. It was a place that Enaam could never have imagined existed. The only words she kept repeating over and over again were, "Oh, it's just like Lebanon!" Being Lebanese herself, she used her homeland as the point of reference against which every other place was measured—and never quite measured up. The air of freedom on the island became her, despite her "high-principled" Muslim morals. Still, she also knew how to uphold her country's customs as to the dress code, for example, by wearing an ankle-length dress, albeit with a plunging neckline, coupled with multi-colored scarves covering her head.

After a seven-day stay in Mykonos, during which both Sami and Enaam had seriously let their hair down, our holidays were coming to an end. We went back to the mainland where we were to spend the last few remaining days at a beachfront hotel in Vouliagmeni; only those days were marked by some quite unusual events.

We were staying at the top-floor penthouse of the hotel and would spend endless hours taking in the view and the August moon painting its trail on the Mediterranean Sea. My mother was with us, too.

During the last few nights we spent there, my mother and I picked up on some distancing, secrecy and seclusion on the part of both Sami and Enaam. This made me quite concerned, giving rise to several unpleasant thoughts and questions inside my head, which, however, were left unanswered. The two of them would stay together in Enaam's room with the lights out for quite some time and around 2 am he would come out on the terrace, followed by a silent Enaam shortly thereafter.

"You know, we were just talking about my Uncle Ali," was the excuse Sami gave reluctantly in response to my mother's intense, stern gaze calling on him to explain himself. Of course, she didn't believe a word he said. On another evening, when my mother and I were strolling along the veranda, Sami suddenly darted out of Enaam's room into the quiet of the night and walked straight up to me. He stared right into my eyes with a frenzied glare and said, "What do you think you're doing?" The next morning, they would simply put on their usual masks and act as if nothing had happened.

The time came when they would be leaving to return to Saudi Arabia. It was the 10th of September and everything was arranged for them to leave that very afternoon. With mixed feelings of sorrow and rage, I was seeing off the man who was inflicting upon my life a 180-degree turn for the worse. Enaam, on the other hand, was floating on a cloud of joy. Not only was she about to leave Greece, which meant nothing whatsoever to her, but she would finally be free to put into action her diabolical scheme towards my annihilation. Her sardonic smirk foreshadowed her future actions.

As for Sami, he could finally rest assured: the two months' grace period after resignation, within which we were allowed to change our minds, had expired in my case and he could finally be certain that I would not be returning to Saudia—although the company had made numerous phone calls during that time, asking for me and encouraging me to return. The "love-stricken" Sami was triumphantly departing for Jeddah.

"I'll be back next month. Now I have to pull some strings and use all the people in high places that I know to get you a special entry permit for Saudi Arabia."

We had agreed that we would be settling in Jeddah, because that was where Saudia pilots were based in Saudi Arabia. I was not to disrupt his career, even though he had done with mine as he pleased. As luck would have it, I was forced to follow him there, all the while hoping that someday another pilot base would be established somewhere else, outside Saudi Arabia.

My thoughts about the job I had forfeited, on one hand, and his promises, on the other, made me change my way of life around that time. Hard as I would try to console myself, I couldn't help feeling as though I had lost a big part of my liveliness. I wasn't accustomed to doing nothing; a secret war kept waging inside me that would not leave me a moment of peace. I kept wondering whether it was really worth it to have sacrificed myself and my career for a man who would be filling my empty days, but in a way that stunted my entire being.

Although young and a graduate of an American college, like many more of his fellow countrymen, at times he gave off the impression of a man wearing blinders, as if he were a traditional, socially underdeveloped Arab from some remote village out in the desert. The ever so chivalrous Sami was ever so slowly beginning to show his true colors.

Between September and February of the following year, he took many trips. Either on duty or as a passenger, he would regularly come to Athens so that we could be together.

During these trips, it showed in our eyes we were so happy to be together far from the prying and ever scrutinizing eyes of Enaam. His coming to Athens comforted me; with Saudia no longer an option, I only had Sami left. And when he wasn't near me, he would spend endless hours talking to me on the phone, at times right through the night, until the next morning. The cost was not an issue.

We had already started to furnish and decorate our home, even though I was far away. He would consult me on every issue regarding the rooms and their décor and he would always adopt my suggestions. In this case, there was no need for obedience or blind submission, because most of the items were bought and paid for by me. You see, I was so excited that I wouldn't think twice about spending my money; I had already invested so much emotionally into this relationship. Every time he would return to Jeddah from Greece, he would be loaded with various objects collected by yours truly, ranging from costly pieces to bottom-drawer items bestowed upon me by my mother by way of dowry.

That was how I had always imagined my dream home: a place with personality and finesse, luxurious but unfussy. My ideas always impressed him because all he knew was that the floors should be fitted with carpets and all rooms had to be equipped with air-conditioning units. You see, for all their black gold, their lives are also different in meaning and dimensions. They do not fuss about what goes with what, because they use their money to get others to do the thinking and figure these things out for them. In our case, however, thanks to my ignorance of how things worked in Saudi Arabia, I had taken it upon myself to provide both the ideas and the moneys for outfitting our home. He was absolutely thrilled with my good taste and richness of ideas. I could tell he admired me for everything I chose, designed and showed to him. Saudi women neither know nor bother to busy themselves with such matters, leaving all pertinent decisions up to the man. In Saudi Arabia it is the man's duty and dowry to his bride-to-be to fully outfit the household that will house his future wife.

As an educated woman, raised in the West, I was so much more than he had come to expect as a Saudi—perhaps too much. Like most of his fellow countrymen, Sami, too, had a rather narrow view of women, the only mission of whom was to bear children. My temperament, personality and cultivation came into stark contrast with the Arabic status quo as far as women were concerned and, in his heart of hearts, that disparity upset him.

As time went by relentlessly, I was getting in deeper and deeper. Sami, with all his phone calls and controlling behavior, was keeping tabs on me even from afar. Every so often, I would experience these inner bouts of anger against the Arabic way of life which he was forcing me to follow even while I was in Athens and he was away. Moreover, with time, he decided that I would not be allowed to meet up with him during any of his future European flights; he had placed me in a confinement of sorts, one that was gradually pushing me towards inexistence. I, on the other hand, could not for the life of me think of anything more natural than two people who want to live together wanting to see each other as frequently as possible.

One day, when I had found out about an overnight stay of his in London while on assignment, I made the decision, without asking him or telling him, to go and meet him there. I didn't appreciate his rules of confinement and wasn't in the mood to enter into negotiations with him. I had missed him and wanted to see him, so I decided to follow my heart and pay him a surprise visit.

That morning, I set out to go to London accompanied by my mother. I had arranged to stay at the Sheraton Skyline Hotel, where Saudia crew members usually lodged, and had booked a room adjacent to his. The moment he saw me was truly a moment of joy. I knocked on his door and his eyes met mine with an expression of astonishment and pleasure. He was stunned because he wasn't expecting me. He asked me whether I had come together with my mother and was relieved to see her—evidently, he assumed this provided some sort of assurance.

During the two days we spent there, his behavior was characterized by remarkable ups and downs. He would throw fits of jealousy alternating with spells of indifference, bouts of possessiveness interspersed with displays of love and affection. One morning, when I got dressed and left the room to go down to the hotel lobby and get a newspaper, Sami darted out behind me, yelling and shouting, chased me down the hallway and stopped me dead in my tracks. He grabbed me by my dress and, tugging on it abruptly, he ripped it down the middle in a flash. Flummoxed and speechless, I found myself half-naked in the hotel corridor, mouth wide open. Before I even had a chance to recover from the shock, I immediately felt his strong embrace around me, as he started to affectionately explain to me just how profoundly he cared for me. I was absolutely thunderstruck by that unprecedented behavior.

Still baffled, I got back to the room where he duly removed my jacket, only to rip that one apart as well. I searched inside me to come up with some explanation, but I was too overwhelmed by these outbursts and violent reactions. "That's how we are," he would say to me often.

"We are either in love or we aren't. We're hot-blooded, not soft as putty"—"we" being the Saudi men and the "softies" being their European counterparts. *Quite an idiosyncrasy*, I thought to myself. *But, who knows, perhaps that is more genuine, more sincere*—obviously, I was struggling to find consolation in any possible version of an excuse.

I very much wanted to believe that these men were indeed extremely emotional, passionate, knew how to love from the bottom of their heart and did everything they possibly could to win a woman's heart… But that was just my wishful thinking. A mirage. What I thought I saw and heard was a long way from the truth. I was living in a dream that would never come true. That explosive behavior was probably his follow-up routine, after the brainwashing, to make me convert to his way of seeing things, adopt his viewpoint, the only correct, infallible and thoroughly objective viewpoint, according to him. By that time, he had indirectly managed to make me submit to his wishes to a great extent; but deep inside me I was hoarding a mass of unanswered questions.

Since he had formally announced our relationship, Sami was now able to speak more freely and openly. His arrogant efforts to have the upper hand were indescribable! We had only been together for several months, but his true character was coming to light… As I later found out, the people of that region are not particularly trustworthy; their overeagerness to be of service, especially to foreigners, is nothing but a sham!

After the London incident, things appeared to run relatively smoothly during the time leading up to our wedding—if only I had known…

Come December, Sami made one of his routine trips to Athens, which had come to be one of his favorite destinations, bearing the "good news." I had been issued the much-coveted special entry permit to Saudi Arabia, so now I could enter the country legitimately, trouble-free and indisputably. There was a whole rigmarole involved in getting that permit; thus only a few privileged Saudis had obtained it and Sami was one of them. By then, our wedding was a sure thing. We had accomplished a very difficult feat: that very different country would open its gates to me and let me. It was quite the exception, seeing as they would normally keep these gates shut to keep the population as homogenous as possible and, at the same time, adhere to the teachings of their God-breathed Prophet. That way, they succeeded in limiting the number of marriages to foreign women to a minimum.

Thus my lot was drawn! The luck of my misfortune!

The event was marked by an unexpected phone call from "Mama" Enaam, calling from Riyadh to joyously herald, laughter roaring, that the marriage license had been issued at last. Before long, I would be falling prey to, and victim of, her satanic schemes… After failing to distance me from her "habibi," her beloved one, once and for all by forcing me to quit Saudia, she was now taking pleasure in the prospect of having me around to toy with me like a cat toys with the mouse before she finally gnaws it to death.

Sami's ambivalence as to where his loyalty would lie was also becoming more and more evident. He was filled with anxiety and insecurity in view of the tough road ahead that he had chosen to follow. The way he had come up with a solution and implemented it to formalize our relationship, coupled with the various hurdles he had to overcome to make it happen, was evidently consuming a great part of his energy. To make things worse, his subconscious was tainted by his Freudian vestige, his Oedipal complex. When far from Riyadh and from the ever-present supervision of his mother Enaam, he was behaving like a "normal" human being; but whenever he returned to his base, he'd magically transform into his alter ego, one that was docile and obedient to a "Mama" he would never think of betraying. In hindsight, I remember him expressing a strong aversion towards foreign women even while I was still working for Saudia. Something about them (us) irritated him a great deal, but I could not put my finger on it and I was reluctant to wring my mind trying to wrap my head around Sami's beliefs, most probably stemming from the closed, theocratic system prevalent in his home country. Nevertheless, it was quite evident that he had been searching for a substitute to his mother; and that he found it in me! Still, his conflicting views caused him to constantly second-guess his decision: Was he right about me or not? And his repeated references to his mother—"You know, Mama did this" or "Mama said that" or "You look a lot like my Mama"—were attesting to his adoration of, and submission to, her. In effect, his household was governed by a strict, closed matriarchy.

He took two more trips to Athens before our wedding, until finally, on the black-letter 8th day of February, the ceremony was officially performed and duly registered.

I was quite ignorant about Islam and he had done little to fill me in on anything to do with it. The only information I did have had to do with dress code: for example, wearing long gowns because women were not supposed to leave any part of their body exposed to the eye; wearing the extra body covering of the abaya; or wearing the *niqab*, which covered a woman's hair and most of the face, with only an opening for the eyes.

"Why do women have to be so concealed?" I would ask him.

"Because that's how it should be; a woman's beauty is only for the eyes of her husband! Otherwise it is considered a sin," he would reply.

I also knew nothing about the custom stipulating that Saudi grooms provided a dowry to their bride-to-be, paying a "price," in a sense, to "acquire" their future wife, in a land where gold was flowing as did oil. Almost in lieu of a wedding dress, brides would be covered head to toe with traditional hand-crafted jewelry made of pure gold and decorated with precious stones, as these were the traditional wedding presents. In addition, the brides would also receive considerable sums of money, classified in various brackets depending on the social standing of the groom. That, too, was another "must" of the marriage contract, which also stipulated financial reparations payable to the wife in the event of a divorce. A Saudi divorce was issued in the easiest way possible: a single "magical" Arabic word spoken by the husband did the trick. He would say "talak" (i.e., "I divorce you") and, voila, you were back to being unmarried, or rather divorced, with no further official procedures required.

Very skillfully and craftily, parsimonious Sami made sure I knew nothing of all of the above.

Thus came the eighth of February. First thing in the morning, Sami, my mother and I flew out to Komotini, a city in Northern Greece, several hundreds of miles away from Athens, which was the only city with a Mufti's office in Greece at the time. Sami was overtaken by a great deal of anxiety and nervousness, reflected on his behavior throughout our journey to Komotini. Like another Rasputin, he kept everything under wraps to make sure I wouldn't know anything, demand anything or expect anything. It was obvious that my mother's presence was thwarting his plans, but the truth is that was precisely the reason she was there with me: to stand by me as a parent.

An episode that unfolded before and after our visit to the Mufti's office to sign our *nikah*—our marriage contract—threw me completely off. *Is this supposed to be happiness?* I'd think to myself. *Or is this how Saudis understand happiness when they are getting married?*

In the presence of the Mufti, other local Muslim officials and my mother, a very modest wedding ceremony was performed in a language I could not understand. A sine-qua-non precondition demanded of me by Sami right there and then was that I convert to Islam. Up until that point, I honestly thought that we were going to perform the wedding in accordance with the rules and rites of his religion only so that it would be deemed valid in his country. But laying that demand on me at that point in time was nothing short of blackmail: suddenly I was to choose between "both Islam and Sami" or "nothing at all." Saying "yes" with my heart clenched, I was accepting what he was forcing upon me in blatant disregard for my individuality and the intrinsic right that everyone has at freedom of thought. The fact of the matter was that I merely agreed on paper, as it were, only because I had been cornered into a fait accompli situation, without really ever changing my faith.

My mother and I filled with mixed feelings and loads of unanswered questions, we all returned to Athens. Still, one thing was for sure: I had been left in the dark regarding any and all benefits of marriage for the woman. Aptly and swiftly and without any pertinent explanations, our marriage contract had been signed. I had been deceived... I knew nothing about my legal rights, thus all my powers and interests were taken over by Sami in a single swoop. I trusted him blindly so I had no reason to question him.

Thrilled at his interim achievement, he started pushing me to set a date for our wedding reception. So, on the 5th of March, we were to hold a gala reception at Asteras Hotel and Club of Vouliagmeni, hosting guests like non less than the Ambassador of Saudi Arabia to Greece.

Despite all the glitz and glitter and the formal character of the reception, inside I was torn about whether I was doing the right thing taking this big step or not. And my second thoughts, stemming from Sami himself, kept on intensifying. I was feeling so worn out! I kept having doubts, something kept holding me back. Perhaps it was my uncertainty of the unknown; perhaps it was my insecurity and lack of reassurance about the new role I was being expected to assume. Either way, Sami's grandiose plans for our immediate future together did not make me jump for joy; instead, I was feeling wary, troubled. Going from leading an active life to indolence, from leading a creative life to stagnation, putting all my energy on hold for months at a time without any means of release; all this left me in a void and sank me into an ever-progressing state of depression... I had failed to trust my instinct.

It was almost time now; the reception was due to begin at 7:30 pm and I was ready to make my way to Asteras. "It will give us great pleasure to have the honor of your presence at our wedding reception..." Nervousness, cold sweat, stress and joy, all wrapped together described my state as my brother drove me to the hotel. I tried to stifle my feelings of anxiety by absent mindedly looking around out the car window, left and right, all the way until we arrived.

"Did you get cold feet?" my brother's voice brought me back from my reverie. "If you've changed your mind, I can turn this car around in an instant."

"No, that won't be necessary," I said to him, smiling. I had made the big decision—*hope springs eternal in the human breast*. Deep inside, I was still yearning and searching for my happiness; no one could take away my hopes and desires that made me view life always with a glow of optimism.

The car stayed on course and we were approaching the hotel. Although March, it was quite cold and the wintery weather was dragging us down. We finally arrived, although much later than we were expected.

"Everyone's waiting for you!" exclaimed the doorman, rather relieved.

I found Sami pacing up and down, anxiety painted all over his face, along with a look of fear that I might have changed my mind and decided not to show up. After all, he had been expecting us for two whole hours!

So, there I was, taking the greatest step of my life!

I shall never forget the look of joy in the beaming faces of all the people we had invited, all those who cared for me. As for me, well, I was a nervous and emotional wreck and it showed. Sami's unnatural, erratic ups and downs had taken their toll on me. There was too much love and passion mixed with too much impudence and mental instability for my taste. So, which one was it? One or the other? Or all of it together? My doubts kept on eating at me…

"Mama" Enaam, naturally present at the "joyous occasion", was laying low. Like a cold-blooded hunter, she was hiding at her stand, watching on, all the while waiting for exactly the right moment to pounce and unleash her annihilating plot against me.

For all our guests, the evening was a case of "champagne wishes and caviar dreams," but for me it was the beginning of my ordeal. The event setting was exquisite, featuring a lovely décor of white and pink roses and a soft background music filling the air with melodious charm. There was happiness all around; yet, I kept picturing myself walking barefoot and torn apart on a bed of thorns. What I saw around me was like a dream I wished would never end; yet, I couldn't feel it with any of my other senses. Like the tormented Tantalus, food and water eluding his grasp, I could see the dreamlike surroundings and yet they felt out of reach. I was swirling through these unprecedented moments of my life as if in a daze, intoxicated by a blend of love and uncertainty. My snow-white bridal gown, painstakingly selected from a Parisian fashion house, gave me great comfort! My white crocodile leather pumps made me feel like a modern-day Cinderella—a month before the event, Sami had my specially made bridal shoes picked up from the Maud Frizon fashion house in Paris. And his wedding present to me was a jewelry case filled with glittering jewels...

But my "Prince" failed to give me our first dance. He had left me alone, opting to give his undivided attention to the groom's side of the wedding party. Which was only natural, seeing as he could not fend off his mother's pressure.

I felt Enaam's persistent gaze piercing through me, a profoundly unsettling sensation. I could sense the brunt of her hatred and jealousy in all their grandeur! She was sitting at a distance from me, at the table reserved for the Saudi Arabian guests. She was wearing a midnight blue evening dress with gold embroidering, her elegantly styled hair highlighted by the gold-stitched headscarf covering the greatest part of her head, her outfit complemented by gold and pearls. Still, she looked quite upset, as if the wedding was a terribly unpleasant event. She wouldn't speak nor smile; she would just dart me, from time to time, with fiery looks of envy.

"Are you happy?" were the only words she spoke to me the whole evening, muttered through clenched teeth, her face devoid of expression. We had nothing to bring us together, everything pushed us apart; but we did have one thing in common. Sami stood firmly by her side, as if to console her. His neglect of me was so obvious that it gave rise to murmurs among our guests.

The band was playing nonstop contemporary tunes and my mother hadn't come off the dance floor for a minute. She was doing her best to release her bottled-up energy in that way; concerned about me, she was trying to turn a blind eye and play down everything that was going on around us. There was too much mystery, too much going on behind the scenes. And once again, I couldn't help but wonder: *What am I getting myself into?*

The lights went out and our guests departed after an unforgettable evening. The reception was over…

We spent the next couple of days at Asteras, a brief stay packed with peculiar outbursts of emotion and passion. Then, after a few more days, we took off to a most unusual honeymoon trip riddled with doubts. I was astounded to find out that, instead of taking us to some exotic islands (which he saved for later), Sami had opted to take us to Paris, a city he hated but knew that I loved. But now, under the circumstances, even Paris, the city I once adored, meant nothing special to me anymore. Besides, it hadn't been that long since I was there the last time.

It was a mid-day in March, the sun was shining and we were setting out on an Air France flight to Paris. But even though this was our honeymoon, we weren't travelling alone. Sami had invited my mother and my aunt to come along with us!

My aunt spoke very highly of Sami, even paying compliments directly to him; and Sami had a need for such a person in his court of jesters to assert his narcissism and self-absorption, which, in reality, were the façade of his deep-seated insecurities and taboos. My aunt was especially fond of him, simply because he knew how to get older people to like him and get on their good side. In front of her, he would put on his best act, while at the same time downplaying my positive traits and hinting at my character flaws.

"Sami is a very nice person and a handsome young man," she would keep saying like a mantra, expressing her utmost admiration of him and making him out to be a much-coveted Prince Charming who had everything going for him: he was dark-skinned and good-looking, young and charming, and a well-off pilot hailing from the land of black gold. Sami would bask in all her praises, flashing a broad smile, overflowing with self-satisfaction. And that was why my aunt wholeheartedly agreed to join us on this trip of trials and tribulations. Throughout the flight, she did not stop fussing over Sami and expressing to him her adoration, not even for one moment. The way she had put him on a pedestal, exalting him all the time, was absolutely outrageous! Our honeymoon was off to a bad start, and I made no effort to hide my discontent.

It was dusk by the time we landed in springtime Paris. We all had long faces, rather agitated, and the whole atmosphere was so tense that it was difficult to believe we were just starting our honeymoon. My aunt's presence was getting more and more unpleasant and the way she continued to lavish her attention on Sami helped drive the first wedge between him and me.

Despair, anger and rage were my predominant emotions throughout the week of our stay there. It was as if the City of Light was experiencing a widespread blackout, new grave questions constantly springing up in the pitch darkness of my mind. My "Prince Charming" was constantly making trouble for me, keeping me on my toes, inciting my fight-or-flight instincts. Every time we would go out to a restaurant or bistro, he would put up an utterly embarrassing scene aiming to humiliate and belittle me as a person just because he knew I had a special bond with France.

On one such occasion, we had just been seated at a Lebanese restaurant, somewhere in the Latin Quarter. No sooner had we given our order to the waiter than the cozy hall was shaken to the roots by the roar of his rough, brazen voice. The patrons around us, although evidently Middle Eastern themselves, were startled and turned to look in our direction. They saw me crying and, before I had a chance to pull myself together, a blonde lady from another party approached me saying, "Don't cry! You have such lovely eyes," in a tone that seemed partly meant to console me and partly to reprimand Sami. Unperturbed and unashamed of his actions, the once ever so affectionate Sami had uncovered the monster lurking inside him. *The human soul is an abyss…*

The days of our honeymoon were like wading through a nightmare and the magical nights in Paris had turned into a thriller of Hitchcockian proportions. My carefree days of the past, when I was still free as a bird, were clashing with my present state, that of a woman ebbing on a life of torment.

During the day I would go shopping on my own dime—Sami was happy to see me spend my money to depletion—and, in the end, he would tear apart most of the things I had bought.

One afternoon, I made my way back to the Meriden, where we were staying, after shopping on Rue Bonaparte. I was very happy with the pieces I had bought and he uttered a few words of praise for my purchases. But as we started to get ready to go out for the evening, Sami caused a major scene out of the blue, during which he ruined my brand new clothes.

"Never mind, I'll get you new ones," he would say afterwards to calm me down.

Every moment gone by was encrusted in a coating of frantic love mixed together with hatred and emotional coercion. The brief intervals of happiness dotting my perpetual misery had helped me not to lose all faith and loosely hope for better days to come. Nevertheless, his repeated mood swings, his maleficent, almost criminal, attacks, which might have been indicative of fear coupled with an over-exaggerated, superficial love of sorts, had me feeling as if I were floating in a vast void.

The comforts of the Meridien did not sufficiently cater to Sami's tastes, so it was decided that we would move to another hotel.

Paris, Sheraton Hotel, on the fourth day of our stay there. After going out for the evening, my nightcap was to be a whole new kind of torture. That night in the hotel room, after fighting with me over an insignificant matter, he savagely grabbed me and pinned me to halt, holding his hand over my nose and mouth so that I couldn't breathe, until I came within a hair's breadth from asphyxiating to death. My nose and mouth covered and my hands immobilized in a lock hold, I was quickly running out of air. My eyes were desperately pleading for mercy as they filled with tears. I do not quite know exactly how and when my torturer dragged me semi-unconscious to the bathroom to splash some water on me. Completely engulfed by his primeval aggression, he had forgotten that my mother and aunt occupied the room next door and would most probably come looking for me. But it eventually dawned on him; and the perpetrator decided to save his own neck. Overcome by the cruel instincts of his misanthropic daze, he had forgotten that this wasn't Saudi Arabia, where things are done so very differently and due processes protect and favor the Saudi man over his wife, all the more so if she happens to be foreigner.

It took a full twenty-four hours of recovery time in the room before I could pick myself up; and it was largely thanks to my guardian angel, my Mother, that I managed to replenish my depleted strength and restore my broken morale. I couldn't find any fitting words to describe to my mother exactly what had happened, while at the same time Sami resumed his role as a paragon of virtue for yet another day. I couldn't for the life of me understand what was happening to me and why I was powerless to fight back; it was as if he had hypnotized me.

And with these frightful and poignant experiences of a "love story" in Paris, our honeymoon was over and we were once again en route back to Athens. So much for my journey to seventh heaven on the wings of love and blissful happiness! In effect, I was an emotional wreck, teetering in limbo, waned by the unprecedented situation I was experiencing, but determined to see this "match" through with all the strength that I had left. It would be an all-out showdown…

CHAPTER FOUR

INTRIGUES – SINISTER CONSPIRACIES

Serious doubts and questions kept eating at me: *Whatever had happened to my career? Whatever had happened to my personal aspirations? Whatever had happened to the happiness I once felt? And why on earth was this wretched man so very jealous of me to want to break me and plunge me into the depths of misery?*

I protracted my stay in Athens for as long as I possibly could—a feeling of foreboding deep inside was keeping me there.

"Well, I for one am leaving," said Sami as soon as we got back from Paris. "I can't wait any longer." Apparently, he had been ordered to do so by Enaam, who had already left Athens and had made sure to stop by Jeddah and check up on our future home on her way to Riyadh. She wanted to be the first to do some "housewarming" of her own special kind. "Come along if you like," Sami's peculiar "invite" echoed in my ears; the whole marriage fiesta was apparently over for him.

On Thursday, he flew on a Saudia plane back to Jeddah. I followed suit three days later, accompanied by my mother who had been specially granted an entry visa by the Saudi Arabian Ambassador, seeing as that country does not welcome visitors even under such exceptional circumstances. The Ambassador had been reluctant to issue her a visa, but he had family ties with Sami and did not want to risk a falling out of favor with him. Sami, on the other hand, was not so thrilled about that special treatment; he'd rather have me there alone to do with me as he pleased.

When we arrived at King Abdulaziz airport, Sami was waiting for us with a broad grin on his face, quite foretelling of his future intentions. He had a sparkling new sports car, one of the latest models, in which he gave us a quick tour around Jeddah before taking us to our final destination: the second-floor apartment at number 38 of Knuz Al Elm Street. I had stayed there before while still an air hostess, but in the meantime he had taken very good care of the place, decorating it with *my* personal items. As already mentioned, standard Saudi custom stipulates that it is the groom's responsibility to provide everything in a household, but my non-Arabic descent had allowed Sami to quite conveniently bypass these rules and provide none of the comforts amply and inviolably enjoyed by local newlywed women. For me, there was no chauffeur and no third-world-imported maids. Instead, I was entering a house of anguish, which I had inadvertently helped outfit to a tee, even though from a distance. And to make things worse, Sami's first order of business was to make sure that there was no telephone in the apartment so that I would be cut off from any and all communication with the outside world. Everything was progressing according to the Enaam-Sami plan.

The house of horrors was ready: fitted carpets, tapestries imported from Greece, curtains in splendid pastel colors, bought by me while I was in Paris, all carefully selected to harmoniously blend in with our home's overall character and infuse it with a breath of paradise. All elements merged to create a sense of harmony—which clearly clashed with the spirit of the house's owner. Painting or any of the fine arts meant absolutely nothing to Sami, so several paintings on the walls, including one by a famous Greek painter, belonged to me, as did several oil paintings and heirlooms that used to belong to my father and now lay scattered around the house. Paired with Italian cast-bronze mirrors and crystal chandeliers, all these elements donned our home with a sense of luxury that seemed out of step with that particular time and space. I aspired to bring an air of culture to the house, enriching it with beautiful artistic specimens from the West and the rest of the world. But alas, I had made the wrong choice of a mate and such strokes of sensitivity would go entirely unnoticed. And as for our bedroom, its decoration in pastels of sky blue and chaste white did not manage to endow it with the tranquility I was hoping for. That room was to become my torture chamber, the altar where I was to be daily sacrificed in the name of who knows what god…

The first few days following my arrival in Jeddah went by in an atmosphere of suspicion and intrigue. Meanwhile, the preparations for our second wedding reception, this one in Riyadh, were well underway.

"Get dressed! Mohammed's sister is on her way here to meet you," Sami announced to me one afternoon, a few days before we left to go to Riyadh. Mohammed was a man of Palestinian descent and a childhood friend of Sami's, who lived in the apartment across the hall from ours. On the surface, there appeared to be a brotherly friendship between

Sami and Mohammed, but in actuality they turned out to be frenemies.

I got ready and waited to receive our guest, albeit with some reservations, because that would be the first time that I would be receiving a woman from the Orient and I knew how curious they would get when it came to western women due to their own confines and influence of Islam. To my great surprise and chagrin, the moment the fully shrouded—save her face—woman stepped into our home, she darted around an exceptionally malevolent glare, seething with unbridled envy, and then proceeded to command Sami in Arabic to drive her to some other part of Jeddah. Utterly taken aback by that woman's appearance and rude behavior, I refrained from responding in the proper manner, seeing as I wasn't very familiar with the must's and must-not's of that society yet. It was quite obvious that hers wasn't a housewarming visit; she wasn't there to meet me and wish me well, but rather to flaunt her contempt because I was a foreigner.

In addition, I could not help being baffled by her "indecent proposal" to Sami, since I knew that Saudi women were strictly forbidden to be accompanied by men other than a first-degree relative, such as a brother or a husband. Hesitantly and guilt-ridden, Sami floundered, then turned towards me and asked me, "Are you coming along?"—although it sounded less like a question and more like a command, as if the master was conveying the mistress's orders to the maid. Although extremely upset by that whole vulgarity, I did go along. Throughout the ride, that "righteous" Muslim woman did not stop speaking heatedly in Arabic, taking full advantage of the fact that I did not understand their language. It wasn't until Sami asked her to, as also dictated by common courtesy, that she began to speak in English and did so until she got out of the car.

Teeming with a pile of questions about what had just taken place before my very eyes, I asked Sami to explain that whole incident to me—although one need not be a genius or an Arabic expert to figure out the gist of the matter. Sami, of course, had all the answers and excuses necessary, taking her side and making me out to be some paranoid, unreasonable foreign woman who just did not understand.

Ebtisam—that was Mohammed's sister's name—came to our place again the following day. That exceptionally brazen woman was ignoring Muslim etiquette for the second time in a row, seeing as Sami was at home with me and women were not to socialize with men in any way or setting whatsoever. In this case, however, the rules were being bent, to say the least. What was to be my story and my show was being played out before my eyes, on the stage of my own home, with others taking the lead and me being an extra.

"You sit down here with your mother and I'm going to make you some tea," rude and wily Ebtisam commanded me, acting as if she were the hostess at my home, solely to have an opportunity to be alone with Sami. Their rendezvous was in the kitchen. Her head uncovered and her hair bouncing about freely, she graciously moved about the kitchen, her motions uninhibited by her loose robe. She was pretending to be a modernized Arabian woman with contemporary views, when, in fact, she was no more than a wretched soul imprisoned in a rigid status quo.

That whole episode wasn't going down well with me, but I gave it some time before I could confirm my suspicions. As she went into the kitchen, I was abandoned in the sitting room, turning a blind eye to the obscurity cast by such backstage events and waiting to see what would happen next. Supposedly unintentionally together in the kitchen, Ebtisam and Sami proceeded to prepare our tea, while free to deliberate amongst them under a shroud of secrecy, but also making sure to raise their voices at some point to convince the unsuspecting bystanders that there was nothing iffy going on.

I wondered if she really thought I was that foolish! More likely perhaps, it was she who was foolish enough to underestimate my intelligence! It was all so crystal clear! She had made the journey from Riyadh to Jeddah, allegedly in order to meet me, and she had made it in such a rush, as if she was somehow running out of time. Her mind was working in devious ways and she was trying to inflict harm upon me in whichever way she could, so long as she could hurt me spiritually and emotionally. What a woman!

The next evening, there she was again! Our doorbell rang and when I opened the door I saw her standing on our doorstep, holding the telephone from her brother's apartment—cable trailing behind her, as this was his landline—one end pressed against her ear as she spoke English into the other end. Without greeting me, she pranced in and plunked herself firmly onto our sofa. She knew her way around our place very well, as she had made subtle a point of insinuating to me the day before.

As soon as Sami became aware of her presence, he made his grand appearance and lashed out at me beside himself with anger.

"Who is she talking to on the phone? Tell me!"

"How should I know? And what business is it of yours?" I answered him despondently.

"Seriously, I want to know!" Sami retorted, sweating profusely in anguish as she continued her act of vengeance, smirking with deep satisfaction. And in that moment I started to get a whiff of the behind-the-scenes backdrop: that of an unofficial harem!

Over the next few hours, I asked Sami to explain to me what was going on with that mysterious woman and what role she played in his life, but to no avail. His beating-around-the-bush responses were all about how I didn't understand and knew nothing yet about their ideal, angelic world, governed by their high respect for laws and morals.

"Stop thinking so much. You are only bringing problems unto yourself." Those were his "wise words" to me. That was what I was supposed to do: step onto the stage of that theatre of the absurd and play along; embrace that insanity in order to preserve my sanity.

"Ebtisam is a nice person and all she wanted to do was welcome you here," Sami continued his sermon, trying to calm me down.

"Why are *you* so interested to find out whom she is talking to on the phone?" I asked him anxiously, to receive the million-dollar answer:

"I simply don't allow anyone to talk on the phone from my house!"

That was his attempt to shut me up and clip my wings once and for all.

The following day was crucial. Brimming with anger and rage, Ebtisam pounded on our door to deliver her final performance. It was time for a face-off! Totally out of control, her face flushed full of fury and hatred, she stood at the open door and hurled a barrage of insults at me in Arabic. Calmly defiant, I chose to ignore her and simply tell her from afar that I would have no more of such visits and that she ought to show some respect and abide by the rules of common courtesy and decency applicable to all people.

She continued to scream and shout on my doorstep, while my mother watched on, unable to intervene—the significant language barrier made it difficult for her to understand exactly what that woman's problem was. As for Sami, he just stood next to Ebtisam, embarrassed, speechless and befuddled by that turn of events.

"She's not a good woman!" Ebtisam cried in frenzy, the veins on her face gorged by her hatred for me.

Remaining calm himself, Sami tried to appease her with a few words in their language. I didn't understand what he told her, but one thing was for sure: He had made no effort to take my side and defend me. He had not acted in the way that would be expected of him. A Saudi woman would have never dared create such a scandalous uproar against a man's wife, especially not in front of him. I had done nothing wrong and did not deserve to be subjected to such degradation and attrition as soon as I set foot there as Sami's legitimate wife. The only thing that she could hold against me was that I was a foreign woman and had nothing in common with them, either culturally or religiously. I had not gone there with any intentions of displaying arrogance or uphold any notions of racial supremacy; quite the contrary, I was always keen to listen and to be heard. But I was being combated from all sides. My only ally and the first to throw herself into the battle for me would be my mother. The danger was clear and present and the war was waging on all fronts.

Ebtisam left with a threatening look on her face, meant to warn Sami of more to come, while I watched on without getting directly involved. My apathy and disdain dealt her the final blow. After her mission ended, she returned to Riyadh.

The situation at home was in a state of turmoil continued for several days, during which I had to endure the outbursts of an irrational man demanding explanations from me when the true wrongdoer and culprit was he himself. Ebtisam's brother, Mohammed, detached and playing his part in a dispassionate way, was providing several groundless justifications for her behavior: "Don't make anything of it," he would say. "Ebtisam is twenty-five years old and still not married. She is seeing a doctor for her nerves." His condescending attitude was his way of striving for atonement, seeing as this had been quite a serious episode by their standards, bearing grave repercussions for both of them had I ever reported it to the police. I, however, was a newcomer in Saudi Arabia and utterly clueless in all things pertaining to family life and my personal rights. The home team was trying to make me let down my defenses. I had to be subdued!

But I was neither born into subservience nor brought up in an environment that fosters it. With my roots firmly grounded in my heritage of classical Greek democratic ideals and my spirit further cultivated in the liberal culture of France, I was standing my ground unshakably and resolutely.

Such was the festive welcome I experienced during my first few days in my new home. Saudi Arabia had opened wide her embrace to receive me—that was what the Saudi Ambassador had said when giving me the entry permit. But the reality I was living was a slightly different one…

Sami took care of all his final preparations before the reception. He took us out to have a look around the Souk, I myself wrapped in an abaya and a chador—it was my first time in proper Arabic attire. It felt rather strange, but I had to accept it; besides, I was accustomed to that image since the previous time I had lived in Saudi Arabia, while working with the airline.

A stroll downtown... The spectacular multitude of fancy jewelry shops were quite the pick-me-up I needed! Mesmerized, my mother and I impulsively walked into one. Sami, the big spender, promptly disappeared, leaving mother and me to do our shopping alone, so that he wouldn't have to partake of any relevant expenses—contrary to what would be expected of a groom. When we met up again, he simply gave us a brief glance and we made our way back home without a word. Where was the supposedly openhanded Sami, when he chose to feign indifference at that crucial juncture of our wedding? "My family will shower you with gifts," was one of the lines he had used to woo me back when I was still my other self, the one that was striding through life with self-confidence. But as it turned out, I never received any gift whatsoever from his family.

"We have to hurry up," he said. "Everyone is waiting for us in Riyadh for the wedding reception." He was talking about my second rite of passage, which was to be performed in front of an all-female Arabic audience...

Part two of their plan had been set in motion. "Mama" of Riyadh was busy orchestrating the upcoming nuptial ceremony.

It was April now and some sweet spring days were infusing me with a breath of optimism. I wanted so much for my dreams to come true, as I had sacrificed my career and the better part of my life for them. That Tuesday night all three of us—Sami, my mother and I—headed out to the airport of Jeddah to catch our flight to Riyadh. And just as we were ready to board the plane, Sami surprised us once again: my mother and I were to travel alone; he had to stay back because he had presumably forgotten to take with him my wedding attire, the same bridal gown that I had brought with me from Athens.

It all seemed very odd to me and yet I refused to believe that this had been a deliberate omission on his part, just so he would buy enough time to board the next flight. Either way, my mother and I boarded the airplane on our own, unaccompanied and anxious about the unknown setting we would face once in Riyadh; surely, the strange, frigid way in which we were seen off did not bode well at all for the way we would be received.

Not long before the airplane landed in Riyadh, I was beset by excruciating abdominal pains that made me lose my color. I was hurting and sweating, so much so that I completely ignored the seatbelt signs that were on, released the buckle on my seatbelt and ran towards the lavatories. The cabin attendant, in state of panic, tried to stop me but to no avail. Once in the lavatory, I felt so weak I almost fainted; yet, I managed to pull myself together as if I had been touched by a magic wand. There was no rational explanation to my sudden illness, but my arrival had been marked by it!

The "welcoming" party waiting to pick us up from the airport consisted of Sami's "Mama," his brother Waleed and a maid. In complete absence of any fanfare or display of affection, we simply and quietly got into the car and drove along wide, long avenues lined with palm trees on both sides, until we arrived at the house.

Once again, I was standing before that great gate and those high walls, safely keeping all the house's secrets inside. The front door opened and a jolly maid met us at the entrance and picked up our luggage. Inside, Abu Sami, dressed in his long white thobe, was pacing around nervously, as if he knew…

Making a half attempt to welcome us, he greeted us hurriedly and awkwardly.

"Take a seat," he told my mother as he showed her to an armchair.

Completely unsuspecting, my mother made to sit down and—thud!—she fell flat on her back. The armchair was broken and gave way under my mother's weight. Enaam burst out laughing profanely, which made me feel utter disgust at her deplorable behavior.

"Would you like to see a doctor?" Abu Sami immediately offered.

It took my mother some time to recover from the shock, the second one she was incurring in such a short period of time—the first one being Sami's leaving us at the airport to fly alone—but Enaam was in a hurry to quickly usher us into the dining room. The tension in the air so thick you could cut it with a knife, we walked into the dinner hall to find the "sumptuous feast" that had been prepared for us was made up of a soggy salad and an indeterminate dish for a main course. I felt sick to my stomach simply looking at them, while in my mind I could hear Sami's voice telling me back in Jeddah, "My mother has cooked a load of food for you."

"When is Sami coming?" I eventually asked Enaam, seeing as it was getting late and there did not seem to be any mention of his arrival. I received no concrete response to my question and that made me ever more anxious and more suspicious. Meanwhile, her sideways glances and deflection tactics had reached new peaks. There was no doubt in my mind she was trying to hoodwink me…

It was well past midnight and I was utterly exhausted by a long and eventful day, but the unexplained would keep me alert. Something was definitely wrong here. Using hand gestures and a few Arabic words, Enaam signaled us to follow her to the private rooms—the rooms where the synthesis of imagination and mystique would come to a climax.

The house was big and labyrinthine, featuring several bathrooms and bedrooms and separate spaces for men and women. Enaam's kingdom was on the lower floor, her "royal quarters" enjoying a great deal of privacy. She did not share rooms with either her husband, who occupied the upper floor, nor any other member of her family. And whenever Sami was in Riyadh, he would spend endless hours in his mother's quarters; he was her obedient servant who would never dream of disappointing her.

When she had shown us to the room we would be staying upstairs, she handed us two nightgowns. "Here," she snapped. The tour was over—but the night would be a long one.

The questions grew louder inside my head: *Why in heaven's name was I being asked to spend the night with my mother? Why would I get no answer whenever I asked about the time that Sami was expected to arrive home? Why had he gotten rid of my mother and me in such a way at the Jeddah airport in the first place?*

My mother and I were unable to fall asleep. I was riddled with anxiety, kindled by Enaam's cunning maneuvers. And suddenly it occurred to me that these sleeping arrangements were quite deliberate indeed: I was to spend the night with my mother and Sami was to spend his with Enaam. The code of silence was to be respected, the hierarchy to be upheld.

My mother and I looked at each other for a few moments. Oh no, I would not just sit there and take this. Nothing and no one had the power to disarm me. I had to react. Enaam's intimidation and fear could only work on weak-hearted women, perhaps the suppressed women of that country and understandably so. But I was neither born nor raised in a culture of pietism.

Undaunted and emotionally charged because I felt betrayed, I was bracing myself to face the impending storm. My mother's love and support gave me strength and courage, her presence near me was decisive in those difficult moments of my emotional, spiritual and moral trial. It was as if time had stood still and space was closing in on me; the air was so filled with that woman's ploys that I was suffocating. No, we could not let down our guard. Both my mother and I stayed put, fully clothed, waiting for the next scene, that of Sami's secret arrival, to play itself out.

From two o'clock in the morning onwards I kept on opening the door of my room and then tiptoeing down the carpeted hallway, all the way to its other end, a vantage point that gave me overview of the house's main entrance, Sami's way in when he would arrive. There was dead silence all around; everybody appeared to be closed up in his or her rooms sleeping soundly. Yet, I had a feeling that my mother and I were not the only ones who were awake; I was pretty sure Enaam, too, was burning the midnight oil, secluded in her private quarters.

At quarter to five, the day was already dawning and nothing had changed; suspense had reached its pinnacle. Thinking I heard something, I once again ran down the hallway to get to the point overlooking the main entrance. Sami had just arrived. Having waited up all the while, Enaam was there, like a misplaced loyal Penelope, waiting to smother him in her embrace. She was claiming him as hers forever!

"Welcome home," she said and he responded to her warm welcome in a tender tone of voice, while the sound of their kissing reached my ears. I didn't actually see it—at that point, the staircase was obstructing my view—but I heard it with my own ears! There was no doubt about it! Enaam had it all planned out and Sami was in on it; that was why she had arranged to get rid of my mother and me as early as possible.

"Sami!" I called out from upstairs in a colorless voice, trying to conceal my feelings of anger and wrath, feelings that any normal person in my shoes would have had at such a moment.

"Yes!" he snapped back in a rage.

I ran back to my room extremely upset and told my mother what had just happened. In a matter of seconds Sami had come up the stairs and burst into the room. To this day I still recall that look of extreme rage in his eyes, as if he was quite prepared to tear me apart, limb from limb! I had messed up their plan. My unexpected interference had botched their scheme in which they had both invested so much! And what a scheme indeed! The forgotten bridal dress, the change of flight plans and all the other pieces of the puzzle I had been trying to put together for so long were now finally falling into place. Their scheme had been commendable, their plot superb; but they had failed to factor in my part: sharp wit conquers evil!

"What's your problem?" Sami shouted at me.

"These nightgowns," I said, holding up the garments his mother had given us earlier. "We won't need them! Early in the morning, we will be taking the first flight out to Jeddah, where I'm going to pack my things. As for the wedding reception, you can do it on your own!"

"Fine," he said and rushed back downstairs. But my reply had marked a turning point in Sami and Enaam's stance.

Before long, Enaam appeared in my room, a guilt-ridden expression on her face. She didn't say much, but for the first time she was recoiling, obviously trying to calm me down and make me change my mind. Of course, she wasn't providing any explanations or excuses, but she wanted to contain the damage, put a lid on the matter right there and then, for otherwise her fate would be at stake. No doubt about it.

Although still with a look of loathe, she was nevertheless backing off. Sami joined in and the both of them argued it was all a misunderstanding, fear visible on their faces. Of course they wouldn't admit to their unholy affair, but they wanted to at least make sure that none of the other family members would get a whiff of the scandal.

That was the warm welcome Riyadh had in store for me. That was the ocean of unspoken joy sprawling at my feet. After a long day followed by a longer night, we finally surrendered to a sleep of exhaustion.

The next day found us waking up sad in that hostile environment. My mother and I were rattled by the whole situation, and yet we were willing to give it the benefit of the doubt. Perhaps it had all been a big misunderstanding… And perhaps that hostility would prove short-lived…

It was already noon and the family was back to normal day-to-day life. There was no evidence of how flimsy the peaceful atmosphere really was. The strained attempts at false smiles were once again the rule of the day; nothing happened by chance, nor was anything even remotely spontaneous.

Sami, in a state of emotional turmoil, was trying his best to hide his feelings behind a superficial expression of sobriety. Meanwhile Enaam was making every effort to portray herself as a paragon of hospitality and as the worthiest of mothers.

On that day I met Mona, the wife of Ahmed, the oldest of Sami's younger brothers. They also lived in that same house with their two children, who were still infants. Mona was petite, short and slim, with strikingly big eyes. She was shrouded from head to toe even in front of her father-in-law. She professed that doing anything else would constitute committing a sin and that her husband forbade any such action. She had a good-natured smile and I received a hearty welcome from her. She had no authority or power and was completely subservient to Enaam. She did whatever pleased "Mama" otherwise she risked facing grave repercussions. Her husband, a strict and reticent man, observed the Koran to the letter and was very close to his father. The family was divided up in cliques, each one adhering to their own beliefs.

At meal time, we were separated into two groups, the women eating in one area and the men in another. "Mama" had personally taken care of the food, which featured traditional *kabsa*—rice with lamb and thickened milk— but there were no forks or knives set on the table. Arabs usually sit cross-legged on the floor and eat their food with their bare hands, picking it up by means of a piece of soft Arabic flatbread. Being exempt from the rule as foreigners, my mother and I were afforded a table and cutlery, but were obligated to serve ourselves... What struck me as odd was to see the maid eating her meal sitting down on the floor all alone, apart from the others, like the odd woman out, or like a child of a lesser God.

There were two days left before the wedding reception, which was in itself a parody. The whole atmosphere did not even come close to having an air of happiness about it; nothing presaged a joyous event. Instead, there was rather a foreboding for something strange and compulsive, shrouded in a veil of mystery. The furtive, collusive dealings between Sami and Enaam filled me with anxiety. I was in a constant state of alert so that I could anticipate their actions and forestall their plans. I was starting to feel the strain both physically and emotionally...

On my third agonizing morning in Riyadh, I woke up in the upstairs room at about eleven. As soon as I got up, I was suddenly beset by odd excruciating pains like knives stabbing me all over my body, which reduced me to the point of collapse.

I was shocked to see Sami sitting at the foot of my bed, gazing at me with a harsh air of indifference, unmoved by my plight, without offering to help me in any way.

My lips were dry as I writhed in pain. I made desperate attempts to move but I doubled up from the searing jabs of pain in my stomach. I felt like it was my final hour, my soul abandoning me as if an invisible hand was tearing it out of my body to finish me off. It was the third time in a very short period of time that I had such a frightfully inexplicable sensation come and go without reason or warning.

It was now twelve noon. My eyes searched around frantically for my mother but she was nowhere to be found!

"I want my mother!" I gasped stammering through my chapped lips.

Without answering me, Sami just left the room.

I was as white as a ghost, barely able to stand and holding onto the door for fear of totally collapsing onto the floor.

After deliberating amongst themselves in Arabic, Enaam, Sami and his brother Ahmed decided to take me to a hospital in Riyadh. They wrapped me up in black Arabic-style clothing and quickly shuttled me into the car. My mother was nowhere to be seen; I had absolutely no idea on her whereabouts!

"There's nothing wrong with her," diagnosed the medic who examined me. "Perhaps the weather has got to her!" he continued, speaking to Sami and his mother who were perched in a corner looking guilty as sin.

"No, doctor, it's not the weather," said I, speaking in English. "I'm accustomed to the climate conditions because I used to work here as an air hostess."

The inexplicable pains had by then passed and so they took me straight back to the house without telling me anything. My mother had absolutely no idea about my absence nor did she know anything about what had happened. She looked at me puzzled as she was completely ignorant of the events and no one had even bothered to inform her; that incident was apparently another secret to be kept under wraps, "sealed with seven seals."

"Where were you?" my mother asked impatiently. And before I could answer her, Sami bust merrily into the conversation to announce his rose-colored version of the events.

"It was nothing at all, just a bit of queasiness due to the heat. She's fine now," Sami said, while a smiling Enaam was summoning us to dinner.

"Come on, the food is ready," she said adding her own note of festive seasoning. She was desperate to once again deflect the conversation.

It was under such conditions that the wedding reception was being prepared, although nothing was giving away there were any preparations for it. Everything was going on beneath a veil of secrecy, nothing done out in the open. As the time drew close the atmosphere grew heavier. Still, I was forming the impression that there would be some kind of ceremonial aspect to the whole affair.

On the day of the event, Mona's mother and sisters arrived for the wedding from Dhahran, another town in Saudi Arabia. They were jovial and congenial, readily showing me their friendliness and how much significance they placed on my arrival and my settling down in their country as Sami's wife.

At dusk, Hari, the maid from Sri Lanka, knocked on the door to my room to let me know, in the few words of English that she could put together, that I ought to hurry up so that we could get going.

"What do you mean? I'm not ready," said I.

No sooner had I finished my sentence than Enaam showed up, holding a bundle of clothes in her hands and gesturing at us that it was time to go.

They had expedited the procedure, making no particular preparation at home, leaving the house exactly as it was. The lights around the house were not turned on as was customary to mark such special occasions. Everything was being carried out in darkness, as if they wanted everything to be out of sight, and the reception was being expedited in a haphazard and hurried manner.

Entirely bewildered, my mother and I got into the car driven by Sami's brother, Waleed, chaperoned, of course, by Enaam, and we all made our way to the hotel where the great reception was due to take place. We drove along the main avenues of Riyadh, until we came to a halt outside an ultra-modern hotel at a point where the town ended and the desert began.

"This way," Enaam declared stretching out her arm and pointing to the elevator.

Sami was to arrive later, escorted by the men, as was customary there; the women with the women and the men with the men. But in his case, the whole wedding party consisted of a harem of women, the only male contingent comprised of only three of his five brothers and their father. Apparently they had decided to only invite close family members that lived in Riyadh; there seemed to be no desire to invite a large number of guests and from out of town, because I was a foreigner and had to be dealt with in a different way. Consequently, it was deemed unnecessary to make a big deal out of the event, so most of the men were excluded from the guest list.

We went upstairs to the suite where I was expected to prepare myself as a bride and, lo and behold, it was a case of total bedlam! A pandemonium of children jumping about up and down the bridal bed made for an absolute mayhem! A group of Lebanese women, friends of Enaam's, were scouring the room, allegedly monitoring the situation; but the truth was everything was an indescribable mess, which painted a not-so-flattering picture of their sense of neatness or mothering skills and demonstrated a lack of respect towards my wedding and my space. I could feel a knot in the pit of my stomach. I felt like they had invaded my privacy, my inner sanctum. I felt so sick I wanted to turn around and leave, because deep inside me I knew that this whole mess was not accidental; it was probably all part of the plan to humiliate me once again. I felt the blood rushing to my head in the face of this blatant display of insolence towards me. How was I to spend the next few hours as a bride in this despoiled room? Their actions and stance made it patently clear that they did not respect me in the slightest. I was just another foreign woman of another faith.

But who was orchestrating all this? Who had allowed these women the right to invade my sacred space? Well, there was no doubt in my mind that the mastermind of this charade was none other than Enaam, my mother-in-law, the woman in control of my life...

Faced with this miserable state of affairs and close to tears, I felt like running away. I was accustomed to a very different way of life... *Oh, how I miss the Western world!* I thought to myself. But in spite of it all, I pulled myself together and managed to regain my strength of spirit. *Enough!* I told myself. *I will not fall prey to these rude, crude, uncouth women.*

A disdainful prompt by Enaam, who was acting like the commander-in-chief among her peers, rang in the moment of truth: I was to once again put on my bridal gown and present myself as *"aroosa"* (bride) at the hall for the wedding ceremony. And so I did.

When I descended to the ground level of the hotel, I saw Sami in the main lobby, dressed like a local nobleman in his impressive traditional Saudi costume, waiting to usher me into the reception area. Amidst that hall were two thrones set on a stage, where the two of us were supposed to sit and be viewed by our wedding guests, an audience made up of women-spectators. That setting made me sad; I felt I was being reduced to a spectacle, an inanimate object to be exhibited before the devouring eyes of these uncivilized women.

They all stood there in their long, elaborate evening gowns adorned with gold embroidery; the more traditional among them had their heads covered with embroidered headscarves, while the more progressive ones wore their hair loose—the latter ones were apparently coming from an Arabic country of more moderate moral principles.

I felt uncomfortable with what I saw in front of me. Sitting on my throne rather embarrassed, head bowed in grief, I felt unable to partake of the charade of alleged joy; instead, I was feeling like a lamb to the slaughter. In the overall gloomy atmosphere, the women's ceremonial ululations only served to exacerbate my irritation. *Oh no! This is la-la land from hell!* I thought to myself, while a fat black woman was serving Arabic coffee to the guests—coffee is the customary beverage at weddings. Her malevolent glare almost made me swoon; I sensed her hatred pierce me to the bone and felt shivers throughout my body.

My mother, who was seated in the front row, was totally bewildered as well. There were many rows of seats, set up like in an auditorium or a theater, and all the women sitting there were gawking, gossiping and criticizing.

I was holding a glass of fruit juice instead of champagne in my hand, because alcohol is strictly prohibited in that land, and exchanged a half-hearted smile with Sami as we toasted. He surely noticed the intense expressions of dissatisfaction and anguish painted on my face. The time passed and there was nothing in that ceremony to remind me of the weddings that I was accustomed to or indeed anything joyous whatsoever. There were only prying eyes and indiscreet looks piercing through me and arguably figuring out that something was the matter with me.

"What's wrong with her?" They kept on asking Enaam. "Why is she like that?"

"Oh, she's just a little under the weather," she would answer hastily, for she was the main culprit for my whole predicament.

Act one of our wedding ceremony, which was more like a dark ritual of some strange cult, came to an end when Sami and I finally left the hall. It was time for act two!

It was about eleven o'clock at night when we moved the party to the hall next door. In a room flooded with lights, the ceremonial buffet was covered with sumptuous amounts of food, mostly rice, piles of it, as well as other local specialties. That setting appeared closer to my tastes, so I began to feel—and look—a little better.

I was the focus of everyone's attention, and I did see a few friendly smiles; some women caressed my hair while others trundled around me in their typically unrefined way, making remarks in their language.

Enaam was acting as though she was running the show. Jaunty and garrulous, she was flaunting around her jet-black evening dress with its plunging neckline—which left very little to the imagination—as if in a beauty pageant! And she was not the only "conservative" woman to be dressed like that. These women were playing hide-and-seek with themselves. Since nothing was really allowed to be visible on the outside, they would toy with the air of mystery they could exude. Never before in my life had I seen such provocative behavior among women. Compared to them, I felt like I was a conservative prude!

The un-shrouded women were literally all over Sami. They would all make their subtle moves, in case any of them would get lucky. All of a sudden, Enaam literally threw one of her Lebanese friends at Sami, shamelessly and unhesitatingly encouraging her to put the moves on him. She, too, was wearing a long dress with an endlessly plunging neckline; she moved closer to Sami, looked at him with a fiery lust and then posed to be photographed next to him. She was one of the contestants!

This was outrageous! I was a newlywed bride being nudged out of the way and the victim of this callous and malevolent woman. I was totally bewildered. What in the name of God did all this mean?

When the time came for Sami to retreat into his hotel suite together with the male members of his family, I was left alone, trying to figure out what to make of everything that was transpiring around me, while my mother had spent the whole night scrutinizing the environs, watching out for any suspicious moves and waiting to step in immediately whenever necessary. If it weren't for her, they would have surely eaten me alive!

In one such instance, my mother confided in me that, while I was busy talking to someone, the Lebanese woman who had posed with Sami was on her way to follow him up to his suite!

"So I intervened," my mother said. "I asked her in French whether she had misplaced something, to which she stuttered in a guilt-ridden voice that she was looking for her comb. 'Is that so?' I said to her. 'In that case, you just stay put and I'll have the chamber maid go fetch it for you.' She left with her tail between her legs; her scheme was busted."

My mother's intervention was pivotal. She was my vizier, the only person who was loyal to me and whom I could trust. The evening came to its close, the lights went off; I had survived…

Far from everyone and everything, Sami and I finally had a chance to be together alone. It was the first time that we had some privacy ever since I had set foot on Saudi Arabian soil. As he was escorting me to our 20th-floor suite after the ceremony, I could discern faint signs of emotion on his face, his behavior towards me affectionate and humane, as if he had finally broken free from something that had been troubling him, affecting his demeanor. Deep down, I was a little worried about my mother, because this was the first time that she would be alone in Saudi Arabia, especially under such adverse circumstances, but I kept my worries to myself. I secretly prayed for us both, hoping for the best…

The next day at noon, the April heat was unbearable. The atmosphere was at a boiling temperature and a thick mist had covered the city of Riyadh. Wherever you looked, all you could see was the sandy yellow desert. I was awaken with a start by some thunderous pounding on our suite door.
"Yes!" said Sami in his language. It was his brother, Waleed, who had come to wake us up on the orders of Enaam.
"*Halas!*" said Sami—which meant alright in Arabic—but in an angry tone of voice.
"What's the matter?" I asked him rather concerned.
"Nothing. Go back to sleep," he said reassuringly.

And yet, his brother returned, half an hour later, once again pounding on our door, this time even harder than before.

"Yes!" Sami howled almost hysterically this time. Then came a brief exchange between them in Arabic, after which Sami turned to me.

"We have to go to the house," he said dryly. "They are expecting us for lunch."

Deep down, he knew that this was just an excuse. "Mama" was calling for her boy and he had to obey.

What an unbelievable nuisance, I thought to myself. *One is not even allowed to enjoy one's wedding night around here!* I felt like a pawn, someone else's plaything. I took a quick look outside through the dark-colored curtains. The desert sprawled majestically under the scorching April sun with temperatures which were known to reach well above 110 degrees. Thank goodness for modern technology that helps people cope with even the most extreme weather conditions! Air conditioning units were the alpha and the omega in Saudi Arabia. Very few people indeed chose to move about during the midday hours. It was as if the whole country was asleep during the day, waiting for life to resume after dusk.

"Beep, beep," Waleed honked the car horn as we drew up to the house, thus heralding our arrival. The gigantic gate flew open to let us in, beyond the towering walls, where the vast flagstone-paved courtyard with the palm tree in the middle was now covered with scattered children's toys that had been left lying about. We proceeded and reached the main entrance of the two-story house. The floor of the entrance hall was covered with shoes, flip-flops and sandals of all shapes and sizes—everyone was supposed to walk barefoot on the carpets.

"*Ahlan!* Welcome!" Enaam exclaimed whole-heartedly looking at Sami, right before she glared at me with aversion.

And all at once, everything changed again. Sweet Sami of our hotel suite was transformed into a cold, detached man, clearly keeping his distance from me. I was Enaam's primary contender and Sami didn't want to displease her in any way. It was a delicate balancing act, in which, however, my feelings were not of equal gravity as his mother's. The position held by the mother figure in Islam is impenetrable, as she is hallowed in a place superseded by God alone. As for Enaam, although illiterate herself, she nevertheless knew to cite the various verses of the Koran that had to do with the role of the mother. It didn't matter to her if her behavior was making another person miserable; that was of secondary importance. All that mattered was that her selfish needs were met.

"Hello, Samia,"—that was how they had renamed me—"How are you?" said Mona, my first affable encounter in the house that day. Mona was permanently covered with a chador as no one was ever permitted to see her, and she hung about the house hesitant and unassuming as ever.

Next, I saw my mother who had been anxious to see me. Very hurriedly she filled me in on what had happened since we had parted the previous night.

"They were rambling nonstop amongst themselves, I really think they were gossiping and having a go at you," she said. "Enaam left the hotel holding her shoes in her hand, and when we arrived here she made me sleep on a bed with used bed sheets in the same room with her. She was so agitated that she did not sleep a wink; she was tossing and turning all night long. In the morning, she offered me some coffee, not in a cup, but straight out of a broken pot! Shameless! I turned her down. I was certain she did it on purpose and decided that I wouldn't put up with her offensive and demeaning behavior."

What a reciprocation of the hospitality we showed her in Athens, I thought.

Hari was without a doubt the only person in that house showing us some interest and willingness to be of help; but even she was blindly subdued to her masters' wishes.

At lunch time, we were once again grouped together in two cohorts: the men, with Abu Sami on the helm, in one group and the women in the other. My mother and I were provided with a table specially bought for our needs. Without much ado, we "foreigners" took our seats and made some polite attempts at socializing with the rest of the women. They, on the other hand, took absolutely no interest in us; no one was taking any care of us and we would quite easily have starved to death had we not taken the initiative to serve ourselves from the communal serving platter that was placed in the center of their circle. You see, we were not allowed to simply get out of the house and go grocery shopping ourselves. The whole system was frighteningly similar to that of a prison.

On the third day after the wedding party came another significant event. Sami's uncle had passed away and, although a newlywed bride, I was forced to partake of their mourning rules and rites. I was displeased with that verdict, but I had no other choice but to follow their decision.

After a short journey in the stifling heat, we reached a house not unlike Enaam's; it too had towering walls around it, enormous gardens, and so forth. In an empty room, floor covered with carpet wall to wall, a large group of women were sitting cross-legged on the floor. They were mourning the dead crooning a haunting dirge while at the same time listening to a tape recording of an excerpt from the Koran. It was quite the let-down! Not only because it was extremely unnerving for me to be in that sad setting, shrouded from head to toe, but also because I would have never imagined that my wedding would be capped by attending an Arabic funeral in Riyadh!

Still, even in their so-called darkest hours of woe, they never let up on fabricating malicious gossip and finding at least some detrimental remarks to make about me. It seemed as though their perception of things was superficial, fatalistic, always connected to the present time and the material side of life. They wouldn't wear black clothes or otherwise indicate they were in mourning; they would put it behind them and simply go on with their lives, as usual.

As for me, I was finding it hard to believe that what I was witnessing was really happening. I was physically present, but emotionally absent. Reading about a culture and experiencing it firsthand are two very different things. Nevertheless, I curled up down on the floor with them, trying to partake of their grief, although in my mind I was going back over the events of my recent past. Then the tall figure of a woman caught my eye as she was standing up in the middle of the room to pray. And I couldn't help thinking: *Isn't prayer supposed to be a humble, private act? Is she praying for her inner peace or is she praying for everyone to see?*

I was actually relieved when "Mama" informed me that we would be leaving shortly to get back to their house—the lesser of two evils, I suppose. Night had fallen, but the asphalt was still so boiling hot that a mist was hovering above the pavement. There were traces of sand scattered everywhere, an unmistakable mark of the desert. We drove back to the house along wide avenues that took us to the other side of the city. The quiet was overwhelming; another day had gone by.

Come Thursday, "Mama" and Sami had a rather pleasant surprise for us. "Get ready," they said, "we're off to the Souk."

Once at the Souk, "Mama" kept going from one jewelry store to the next, giving the impression that she was preparing to buy a great gift of some sort. Still, in the end her passion trumped etiquette. She kept changing her mind and manner, dragging us along with her, here, there and everywhere. After the jewelry stores she moved on to the silversmith's, but eventually she ended up buying two meters of fabric and a pair of sandals out of the basket of a street vendor.

Back home, she was expecting visitors. She had invited her lady friends to come over and take a closer look at me and give their two cents' worth. She wanted to solicit their impressions about the alien constituent that had so drastically changed her life.

Generously endowed, as they were, with a sense of discretion and courtesy, their opening question about me to Umm Sami—the mother of Sami, as they called Enaam—was none other than: "How old is she?" Time and ageing carried with them the dreaded threat of swiftly being put out to pasture and it was something that women were powerless to fight against. I was quick to pick up the thread of their conversation and to get the gist of where they were coming from. It was quite simple for any intelligent person to catch on! Without a shadow of a doubt, I was clearly an undesirable, whether that sentiment was masked by a forced smile or whether it was openly displayed. Certain of herself and the eventual turn of events, Enaam seemed to be reinforcing their disapproval of me; in fact, it was actually her that was setting the principal tone and the rest were just attuning themselves to it. It was as if my separation, divorce even, from Sami was just a matter of time to them. Of course, in their minds and patriarchal society, that wasn't such a big deal, since a single word out of the man's mouth sufficed to end a marriage. Under the circumstances, a woman, especially a foreign woman, didn't stand a chance.

The unremitting maneuvering aimed at breaking me went on. They wanted me to submit to their point of view. The relentless confrontation was well under way. I, on the other hand, kept my chin up and put my foot down. I had no intention of backing off. And that stance took a great deal of courage, determination and strength, seeing as, in their minds, I was a possession belonging to a master, my husband.

At some point it was announced to me that Sami would be leaving for Jeddah on his own and I was to stay back in Riyadh, under the watchful eye of Enaam. That was what they had decided; only this time their plan fell through. I reacted exactly as I should have, so Sami, for all his harshness, was backed into a corner and forced to give in, even though his "Mama" kept on trying to brainwash him into leaving me behind until the very end.

We had spent one whole week in Riyadh and that nightmare was finally over. We were boarding the plane to get back to Jeddah.

"You and your mother go ahead and I'll be with you in a minute," Sami said to me as soon as we landed.

"Go ahead where?" I retorted slightly annoyed, as we proceeded towards the exit. Then I turned around and saw him flirting, all smiles, with an air hostess that was a former colleague of mine.

"Sami!" I called out from within the crowd.

I was beginning to get a taste of what it meant to be a "possession." But I could not bow my head in blind submission; my instincts forced me to rebel. All the values and principles that I had acquired throughout my life could not simply be rubbed out from one moment to the next. I had to muster up all the powers I possessed in my body and soul to fight a battle which I could see would be hard, unjust and unequal.

"I've told you before and I'll tell you again," said Sami on our ride home from the airport. "Even if you see me flirting with someone, you are to lower your eyes and keep quiet."

What came out of his lips was a heavy blow indeed; yet I have to admit, that was the second time I was hearing these words within a very short period of time. The first time he had said it, I hadn't taken it at face value, thinking it was part of his tactics of intimidation, aiming to estrange me from my Western ideals and induct me into submission. But this time, it started to dawn on me that he actually meant what he was saying. My argumentation and debate skills in my attempt to try to reverse his dated notions were met with his unyielding obstinacy. And it was in such a climate of conflict that we arrived at 38 Knuz Al Elm Street.

It felt good to be "home"—for all intents and purposes, the apartment at 38 Knuz Al Elm Street was the closest thing to home I had at the time. It was a familiar place, in which I had invested both emotionally and materially, contributing to its design and décor with both my personal items and my personal taste. That was the one domain where my word was law. Riyadh meant absolutely nothing to me—nothing but a bundle of unhappy memories. In Jeddah I had far more freedom. Enaam was not there to monitor my every move and every breath. Even so, she had somehow managed to extend her tentacles even this far, to the other side of Arabia.

An important thing that was missing from our home in Jeddah was a telephone. Sami would very adroitly and with various unfounded excuses evade the issue; yet the truth lay somewhere else: His real purpose was to cut me off from every means of communication. It was a precautionary measure dictated by his instinct, as if he knew what was to follow. His real self was beginning to surface, little by little, day by day.

Back when I had abruptly given up my job with Saudia, after my resignation had been orchestrated almost overnight by Sami and "Mama," I had been forced to move some of my personal belongings to Sami's place in Jeddah. Among the items I had moved there were some electronic devices, which I now tried to retrieve. I looked for them around the house for several days after the celebrations and festivities were all over, but they were nowhere to be found.

"Sami, do you know where my stereo is? The one I had left with you for safekeeping?" I asked him.

"Oh, I gave it to Halil!" he replied flatly and in a harsh tone of voice that left no room for further questioning. Still, I insisted.

"I want to know what you've done with it and how it ended up in the hands of Halil," I said. Halil was a bosom buddy of his; I had met him in the past and did not think very highly of him. He was Sami's snitch. He would feed him information and Sami would help him out financially, supposedly out of brotherly love. And Halil was not the only one; Sami did go to great pains to ensure that there were many such yes-men in his court of jesters!

I got very angry at him when I realized how his lack of consideration for me had given him a free hand to so easily squander my belongings here and there without an ounce of respect for me.

"What gave you the right?" I went on ranting and raving indignantly.

"It doesn't belong to you anymore—and that's the end of that!" he brazenly blurted out. That was his way of keeping me from claiming anything as my personal possession.

"Go and fetch it right away or else I will go and get it myself, got it?" My mind was made up; I would stand my ground. Feeling betrayed, I decided I had to stand up to the man who had once made me trust him so unconditionally. *Submit blindly? Cease to exist? No, siree! Not me!* I would not give in to this degradation of my personality, aimed at robbing me of my free will.

Enraged, Sami yelled and shouted at me, trying to overpower me and enforce his will. Then he left the house like a frenzied maniac, only to return a short while later. He had brought back my stereo. But before I could celebrate my small victory, he set it down on the floor, grabbed a thick piece of wood—part of some Indian decorative item—and started to pound at the speaker until he broke it.

"There's your stereo," he snarled after he had forever marked it with his malice.

Although furious myself, I did not respond in the same manner. All hell would break loose if I was more like him. His screams must have carried right to the other end of the desert. I just stood there, dismayed, stoically waiting for the storm to pass. But in my mind I couldn't help wondering whether this was just a transient outburst or whether I had overstepped my bounds and broken the rules that had to do with the concept of the woman being regarded as an object and the man as the undisputed lord and master.

And just as I stood there, numb, he dealt me an underhanded blow. He pushed me so hard that, my body unable to resist the impetus of the shove, I fell down, crashing head first onto my stereo. I found myself passed out flat on the floor, but was quick to come to, awakened by the weeping of my mother—who had witnessed that whole episode—and the first aid she was providing me. *(What a terrible thing for a mother to witness! I would never want to be in her shoes!)*

Sami was weeping too, not out of concern for me, but because he was shocked by the thought of what would happen to him had my injury been fatal. The laws of the Koran are very harsh indeed and such an act carries the ultimate punishment: death by decapitation! Executions were performed on Friday, a day off in Saudi Arabia, staged publicly on some square, in the presence of large crowds, to set an example.

Sami was terrified for his own life; his fear bore no trace of concern or compassion for his fellow human being who, it just so happened, was also his wife in that particular case. All he cared about was to save his own skin; the lives of others were of no consequence.

Relieved to see me open my eyes, he scuttled to the fridge to fetch some ice and place it on my injury. There were no ice cubes in the freezer, so, in his state of panic, he grabbed a frozen chicken and placed it on my head. When the incident appeared to be over, Sami breathed a sigh of relief. The danger was over, the weeping stopped and the tears dried. And by the following day he acted as if nothing had ever happened.

Nothing seemed to be able to knock some sense into him. In spite of everything, he still stuck to his guns, holding on to the beliefs and attitudes that he thought were ascertaining his masculinity. I was always in the wrong and he was always right. As far as he was concerned, everything I had come to know in my life up to that point was absolutely groundless. Everything was erroneous, a utopia.

April was a rather slow month in the air transport business and Sami didn't have much work. Being simply on call, he would spend most of his time at home with only a few minor exceptions.

The atmosphere at home was electric. Tension running high, my mother and I were constantly walking on eggshells. Still, Sami would keep picking up fights, making a big fuss over any minor issue he could think of. I could not understand what the purpose of it all was. This was a man who had appeared to be so passionately in love with me back when I was in Athens and he would fly back and forth to Greece for five or six months straight, sometimes even twice a month, each time bringing some of my things back with him to Jeddah, where we were supposed to live together in peace and harmony. He had even confided to my mother's sister that he wanted to have six children—that number was quite significant, seeing as it was the same number of children his mother had.

"What I had to do with you is done," he said to me one day, as he was casually going through his things in his den.

That was the first time he was delivering such a brazen, forthright message to me.

"What do you mean?" I asked filled with anger, which I did not let on.

"I mean what I said!" he responded with arrogance and the power granted to him by his position. He was a Saudi man, in his home county, and I was powerless foreign wife, that could turn to no one for support.

I went back to the living room, devastated by that unexpected message. I was only married for two or three weeks and already I had to start thinking what would become of me. Many people had envied me for my apparent good luck, but nobody knew what I was really going through. It was a travesty: my people in Greece thought I should be counting my blessings for getting married to a handsome, well-off Saudi pilot, while his people in Saudi Arabia were cursing me for being the lucky winner of the prized groom, thus thwarting the good luck of some local contender. It was utterly absurd. Everyone could see that I was living in a big, luxurious apartment, filled with carpets, paintings, tapestries, but no one could have known that I had bought everything in it myself, since Sami had cunningly and improperly—by their standards—allowed me to deplete my own funds to furnish our home, thus not only ensuring that everything was in good taste, but also that I would be financially weak and easier to subdue—two birds with one stone. Just as no one could know that there was no telephone in our home, so that I could have no contact with the outside world. I was a bird in a gilded cage. That was the rosy life he had once promised me…

That would have been unheard of if I were a local bride. Even the brassiest of Saudi men would inexorably provide all the furnishing of a newlywed couple's new home as dowry. But there was a quid pro quo: the dowry was given in return for something; it was the price the groom paid to "acquire" the wife. Hence the wife was thought of as the husband's property. That was how the Saudis regarded the institution of marriage.

Of course, my case was dealt with in a totally different way. I was a foreign element and that left ample space for unorthodox maneuvering. My ignorance and perceived weakness could be fully exploited. As I have previously mentioned, I was completely unaware of the Arabic institution of the dowry and all its implications; I had been deliberately kept in the dark, isolated by the secrecy of my surroundings. What's more, I could sense a primordial hate expressed towards me, stemming from the fact that I was Christian. I truly believe this was part of it. Sami had accomplished a major feat: he had converted a Christian to Islam. So now he also wanted to crucify me to feel even better about himself.

I was not a narrow-minded person. I wanted to expand my mind in any way, learn my lessons from my mistakes and misfortunes on any given day. So I gave him the benefit of the doubt; I figured that he, too, was the victim of a closed-type pietistic society, putting blinders on him, even though he had studied in America and traveled around the world. He appeared to be unaffected by the outside world; on the contrary, he would passionately reinforce his Saudi viewpoints, as if his country was the navel of the earth. But when he was abroad, he knew full well how to pretend—that, too, being a part of his tactics.

To escape the sorrow and uncertainty of my environs, my thoughts would often travel a few hundred meters away, to the compound where I had lived some of the best moments of my life. That was my way out of my captivity; my thoughts were free...

Dusk was my favorite time of day. The serenity of it caressed my soul. As the sky's iridescent violet shades blended with the monochrome of the vast desert, the muezzin's call to prayer painted the air with a note of sanctity. Those moments were so enchanting it was as if time was standing still, right before the day gave way to night. My mind would be carried away on the wings of my imagination, landing me in some city's bustling downtown or seeing myself off to a faraway trip. My thoughts were galloping all over the world; I'd be everywhere all at once; out in the streets, or on a square or amidst a group of the faithful leaving their work to go pray; and I would be a simple observer, captivated by their zeal. I was fascinated by that instantaneous picture, even if only in the sphere of my imagination.

These thoughts counterbalanced the instability and insecurity of my daily life, and encouraged me to face up to my tyrant. He was my "lord and master," as he loved to be called. The staff of their house in Riyadh would address him as "Captain"—that was another aspect of that culture that I didn't know: there were proper forms of address depending on the social status of the addressee by which everyone, including that person's inner circle, was supposed to abide. Especially the eldest son was held in particularly high esteem, according to mores and customs that traced their roots many centuries back.

Spoiled to egocentrism, Sami thought so highly of himself, he maintained his word was law and no one was entitled to talk back to him. That was, of course, irrational and I couldn't put up with this irrationality. Yet, it had only been a short time since I had fallen from the zenith to the nadir. Where had all my dreams gone? My initiatives, my bold decisions and self-management of my life for the better? Now, I was not only forced to share my life, but also to watch it being shattered into a thousand pieces, trampled and crumpled until there would be nothing left of my old self.

No way! I told myself courageously and, at that moment, I felt a tremendous force surging inside of me. I was ready to face anything the future would bring. Even if it meant I'd be walking a tightrope.

"Where is my Chinese porcelain vase?" I dared asked Sami one day. That piece of genuine china was one of my personal belongings that he had brought back with him from one of his trips to Athens, and now I couldn't find it anywhere.

"You want your Chinese porcelain vase?" he asked while at the same time retrieving it from the hiding place where he had stashed it.

"Here you go!" he said and dropped the vase onto the floor, smashing it in a million pieces, a blasé look of meanness, hate and envy in his eyes.

I wept so much! I had personally chosen that vase with great care and love during one of my trips; yet he seemed to enjoy destroying everything that I loved. He proceeded to break several more of my select items. And when I yelled at him in anger and despair, he came up to me and hit me with several powerful slaps in the face. He then grabbed me by my hair and started to threaten me, shaking his index finger at me, that if I dared cry, he would ruthlessly break the rest of them in pieces too.

"These items are in *my* house, they are not *yours*, and I never want to hear the word 'mine' come out of your mouth ever again. Nothing is yours!" he hollered.

With this atrocious and primitive way he was imposing the law of the strongest that dominated this patriarchal society, where woman is nothing but a valueless object to be used at her master-owner's will and be tossed out at any moment. So I, too, was forced to accept everything without any right to object or even to pose any questions. But there was a crucial difference: The local women had apparently been trained, or at least accustomed to bow their head showed their blind subjugation; but I was not a local. I didn't know to bow my head and simply nod a "yes" or "no" in submission. My body might be suffering, but I refused to subjugate my spirit. I had to be patient.

Day after day, more and more truths were coming to the surface. The masks were coming off! With every passing moment my rose-colored glasses would lose their hue and I would discover yet another horrid aspect of that man's personality and that of the people surrounding him. He was a hypocrite, a split personality, moody, selfish, arrogant, unpredictable, a liar, harsh, with a touch of a bad sense of humor... All these elements composed the person called Sami. When I had first met him he was not religious person at all—or at least he pretended not to be, in his effort to appear as a man of his time. But in Jeddah he took to praying, pretending to be the good Muslim. And after prayer, he was back to being a tyrant. The expressions on his face were alternating as fast as the screenshots in a film reel, reflecting his disturbed soul. He was always negative about everything, shunning every word I had to say before it even came out of my mouth.

"You think too much," he kept telling me. "Thinking takes you to an impasse. Stop thinking!"

He meant that I would have to accept everything without any objection or reaction; that I'd better stop being a thinking human mind; that I should be a robot, submitting to his every whim; and, most importantly, that I ought to feel guilty and responsible for anything that went wrong. "And the guilty party always pays the price," was the great philosophical statement he had come up with by way of solution to the insurmountable problems he was creating for me.

Our first family outing to the market place was quite the change for us. My mother was still with us, although the time of her return to Athens was drawing near.

"Let's go out to get some fresh air, get out of this house for a while," I said to my mother, but it was self-explanatory that Sami, my "guardian angel," would be escorting us. For a woman to go out on her own was unheard of. The status quo stipulated that the woman must be accompanied by her husband—and no one but her husband—and be properly dressed, i.e. fully covering her body and hair. That was the only way I could step out of the house. The attire had to be such that the outline of the body would be indiscernible, even its general shape, in order not to attract the men's attention. Men did not have the right to meet any other woman than the one chosen for them by their family. And the only premarital association they could have with her was to see a picture of hers. That was how marriage was done in Saudi Arabia. And if anyone chose to defy the rules, he would bear the consequences. The Saudi society is very puritanical and very set in its ways, quite unreceptive to foreign bodies.

On that afternoon, Sami allowed me to leave my face uncovered. Jeddah was considered more cosmopolitan than other Saudi Arabian cities. Dubbed as the capital of Western Arabia, it was home to many expatriates working there; hence, for the time being, I was allowed to go out with my face uncovered. I clearly stood out among the local women and Sami would not take his eyes off me. Every step I took, he was watching me—and over his shoulder. Every time I would glance slightly sideways, I was charged with a mistake and a sin. I was supposedly trying to lure other men, appealing to them with my eyes, and that was considered a seduction. When I first heard of it, I felt like laughing at the nonsense he was telling me; but on second thought I decided to contain myself, lest my laughter triggered one of his outbursts.

The combination of extreme heat and humidity was suffocating and exhausting. When we got to the center of the city, close to the port, the stench from the drainage system was unbearable. For all that country's riches, some things were clearly demonstrating that this was still an underdeveloped city.

As we were walking from the parking lot to the shopping mall, I was quite astounded to see two Saudi men holding hands tenderly as they walked in front of us.

"What's up with that?" I asked Sami curiously. "Is homosexuality allowed in your country? I am very impressed," I continued. "You won't permit friendship between people of the opposite sexes, yet you accept this sort of relationship between men?"

"This isn't homosexuality. They are friends and they love each other. I hold hands with my best friend, too," said Sami.

"I've only seen girls hold hands like this," said I and ended the conversation before I got into trouble.

The King Abdulaziz mall was the predominant edifice at the market place, an ultra-modern building hosting numerous luxury stores. A couple of steps down the road, the narrow souks were adding a touch of local color to the scenery. The souks were lined with jewelry and goldsmith shops one after the other; the scintillating genuine pearls gathered together in small bags and the sparkling gold hanging everywhere, both inside and outside the stores, made me feel as if I were magically transported in one of those Ali Baba fairy tales…

And yet, everything was real. Full costumes made of gold, golden belts, bustiers and headdresses, like those worn by Cleopatra, decorated the shop-fronts addressed primarily to newlywed women—it is a Saudi custom to flood the bride with loads of gold. All the jewelry stores were brimming with people. I was astounded! They all seemed very well-off and absolutely trouble-free.

Sami was commenting and explaining to my mother everything that was going on around us as we entered one of these stores. We were bedazzled, excited and full of curiosity. Up until that point, it had been the three of us strolling around the market, Sami constantly keeping his eyes locked on me; and yet now, all of a sudden, his sly instinct had kicked in and he had disappeared! That was the second time in a very short period of time that he was doing the same thing. The man who had once promised me so much was now repeatedly shattering all his promises to pieces. Just my luck!

Thirty minutes later, when my mother and I had indulged our modest desires and I had paid for our purchases out of my pocket, I heard Sami's angry voice asking me if we were through yet. Without any further discussion, we up and left. He looked quite annoyed for reasons that he only knew himself. And all the way to the car, he didn't stop warning and threatening me.

What had I done this time? I had done nothing wrong! My dignity was beyond reproach. Nevertheless, Sami would fabricate stories and slam me with accusations that would follow me everywhere, along with his fear and hysterics, until I would be left, guilt-ridden, in his mercy.

"Who were you smiling at? Just wait and see what that'll get you!" he'd scream and keep on hurling threats at me while he drove like a crazy person.

My mother and I were utterly confused and deeply concerned, but could only just wait to see what was coming next.

When we reached our home, Sami slammed on the brakes bringing the car to an abrupt stop. Another day out had been crowned with success...

The situation was inexplicable! It was the first time in my life that I found myself knowing that I am not the master of me, that I do not belong to me! I could feel a breakdown approaching. I felt emotionally bruised and weak inside; it was only my mind and prudence that kept me going and thinking soundly at any given moment. It is a dreadful thing to feel like you don't belong to yourself but are instead governed by someone else you who controls every aspect of your life and deprives you of any right, including the right to smile, read, express yourself freely or pretty much anything else. It appeared that I had no inalienable rights anymore and was to function in accordance with my master's will. In that country, it was up to the master whether to keep you, play with you, domineer you, or leave you and simply toss you out!

The sun was rising. Another breaking day was finding me at the easternmost part of the world I had ever been in, at some edge of the city, close to the desert line. It was late April and the heat was already unbearable—summer presaged its advent. Sami was still mostly at home with us, since he had not returned to full duty yet. Time seemed endless, insensible and tough. The conspiracies between him and Enaam continued to play out. Their goal was to get rid of me for good without prejudices or any cost. In addition, he constantly being pressed with criticism and negatives remarks to isolate me, while Enaam's ultimate goal was to make Sami get rid of me and uproot any feelings he might have for me from his heart. The fiesta was over, the lights had gone off, and it was back to the salt mines. Or so Enaam thought and was trying to command Sami to implement. Her hold and impact on him was tremendous. She dominated over seven men in their house, all of whom would obey her and soak up all of her decisions like sponges; they were there to execute her orders. She had regimented her six sons and her husband like an army who functioned for her sake and according to her desires. She was a real tribal chief, but her motives were paltry and she used intrigue and cutthroat instincts to satisfy her self-importance and her desire to be in the lead among all other women.

I had now been in Saudi Arabia for quite some time and, to keep on living there, the law required me to obtain a special residence permit, as without it I could be subject to arrest and thrown into a Jeddah dungeon until I could prove my origins and the reasons I was in the country.

One morning, Sami left to allegedly go and take care of the necessary paperwork for my residence permit. His late return at noon made me suspect he was rather scheming my banishment. He artfully tried to mask it with a lie, vaguely telling me about some "iqama visa" he was attempting to obtain for me, without providing any clarifications as to what that was. I was starting to get really worried and confused!

"You know", he said, "I went to the proper authorities here in Jeddah, but it turns out you cannot obtain the visa here. You have to go back to Athens and apply for it at the Embassy of Saudi Arabia. They are the proper authority to issue it".

Naturally, I raised my objections, but he immediately tried to assure me and put my mind at ease. In the end, he convinced me that this particular visa was indeed only issued by the Saudi Embassy in my home country.

At that point, my mother and I had been there for almost a month and, according to my master, her time had expired and she had to leave. As I later found out, he could have easily obtained an extension for her, but at the time we were not aware of the pertinent regulations. And in his attempt to terrorize us, Sami was making out the Saudi state to be a frightful monster-state, eager to devour anybody and anything.

"Your tourist visa is expiring," he said to my mother, "and you have to leave! And you will go with her," he continued turning to me. "You need to take care of your visa at the Saudi Embassy in Greece." Just like that, he had solved the problem!

It was early afternoon at the end of April when we left Jeddah headed to Riyadh to say good-bye to his family. From there on, Sami would be escorting us on a direct flight to Athens.

The script was well thought-out and, this time around, it even included a couple of lines for his father.

"Yes, that is where you will apply for the visa. In Athens, not here," Abu Sami ascertained in a sullen tone and just a few words.

He was being used as the ultimate deterrent; his words had a special gravity and I was expected to bow before them.

Enaam was floating in an ocean of happiness; it was only a matter of hours before everything would go according to her satanic ploy and she and Sami could get rid of me once and for all, without me being able to claim anything. According to her script, I would leave without grumbling or arguing and, being a foreigner, I would never come back. But they were overseeing a crucial little detail: I had a brain in my head and wasn't afraid to use it. The yoke of the master-husband whose word is law might apply to a different audience, but not to me.

It was around noon on a Thursday. The burning sun had reached its peak, the blurry sky reflecting the yellow sheen of the desert as far as the eye could see. What a contrast to the clear blue Greeks skies! The atmosphere was heavy and tense, sorrow was taking over me. Intuitively, I could sense what would follow, as Sami was driving us to the airport accompanied by Enaam. I was carrying nothing but a small suitcase, leaving all my other belongings back in Jeddah.

After we went through the check-in and luggage drop-off process, Enaam pointed us in the direction of the women's waiting room—even the airport was a segregated place—and we hurriedly exchanged our brief good-byes.

When we boarded the plane, we were met by Sami, waiting for us all dignified and regal in his uniform. A smile of triumph was lighting up his face, as if he couldn't wait to finally be released from a heavy burden that had been weighing him down. All through the flight, he kept going in and out of the cockpit, keeping an eye on us. At one moment, he came close to me with an affectionate smile.

"Happy birthday, my love!" he said, offering me an emerald jewelry set. Wasn't he a man full of surprises! He had remembered my birthday…

"How did you like Riyadh?" he asked my mother in pidgin Greek.

Still, she had grasped the hidden meaning of his question, which was really referring to his home and family.

"Not at all!" she answered him brusquely and resolutely.

Sami smiled a sardonic grin and returned to the cockpit. Her answer had surely come as a surprise to him; it was boorish and debasing for his tastes. But my mother was justified in her urge to spontaneously share her true feelings with him; all she had experienced throughout her time in Saudi Arabia was the bitterness and frustration.

After a four-hour flight, we finally reached Athens. It was Good Friday afternoon. It would take us some time to recover and rediscover ourselves, adjusting back to the rhythms of our culture and religion, which I had never given up on deep inside of me. Time moved back ahead to the present.

Sami escorted us to our home. I could tell he was nervous, trying to find a way to leave us there and go to his hotel where he would stay until the next flight out to Saudi Arabia. Ill at ease and rather embarrassed, he was hoping to gradually sever all ties and simply return me like an unwanted package. On the surface, he appeared to be succeeding in his mission. His anticipation ran so high he could not hide his feelings of excitement about the fulfillment of his mission.

I, on the other hand, had not suspected his dark intentions at the time, so I asked him if he would go with me to the Saudi Embassy in order to take care of my visa. He turned me down, which I found quite offensive. He said that he had no time and that I had to take care of it by myself. What was more natural than a wife asking her husband for a little help and support? And yet, he wouldn't give it. He was clearly preoccupied with other matters!

During the two days that he stayed in Athens, his behavior was intentionally frigid, aiming to foster the negative environment necessary to advance their self-serving plans. He was completely disinterested in me and regarded his stay in Athens as forced labor.

So, he left for Jeddah as an apathetic, simple acquaintance, having dropped me off at my destination. Cold, indifferent, free of regrets, and irresponsible, he simply dumped some ballast and was on his way. I was nothing more to him than an item—and a kitchen item at that.

One of the following days, I went to the Embassy of Saudi Arabia. Indeed, I met the Consul General, who was quite welcoming—he was, after all, one of the guests at the wedding party in Athens—but also sure to let me know that neither the Embassy nor he was the competent authority to issue that type of visa. That was where I found out that the "iqama visa" they had been talking about was actually my residence permit. The Consul looked quite perplexed and kindly referred me to the Ambassador, Abdullah Malhouk. I explained my issue to him and, after he had listened to me carefully, he authorized my entry visa "for the sake of my mother," as he put it.

"Your husband knows that the residence permit is issued by the Ministry of Interior in Saudi Arabia. It is a simple procedure and a matter of two to three days tops."

I almost fainted at the Ambassador's office. That was when their deceitful scheming first became clear to me in all its grandeur. I was not prepared to let them have it their way and never return to Saudi Arabia to collect my belongings, including jewelry and other personal items of both sentimental and financial value. Was I to let him keep all my beautiful household items so that he could pass them on as dowry to his next bride? And all that, just because I was a foreigner who wasn't familiar with the local rules of matrimony? Was I to unprotestingly endure the deceit and fraud perpetrated against me just because I had a foreign passport? What bothered me the most was the mockery, the deception, the humiliation.

I was not prepared to give up on this fight. I was now aware of the ridicule I had suffered, the utter disrespect to my personality and wound to my soul. These people had violated me, destroyed me, leaving behind the ruins of me, just for a change, just for the sake of "having a little fun," as they often used to say amongst themselves.

It was only with God's help that I was issued an entry visa. And as soon as I was, I began to brace myself for every possible outcome. Sami was back in Jeddah and had been calling me time and again, eager to hear what would put him at ease. But the news he got instead came as a shock! Instead of being rid of me once and for all, I announced to him I would be going back to Jeddah. He tried to contain his reaction, muttering he'd be waiting for me to return.

Armed with courage and self-conviction, I embarked on my return journey to Jeddah. I had recharged my batteries and replenished my strength and I was certain I was in the right.

It would be the first time I would be all alone in Saudi Arabia, forced to face everything and everyone on my own, but I tried to stay positive. So, I arrived there a very different person than the one they knew before. This time around I was neither carefree nor naïve!

Sami was waiting for me at the airport dresses in his traditional Saudi thobe. His welcome was quite decent, while I was trying to strike a delicate balance and, after a brief, diplomatic exchange, we had put the visa issue behind us. Besides, he didn't have much to say; his sly attempt had simply fallen through!

His driving was nervous and mechanical. Time and again he'd clear his throat as if to say something, but he didn't know how to! Eventually, while turning the wheel of the car, he frowned and said, "Have you thought long and hard before returning to Saudi Arabia?"

I gave him a quizzical look and responded, "I don't understand. What's there to think about? Is this supposed to be a warning? Whatever do you mean?"

"I mean what I said!" he answered curtly.

And in that festive atmosphere of tender love and care, my kingdom was about to open wide its embrace to receive me for the second time!

CHAPTER FIVE

THE INFERNO OF KNUZ AL ELM STREET

I was all alone. Just me and my surroundings, barren of any sound. He was not there. He was travelling for countless hours and days at a time, and I was all alone at home. Yet, I was under strict orders that governed my life and my behavior. I was not allowed to receive anyone or talk to anyone. Men or even relatives were not allowed at home under any circumstances. "Even if you're dying," he once told me, "you'll figure out a way to save yourself on your own." I was not allowed to go out nor come into contact with the outside world in any way. I was under house arrest…

One day, when Sami was away on a two-day assignment, I was feeling extremely bored and lonely. I had nothing to do and no one to talk to, and the hours went by so slowly that the day seemed never-ending. It was just me, myself and I in the heart of the desert. And as the day progressed, the silence was getting to me. I was overcome by an inexplicable fear that made me feel weary and anxious. I began to take inventory of my possessions and putting them in some sort of order. In the end, everything was in its place and I was alone amidst all these objects.

I started to pace around the apartment—it was a big place so it was quite a stroll from one end to the other. I looked out the window; the windows of the houses across the street appeared to be closed. Surely there was life behind those windows, only it wasn't visible from the outside. The streets were empty too, there was no one out. It was like a ghost city, a deserted place. I wanted so badly to go knock on the door of a neighbor, simply to say "hi" and talk to another human being, just to make sure that I was not the only person living in that area. I yearned to hear the sound of my own voice, to assert that I existed, that I wasn't merely a shadow of myself. But even the thought of something like that was forbidden. It was no use brooding about something I was not allowed to do. I kept on dawdling the day away, becoming all the more painfully aware that I was in the middle of nowhere.

Night fell. Nothing changed in the surrounding scenery, except that now it was dark. I turned on every light around the house to feel a little better. I cannot explain why but I had started to feel really scared. Perhaps it was the darkness or perhaps it was loneliness or perhaps it was the combination of the two that were causing me that disturbing feeling of fear and insecurity. I had been alone many times before during my travels, but that experience of being in the desert was unique. Loitering about, I wished there was a way to make the hours of the night go by faster and speed up the advent of daylight. I went to my bedroom and lay down, trying to relax and let go of all my negative thoughts and feelings. After lying on my bed for some time, I was alerted by a strange sense of foreboding. I got up in a panic, feeling as if the room was closing in on me. I had to get out of there as quickly as possible. I picked up the bedsheet, left the room, shut the door behind me and ran as fast as I could. An impalpable fear had beset me. But where could I go?

My instinct led me to the entrance hall, right behind our apartment's main entrance. I curled up and spent the rest of night sleeping right there. At that moment, I had rejected our cold bedroom once and for all!

The merciful light of day found me sleeping behind our front door. The nightmare that I had experienced the night before was a thing of the past.

When Sami got back from his assignment, I felt relieved; at last, I was not alone anymore. I shared my concerns and my inexplicable fears with him and he laughed in my face. Of course, he was right, as always... The only thing that mattered to him was that I be obedient and follow the commandments he had bequeathed to me.

Nevertheless, he gave it some thought and, after a while and upon consulting with his kith and kin, he decided that I was better off staying with his family whenever he would be away on assignment. So, every time he would be going on a trip for two or three days, he would pack me up and drop me off at the Jeddah airport for one of his brothers to pick me up and drive me to Riyadh. The respective brother would keep close tabs on me, load me onto his car and deliver me like a parcel to my end destination: the fortress-house in Riyadh.

As one may imagine, things were all but rosy for me in Riyadh. Enaam was constantly keeping an eye on me like a watchdog, staying close to me the whole time so that she could control everything about me, down to my breath. It was smothering! I had nothing to keep myself busy there, except reading, for which I made sure to steal some time alone in the room of the upper floor. Sometimes I would also chat with Mona, although our conversations were kept short, seeing as everything we said was filtered and censored by "Mama." If she heard something she did not like, she would report a vilified version back to her sons and have them implement the proper punishment. The same was the case with Hari, the maid. The two of us were quite friendly to each other; she was the only person taking care of me, always willing to offer me something to drink or eat in that otherwise hostile environment.

Before long, Hari and I had come up with a sign language of our own, a secret code of communication. A simple look or a nod was enough for Hari to understand what I wanted and cater to it. She knew when I was hungry, she would read it in my eyes, and she would sneak me some fruit or a piece of flatbread wrapped in a piece of paper into my room.

Hari was a poor young woman who had left her far-off land to come serve these heartless people twenty-four/seven for a measly salary. She wasn't so much an employee as she was a slave: she was not entitled to any leave or time off at all, constantly catering to ten adults and two babies, which she was bringing up almost single-handedly. The treatment she suffered by these people was nothing short of cruel; she was always sitting down on the kitchen floor, like an animal, waiting for their next command. She was not allowed to be in the same room with her masters even for a moment. To them, she was a servant, a "dog's daughter" like they used to call her if she fell behind with one of her chores.

"How dare you speak to her like that!" I indignantly lashed out at Abdullah, Sami's youngest brother, one day. "She is a person. She has a name!"

The whole family turned to look at me with revulsion. How dare I defend the help! Their hateful glares were quite telling of the future surprises they had in store for me...

Meanwhile, I could understand enough Arabic to be able to communicate with Hari, who loved me and felt for me like a second mother, and confided in me all her grievances. Her room was next to mine and sometimes, when she would suspect something was wrong, she would sneak into my room, careful not to be detected by the household's master, to check up on me. Eventually Enaam got a whiff of our mutual fondness and took action.

"Wait till you hear what she did to me!" Hari told me one day very upset. "She woke me up at five o'clock in the morning so that I would be so tired later on that I wouldn't be able to hang out with you at all. My arms hurt like crazy from all the work she had me do," she said as she showed me the pain relief patches she had applied on her aching shoulders.

Hari was treated cruelly and exploited beyond imagination. She was hardly ever afforded a breather, constantly on duty and at their service, and yet she was always smiling and keen to be of assistance. Much like myself, Hari meant nothing to them; she was an old, used up object and there was nothing to prevent them from tossing her out if something went wrong. Still, she was expected to inviolably abide by their inhumane rules and do so unprotestingly. She wouldn't dare escape and flee back to her home country; she had to stay there and suffer their bondage. In me she found the compassion, understanding and humanity that she longed for. Above all, I was to be trusted. I lent her a listening ear and she bared her heart about anything and everything that mattered; such as, for example, the latest facts concerning Mona—a household "fixture" whom I now realized I hadn't seen much during this stay of mine in Riyadh. She had disappeared.

"Where is Mona?" I had dared ask "Mama" at one point.

"She has gone to Dhahran to visit her mother," Enaam had replied appearing content on the surface, but with a look in her eyes that concealed hypocrisy and guile.

Living in that house was torture for Mona; the perpetual tension and strife was taking a toll on her emotional wellbeing. Like me, Mona was under constant scrutiny too, suffering from Enaam's calumny of her to her devout Islamist son Ahmed.

"Don't listen to her, she's lying," Hari secretly entrusted to me when no one else could hear. "Mona has been sent away. There was a big fuss. 'Ahmed, beat her and kick her out! I will get you another wife. And as for the kids, I will get you Filipino maids to raise them!' That was what Enaam had commanded her son."

Mona had suffered numerous persecutions in that house. She had been through Cyanean Rocks time and again, thanks to that tyrant hailed as "Mama" or Enaam. But Mona would bow her head and submit to the cruel, relentless status quo of the family she had married into. She had no other choice, no power and no way out; she was entrapped in a system full of injustice and gender discrimination. Women of that culture had been trained to endure just about anything by their master-husbands. Only smarmy subservience, if anything, helped them get by.

And while that was the general atmosphere in Riyadh, my life back in Jeddah was not much better. Of course, returning to Jeddah meant that I was out of Enaam's immediate supervision, but she had found ways to learn every detail about my life, even from afar. She would make frequent calls to Mohammed, our neighbor from across the hall, and she would even send Sami's best friend Halil to spy on me and report back to her. Telltales swarmed all around, eager to squeal, just like in the dark fairy tales I used to read about such places and times of yore as a child. Danger was clear and present!

Around that time, for reasons still unknown to me, Sami decided to take me on a short trip to the United States so that I could meet his two brothers who were studying there at the time. From my viewpoint, that trip was a godsend. It would give me a chance to get out of that place, get back in sync with modern life, and feel like a person of my time. I was sick and tired of the intrigues and conspiracies of his closely-knit family who were sapping the strength out of my soul, dragging me down to their level and hampering my development as a human being. Sure, I was there to give it a fair shot, but I could use some recharging.

We began to prepare for the trip immediately; Sami had only a week off from work, so we had to be on the next flight out to New York. Thus, on a Tuesday of June we embarked on the eleven-hour flight to the United States of America. To me, this was a routine flight I used to work on as an air hostess; skies were clear and there was nothing to alert me as to any dangers ahead. Meeting his brothers was quite the innocent and legitimate justification.

We spent two days in New York before taking a flight out to Minneapolis, Minnesota, which was our final destination. In New York, Sami was looking rather listless and concerned, as if he was reluctant to do something he nevertheless had to do and get over with. He was cold and distant towards me and that made me feel worried and suspicious.

By the time we arrived in Minneapolis, Sami was in a much better mood. His third brother, Abdul Aziz, was waiting for us at the airport. It was already dark and he drove us to his place, where we would be put up as his guests. He was acting all cool and congenial, but I could tell there was something insidious and conniving about him under the surface. It seemed that his stay in the United States hadn't changed him the least bit.

The next day was sunny and summery. The surroundings were lush and inviting, so the two brothers decided we would all go out for a walk in nature to admire the lakes of the town. The two of them were talking in their own language nonstop and so fast that I could not understand what they were saying, which made me feel uncomfortable and charged the atmosphere in a negative way. Not too far along our walk, Sami suddenly got mad at me for some inexplicable reason and started to shout at me and chase after me into the woods. I was so afraid I was running as fast as I could to get away from him, sensing the serial-killer-type ferocity of his chase. Dripping with sweat out of panic and fear, I kept running and running, past the lake and up into the forest that crowns the crest of the hill. Some scattered groups of people that were relishing the serenity of nature got alarmed when a woman's silhouette running through the forest to escape from a threat caught their eye.

Sami kept coming after me like a man in frenzy. I could feel the horror drawing near; I had no time to think, the danger was eminent. The sudden appearance of a young man chasing after his ball put an end to Sami's pursuit. Quick to mask his intentions as he caught up with me, Sami masterfully pretended to be the loving husband who was merely playing tag with his wife. In an impressive display of lightning-fast reflexes, he threw his arms around me, in fear of being made for what he was really up to and facing the consequences of that country's laws, which clearly protected the persecuted and the attacked. Cognizant of the actual state of affairs, yet an unperturbed spectator of the incident, his brother simply stood and waited, completely unaffected, at the spot where we had begun our chase. Sami escorted me back soaking wet and out of breath. I tried to understand exactly what was going on and what his goals were, but in his crude as usual manner he once again silenced me.

Throughout the ride back in his brother's car, Sami didn't stop insulting me, degrading me and abusing me even for a moment—at some point he even pulled at my hair! Abdul Aziz was driving, I was riding shotgun and Sami was sitting in the back seat to be able to fully control my moves. I started to cry. I felt like opening the door and jumping out of the car. I cried for help but help was nowhere to be found. I was on my own...

"Stop the car, I want to get out right this moment!" I briskly said to his brother. I thought I should get out of the car and run to a police station, but I had neither my passport nor any other identification document on me. Sami was keeping all of that.

My pleas left unanswered, my despair was prolonged until we got back to Abdul Aziz's place. His brother was at home with a friend of his, a young American woman, but even her presence there did not stop Sami from raising hell.

"Why won't you talk to your brother?" I said to Abdul Aziz in exasperation. "Please, tell him to stop. I want to leave. He is really dangerous!"

"I know my brother!" was his impassive and cynical response.

And before he had even finished that sentence, Sami got up and started to chase me around the table, wielding a knife. I was crying for help, but no one was intervening. They simply stood there and watched on. It was a live horror show and free of charge! I don't know if it was in the script or not, but at that moment the telephone rang. It was Enaam, and her phone call put a (temporary) end to the madness.

I wished someone would tell me what was going on and what their intentions were. Why had he made me travel so far away only to suffer in much the same way as I did back in Jeddah? And what was his brother's part in all this? Was he really approving of Sami's heinous acts?

All these questions kept going through my mind over the next few hours. I could not for the life of me understand the purpose of being brought to the United States. I stayed awake watching every move that might determine my fate or was simply suspicious. I was living a horror that only a sick mind could conceive.

Their efforts had fallen through once again, so then they tried to cover their tracks, Sami by invoking his great love for me as grounds for his actions and Abdul Aziz by maintaining that he trusted his brother. I, however, was sure that something else was going on, and no one could convince me otherwise.

The final act of our trip to the States—and yet another trial I had to go through—was played out at JFK airport in New York. As we were walking along the vast corridors towards the boarding lounge, Sami suddenly scolded me for some insignificant reason and then took to his heels, sprinting away through the crowds. Needless to say he had on him all our travel documents, including my passport, as well as any travel cash. I was left all alone, with nothing on me. That moment I heard the announcement of our departure, so I followed my instinct and started to chase after him. I was running as fast as I could, jostling my way through the crowd, no time for apologies. I had to catch up with him no matter what; otherwise I would be left all alone and with no ID in the jungle of New York. I was scared to death even thinking about it. All my reflexes went on overdrive. I ran like crazy and, in the end, I made it. I had no idea in which part of the vast airport I was; all I remember is that I felt like I was in the set of some American action thriller movie. I cannot begin to describe my feelings at the moment when I finally caught up with him, but the first thing I did was ask him to give me my passport. He wouldn't, but there was no time to waste as our flight was already boarding. Once again, I had no other choice but to follow him, no questions asked. Under the circumstances, I was much more frightened of the unknown…

Just as we were stepping into the aircraft, that whole episode seemingly behind us, I finally acted on my indignation: all my piled up anger, my fury, my deep sense of betrayal, my urge for revenge, it all armed my right hand with unbelievable energy, released into a catapult-like slap on his cheek. It was as if all the strength I possessed had been funneled into that irrevocable action, that incredible slap that I will never forget. It was my way of vindicating myself, even for a brief moment.

Sami did not say anything. He just smiled, as if thanking me, and got on the plane, calm and content, like a gentleman. I guess my reaction had struck him dumb! These men have probably never even imagined this kind of behavior coming from a woman, seeing as in their country men are the lords and masters and their word is law.

The storm having blown over, our return trip continued in relative peace and quiet. Still, I could hardly relax. I stayed vigilant; the nightmares I had been living had turned into an integral part of my life. A deep-seated inexplicable hatred appeared to be ingrained deep in these people's hearts and minds, and these feelings appeared to be projected on me, not me personally, but me as an exemplar of the female species, on whom they could materialize their plans.

The trip back was a long one. The seats we were assigned were in the middle section of the aircraft and several seats around the plane were empty, so Sami could move about relatively freely. He still wanted to toy with me until I surrendered completely, but I was holding up and he did not like that.

After the meal had been served and the used up trays had been picked up, Sami kept hold of his knife and fork.

"Why are you keeping these?" I asked him.

"You'll see!" he replied impudently.

I leaned my head back; I was exhausted, mentally and physically. Reassured by the presence of the other passengers around us, I managed to calm down and dozed off for a little while. I don't know for how long I slept, but when I was woken up by some turbulence, I briefly peered through my eyelids and saw Sami glancing at me sideways, so I pretended to be still asleep. As if he had noticed or read my mind, he woke me up with a rough jolting of my hand.

"Well, what did you think of our trip?" he dared ask me to feel out my intensions.

"It was awful, it was torture, a nightmare!" I replied in despair.

Before I had a chance to finish these few words, the knife in his hands was pressed against my stomach and he was threatening me:

"I don't ever want to hear you speak like that, ever again!"

He wanted to terrorize me. I looked around to see if some other passenger's eyes would meet mine, but no one was looking in our direction. Reluctant to either speak or pick a fight with him, I kept my mouth shut.

After a seemingly endless flight, the airplane finally touched down on Saudi Arabian soil and the air hostess announced that we had reached our destination. *I'm fresh out of destinations*, I thought to myself feeling miserable. The way I had been treated by Sami during that trip made me feel like I had been led by the nose, like I was a "package" that had been taken half way around the globe and back for absolutely no reason at all—although perhaps I was beginning to understand... That strange dream, the one with the black cat, that I had while still an air hostess and floating on oceans of happiness, was now beginning to become clear to me. The black cat was a symbol for what came into my life to knock everything over, smash everything to pieces, turn my happiness into unhappiness, my joy into sorrow, white into black... At that moment I became a strong believer of fate, kismet, everyone's inescapable destiny. And yet, I didn't want to let this belief sink in. I would not give up. I would fight tooth and nail for my own ideals. I had done nothing wrong, although my karma indicated otherwise. But I would change that fate around. I would take my risks and fight my battles...

A period of calm after the storm followed our return to Jeddah. God had heard my prayers and unpredictable Sami, as if touched by a magic wand, was acting normally! It was Ramadan, the holiest of months for Muslims, and perhaps this was part of the reason why he was being calmer. For the first time I saw him eagerly pray four times a day and exercise fasting to the letter. Could it be that he was seeking atonement, asking his God for forgiveness, or was he asking Him to satisfy his own selfish demands? Only he could answer this question and he would do it through his thoughts and actions.

One evening around sundown, on one of those rare, peaceful and joyful moments that we spent together, we were startle by the doorbell ringing. It was Halil! He had come to announce to us that Enaam and Waleed were due to arrive in Jeddah any minute now and that Sami was supposed to go pick them up from the airport.

I had never seen Sami so upset and confused before. Utterly bewildered, he turned to me and said, "My mother and my brother Waleed will be here soon." Then he got ready and took me along with him to the airport. He looked extremely worried and nervous. It was as if Enaam's sudden visit was stressing him, as if there had been some sort of ultimatum, to which he had failed to respond on time. It was clear to me that this visit by Enaam was not of the maternal or even friendly persuasion, but before I could figure out exactly what the matter was, she showed up at the arrivals.

Short and fat, covered head to toe in her black chador, she was trying to walk somewhat briskly in an attempt to appear airy and delicate despite the overall impression of stubbiness. Enaam, Waleed and Sami exchanged their greetings, but she only "remembered" that I was there too after several minutes, when we were already heading towards the car. She was looking for any chance she could get to humiliate me and devalue me. Surely the news about our trip to America had not appealed to her at all.

"How are you?" she asked me coldly in Arabic.

"Fine!" I replied in just one word.

"Fine?" she repeated in a sarcastic, envious slur.

Right after that, I began to grasp the reason for her visit. Something was definitely cooking; no good would come of it. In my mind, I prayed to God to give me strength, to guide me and to protect me.

Enaam's visit had to do with me. I knew it, I could sense it! The frigid look she gave me had made my blood freeze! I had to be as strong as I could, bracing for the worst. That woman really had it in for me, she was out to get me and force me out of their lives. I could only attribute all this hatred, jealousy and meanness coming from her to a rather limited, culturally warped intelligence, which she would usually only put to work to inflict harm.

It was already dark by the time we got home. Enaam immediately made herself at home—or rather she took over the place—assured by the familiar environs and the presence of her beloved son Sami, and then the three of them began to chitchat in the living room.

I withdrew into the kitchen: that was my domain par excellence, the part of the house that "belonged" to me so I could slave away in there preparing all kinds of delicacies for my masters of Riyadh! Nobody gave a dime about me; I was an invisible maidservant, a domestic worker, with an expiration date.

I prepared a Greek dinner and, taking on the duties of the butler in addition to those of the cook, I even served them.

Their first evening there was rather uneventful, which sort of confused me because it didn't confirm my fears and suspicions. Perhaps it was because I spent most of the time in the kitchen that I didn't have the opportunity to witness much of their scheming. Or perhaps this was part of their tactics: the calm before the storm, a temporary ceasefire to be followed by carpet-bombing so that the enemy will most surely be obliterated.

It was the holy month of Ramadan, when life essentially began after the sundown. The day became night and the night became day, as people would gather to eat and drink and socialize from nightfall until the next dawn. People would do all their chores after sunset and even the stores would stay open until well after midnight. It was all about the night during Ramadan. During the day the faithful would not eat anything and pray devoutly five times, but come nightfall everything was allowed. I couldn't help feeling this Muslim month of fasting was more about the superficial than the substantial. In my opinion, that was the way of many Muslims: adhering to the ritual without delving into the depth of things, searching for the innermost meanings. That was miles away from the soul-searching, purification and redemption that I had come to associate with fasting in my religion.

It was late in the afternoon when I came out of my room the next day. Given the circumstances, I was forced to abide by the rhythm of the rest of them. But even during my sleep I would not feel entirely free. But if just so happened that I was awake before Sami was, I would lie still on the bed waiting for "my master" to wake me up and set me free. If I ventured to get out of bed before him, he would stretch out his arm and pull me back down. And he'd know every single time, even though he was supposedly a heavy sleeper. It was as if he kept an eye on me even while he slept. I was a prisoner even in my sleep. Unspeakable situations...

"You'll stay put!" he would tell me and I would flinch and stay put and wait for time to go by, counting my breaths along with the seconds on the clock, as if I was performing some yoga breathing exercise. I would fall into torpor of sorts, avoiding even to swallow—such was my emotional torture.

It was six o'clock in the afternoon when the "grand master" decided to get up, come out of his chambers and proceed to the reception area where he would meet "Mama" and Waleed. Enaam welcomed him warmly, but the grin on her face was rather sardonic!

Food preparation was well underway. After fasting throughout the day, soup was the perfect starter to prepare the stomach for the main courses to follow. Food was prepared according to a special ritual during this religious period.

Enaam had taken it upon herself to prepare our meal, infusing it with a heavy dose of Ramadan, as she was quite the devotee... When all four of us sat around the dinner table, the atmosphere was rather tranquil. There was nothing there to foreshadow the storm that was about to hit any minute.

Unwary, I suddenly saw Enaam starting to yell at Sami. It was quite disconcerting to see Enaam fighting with him, but, given my precarious position, there was nothing more I could do than silently witness the altercation. But before long I realized that this furious outburst was exclusively about me. When her attack was turned directly against me, I was appalled by the randomness and unpredictability of it all. It was the worst assault launched against me ever! I felt the adrenaline pumping through my veins at the view of that woman charging against me like an untamed animal eager to devour me. She was now standing, scowling and menacing, spewing out her meanness and fury in my direction, yelling with, oh my god, what a scream!

"Are you talking to me?" I asked her in my poor Arabic while my face was flushed with increasing anger and rage.

"What is it that you want anyway? Get out of here! Go to your home! You are a stranger!" she went on yelling at me those precise words, which were entrenched on my memory.

"Fine, I will leave right away!" I replied unswayed, hiding my pain inside and unleashing all my fury. "Please get me a telephone so that I may call my mother or my brother to pick me up. And thank you for everything!"

Enaam took it down a notch when she heard me mentioning my family, but then she resumed her assault.

"Why are you snooping? Why do you want to know where Sami sleeps when he is in Riyadh? Why did you ask Mona about it?" she asked.

Undaunted by her confrontation, I replied boldly: "Of course I want to know. Why would you have a problem with that? Sami is my husband and I have every right to know. He is the reason I am here, having left everything behind for him, including my career. I had put my faith in him and I would never have imagined that I'd have to share or claim my husband from another woman. I am his wife and we belong together! Please, I do not want to carry on this conversation with you!" I said shaking, while she kept up her ululations.

I stood up and left and locked myself in my bedroom. The last image from that scene that was imprinted indelibly on my mind was Sami's stance in all of this: sitting back on the couch next to Enaam, who had not stopped yelling, he had been enjoying the spectacle of her attack against me and our battle like an uninvolved spectator. His faint smirk revealed that he was on her side. Of course, what else could I expect? Sympathy? Compassion? Understanding? Nope. The situation was clear to me.

Locked up in my room I wept and sobbed for quite some time. Eventually I fell asleep feeling utterly ragged and exhausted. They wanted to destroy me, obliterate me physically, mentally, emotionally. What God was dictating so much hatred, meanness and envy against me? Why bother fulfilling their religions duties as devout Muslims, when at the same time they would behave like followers of some dark cult, thus offending Islam itself?

Several hours went by... In my nightmarish torpor, I heard Waleed knocking at my door.

"Samia, open the door!"

"No, I won't, I don't want to speak to anyone!"

I had said exactly what I was feeling and there was no point saying anything more.

Waleed left only to come back a few minutes later.

"Samia, open the door, I want to talk to you." He was persistent.

He had been sent to play the role of the intermediary, protecting the interests of his family because they were afraid of the consequences if my family found out about that situation. Nevertheless, Waleed was the only one I would allow anywhere near me at that moment, because he had not showed any clear prejudice against me during the incident. Still, this new tactic of rapprochement was simply a means to tone down the situation; it did not necessarily mean that they had reconsidered their stance.

Eventually I gave into Waleed's plea, since he was so gently and diplomatically trying to approach me. I opened the door and Waleed proceeded to talk to me for some time, trying to convince me about how much he and his mother really liked me!

"You just need some rest," he said and his words sounded to me like lines from the theatre of the absurd. It was they who had wrecked my nerves and brought me to my feet, and now they were feigning concern about my health and well-being! What a joke!

"I have done you no wrong! Why do you keep treating me like that, why are you violating my personality?" I kept asking him through my sobs.

"Listen," he said. "My mother wants to talk to you."

"No, no, I don't want to face anyone, not after that attack!"

Once more, Waleed left the room only to return again a few minutes later. Pretending that he was alone, he once again convinced me to let him in; only this time Enaam was with him. I was startled to see her standing there, a half-apologetic look on her face, trying to appear friendly to calm me down, without saying anything at all. I believe that it was for fear of retaliation from my family that they had taken a step back; I still had a family that was ready to intervene at any given moment, even from faraway. Or perhaps their recoiling was attributed to the fact that we were expecting Mona and Ahmed to arrive soon. Either way, it was hard for me to read Enaam's change of behavior. Only a few minutes ago she had been trying to get rid of me at any cost, while now she appeared as though she wanted to make amends. Could it be that my reaction had touched a nerve? Or where they indirectly attempting to woo me into greater submission? Perhaps this was just their attempt to shut me up and prevent me from seeking reparations...

Ahmed, a devout Islamist following the Koran to the letter, was expected to arrive in Jeddah with his family any minute. Then they would continue their journey on a pilgrimage to Mecca because of Ramadan. Conflicts were not allowed during that religious month and perhaps that was one of the reasons for the temporary truce.

As soon as Ahmed and Mona arrived, Enaam behaved as though everything was as usual.

"Come, Mona, let me show you around Sami's house," she said to her other daughter-in-law, placing special emphasis on her last two words, although she knew that almost all of the items in that place were actually mine. She was blatantly ignoring me. It was her standard way of making it perfectly clear that I had no place there and was not worthy of her son. I was of negligible value. Enaam was showing Mona around the apartment, boasting about her son's exquisite taste! Mona was dazzled, expressing her approval of what she saw with vocal exclamations. If only she knew...

Enaam had also taken over the culinary duties, eager to pass for the good hostess and master chef. Shortly thereafter, the four of them would leave to go on their pilgrimage to Mecca, leaving a pile of dirty pots and dishes behind and me to clean up the kitchen. It was as if Enaam had made sure to use every single vessel and utensil in the kitchen to prepare that meal! And that was just another example of her signature pettiness.

She put on her white abaya and white chador—a vision in white, head to toe—as white was the color symbolizing purity and purgation. She even had the nerve to ask me to borrow a white handbag to match. Leaving the infidel sinner—me—behind, the sparkling paragon of virtue and kindness was light-heartedly on her way to the great pilgrimage in Mecca. What a hypocrite! Her previous impious behavior notwithstanding, she would now take to praying with devotion. What was the use of that?

As for Sami, the man who had made all this possible, he was merely keeping his distances and insidiously let his mother dig my grave, allowing her to do his dirty job for him.

Flauntingly leaving me stuck with doing the dishes, they all left without so much as a "good-bye." It was early in the evening. Sami escorted them to the rental limo, and when he came back home, he offered for the first time ever to take me for a walk on the beachfront. Apparently, he was trying to make me forget or even forgive everything that had happened in that house earlier. He also wanted me to calm down and forget all about the mess in the kitchen and the tortures that I had suffered in order to keep my mouth shut. He was all alone with me now; he would no longer be entertained by the insults hurled against me by his beloved "Mama."

The stroll he had suggested was the standard constitutional of the locals: a long walk along the promenade, lined with spread-out carpets and men enjoying their hookah and hot tea, each one surrounded by two or three wives and a bunch of kids playing or gazing at the pitch-black Red Sea…

All alone amidst all that trouble, far from my family and friends, in a foreign country filled with people who had blinders on, as I saw it, people living displaced in time and space, I had to find a way to exist. I had been afforded not an iota of understanding, compassion or remorse from them; instead, I was always the one incapable of understanding them, supposedly misunderstanding these pure at heart, well-intended, friendly people...

I turned in on myself looking for inner peace. Any discussion appeared to be pointless. Sami was probably feeling guilty and trying to approach me and elicit my thoughts. While Enaam was still here, he was just an impassive observer, simply accepting all of her decisions. That behavior had made me detest him; he was sneaky and a coward. As for that woman, I was left speechless by her cold-heartedness. How could she so callously pretend that she was faithful and pure, especially during the period of Ramadan? And now she was heading to Mecca for *Umrah*, a "secondary" ritual pilgrimage that Muslims would do throughout the year. If you asked me, she was probably going to Mecca for the fun of it, rather than to attend to her religious duties.

She stayed in Mecca for two days and then promptly returned to Jeddah to complete her scheming before returning to Riyadh. Naturally, I was blissful to have her back; I was floating on cloud nine. Especially now that she was returning after being "enlightened" by her pilgrimage, her aura was brimming with divine substances that captivated me...

The two of them resumed their game playing, just like that first night I had spent in Riyadh with my mother. When night fell, Sami and his mother retreated to one of the bedrooms to "talk in privacy." They had made me part of their hide-and-seek, as I was trying to find them. Later that night Sami slipped out of our bedroom like some kind of thief, attempting to sneak back into Enaam's quarters.

"What are you doing there?" I yelled at him from the other end of the hallway. He was not aware that I had been watching; he turned around and smiled at me in an attempt to disguise his guilt.

"Oh, there's something I want to show Mama," he said.

"And why do you close the door behind you?" I asked him rigorously. That picture brought back to life an image from a few months ago, when I was accepting some facts because I had no idea about their relationship and didn't want to admit it to myself.

After our little chat, Sami pulled himself together, entered Enaam's room and left her door open. I could see Enaam sitting coyly on her dressing table stool, her hair covered up like a good Muslim, her eyes folded on her lap, as if she was about to deliver a sermon.

What a performance! Did they actually think I would buy any of this? Apparently they were underestimating my intelligence, yet this was another dark side of theirs that was stoking my suspicions…

Late in the afternoon of the following day, after the end of the daily fasting, they decided that we had to pay a visit to his friend Halil and his wife. They were newlyweds and Enaam wanted to see Maha, the bride, who, it just so happened, was some sort of distant relative of theirs.

A few moments before we left the house, Sami and Enaam surprised me once again with an unforeseen attack. The duet came at me full throttle because I had allegedly not put on my chador in the proper way. I was standing in the middle of them, Sami insulting me from the right, Enaam rooting for him and reinforcing the insults from the left. Once again, they were belittling me to oblivion… My ears were ringing, I couldn't take it anymore. I wanted to die, to stop hearing or knowing any of it. God, I was in hell! These were moments and images that were imprinted on my soul forever, memories painted in indelible colors that would always be there, even long after time would have healed the wounds from this madness. It was a concert of hatred and meanness by hypocritical pseudo-pious people, hiding behind their religion, choosing and picking from it only those aspects that served them well…

I burst into tears, unable to withstand all that hate. I was all alone amidst the demons of the desert. They were harsh, rigid obdurate people who took pleasure out of watching me suffer and tearing me into pieces.

"Get up," Sami brutally commanded me, showing off in front of his mother. "We are leaving."

Although an emotional wreck, I was forced to go with them to their friend's house. My head was buzzing, I could not think nor hear anything; I was living my drama, desperate and helpless. I had collapsed! Why was this happening to me? What had I done? I used to be a happy girl who gratefully enjoyed every moment of the life that had so generously been given to me by God. Why then had life turned its ugly face on me?

I was lost in my thoughts when we got to their house. Enaam and I sat down with Maha, separately from the men.

"Hello, Maha, how are you?" Enaam asked her with an air of importance as she was stepping in.

I was visibly upset, my eyes red from crying.

"What is the matter? What's wrong with you?" Maha asked in a low voice, looking at me and trying to find out what was going on. I simply pointed my index finger at Enaam and started to cry again.

"Would you like to go lie down in my bedroom?" Maha offered, while Enaam was looking at us intently lest she missed any part of our communication.

"Yes, thank you," I replied and went to the room next door to free myself of Enaam's presence.

I could not help myself, I kept crying nonstop. I was feeling extremely vulnerable, overwhelmed by all the adversity I was faced with. I wished I could simply disappear and not have to see them anymore. I felt like the walls were closing in on me. I was yearning for some peace and quiet, my long lost inner calm. I was going through indescribable horrors. The surroundings, the desert, it all was driving me crazy. I felt entrapped and forced to face up to terrible human monsters that were out to get me. For the first time, I felt my strength abandoning me. Yet once again I managed to pull myself together. I was not going to give her the satisfaction to perish. The more she would see me crawling the stronger she thought she was winning. I had to resist!

Maha was secretly stopping by the room to check on me on her way back and forth between the kitchen and the living room.

"Are you alright?" she would ask me, hoping to comfort me.

"It's her!" I would respond through my sobs.

Once again, I had been completely humiliated. Their condescension had shattered my dignity to pieces, all in the name of their petty motives and aspirations. My thoughts all blurred and confused, I had nothing left to do but wait until the next morning, when Enaam would leave and I would be free again, delivered from that living nightmare that tore me to pieces just by thinking about it!

Enaam was gone, but she'd left wreckage behind! Sami had surely received precise instructions as to how to handle me from then on and there was no way he would let her down.

My torment had just begun! A triumphant Enaam had returned to her home turf, remotely pulling the strings of puppet Sami in the way she knew best. The rival was I, the battle was on and they had home advantage in this match between good and evil.

The Ramadan was nearing its end. After an entire month of fasting and praying the Muslims were going to celebrate. All stores and public services remained closed and family members were paying visits to each other, exchanging expensive gifts intended mostly for the women and children. The end of the Ramadan is the greatest holiday for Muslims, so everyone was giving it the importance it deserved.

But the celebrations did not include me; once again, I was being discriminated against. Sami took me to Riyadh to exchange wishes with his family—I could not avoid it, I had to do as he asked. At times like these, they would flaunt me around as a member of their family, just for appearances, for fear of being talked about in a negative light, as is often the case in closed societies. Gossip and criticism were there favorite pastimes. They would spend hours on the phone with friends and relatives, analyzing everything and spreading the news like a wildfire from one end of Saudi Arabia to the other. It was a whole concept and philosophy of life: given the restrictive social conventions, the telephone offered a wonderful means for release and interpersonal communication.

I arrived in Riyadh at noon. The first person I saw when I stepped into the house was Abu Sami, who happened to be lounging in the big hall. Enaam had retreated to her room.

"Many happy returns," I said to him and, seeing no one else around, I proceeded to go upstairs to the room on the upper floor.

Stuck in that same place and situation again, I was simply waiting for time to pass. I was not able to do much, I was under strict confinement. And the thought that later on I would have to see Enaam and wish her well after all that had transpired in Jeddah filled me with stress and anxiety. I steeled myself and decided to take the high road. I was not about to give her any grounds to steamroll me once again. Besides, being at their house put me in a disadvantage.

"Many happy returns, Umm Sami," I said to her with a broad smile on my face in front of her close family and some of their relatives.

"Same to you," she replied, feigning a smile herself, while Abu Sami swiftly slipped into my hand an amount of riyals as a festive gift. I was startled by his gesture, but the truth was it was custom and the presence of their relatives that had forced them to do it. Everything had its place and meaning.

When I kindly asked for their permission to make a phone call to my mother in Athens, Enaam intervened rather perturbed, saying it would be wiser if Sami were present too during my call. I got the message! Fearing for a scandal if I told my mother everything, she needed Sami, who knew enough Greek to get the point, to monitor my conversation. So, they had found a way to gag me! By censoring my communication with the outside world they were depriving me of one of my basic freedoms. It was a matter of time until I would completely lose my sense of self, of who I was, what I wanted and what I expected. The latest incident in Jeddah had weakened my morale and worn down my strength. My moments of peace were few and far between, like shiny little oases of breathing space amongst endless hours of exhaustion.

After our return to Jeddah, life resumed its "normal" rhythm. Our home was almost constantly in a state of panic; Sami would make a big deal out of every little thing, creating explosive scenes which would end up in drama. He was determined to subjugate me as a person and he would achieve this by sinking my morale to the point where my spirit would have surrendered so my body would obey. His usual adage was something to the effect of "Why did you turn your face to the right? Who were you checking out to your left? What did you mean when you said that?" And after the initial questioning, I would be put me on the stand, charged, tried and found guilty, with no right to a defense, all so that I would be subjected to emotional and bodily torture. None of my questions were deemed adequate by my prosecutor and he would resume his grilling until he got the answers that would confirm his suspicions. Beyond any logic and reason, I was being subjected to a trial as if I had perpetrated a crime—the crime of looking or smiling! Guilty as charged! After my trial, I would be subjected to a protracted catechism, aiming to reform me: I was not allowed to read or write, or to speak French or do anything that had to do with France! Did I really exist or was I merely a shadow of myself?

    One rare afternoon, he actually offered to take me downtown to the shopping center to buy shoes. There were fine luxury stores for the expensive tastes of the Arab customers and I asked Sami if we could go into one of them. The store personnel were always men and, very politely, they would only address the husband in serving their clientele. Coincidentally, the member of the staff who came to our assistance was French, so I spoke to him in French—big mistake! Sami got so furious that he started to yell at me amidst pairs of scattered shoes and in front of the very perplexed staff. Then he grabbed me, dragged me out of the store and shoved me back into the car. I was speechless and Sami was driving like a madman at warp speed, while at the same time grilling me again with his usual barrage of question. Why and how had I spoken French to the staff? For one, it was utterly offensive that I spoke and, secondly, I certainly knew that man from my time in Paris! That was Sami's version of the story and the only one that mattered.

Once we got home, he proceeded to beat me all night long! I had to pay for my sin. I was screaming and yelling for help, imploring him to let go of me, but was unaffected by my pleading. As for our neighbors or passersby, no one would dare intervene in such a situation. I was, quite literally, "a voice crying out in the desert." I was all by myself, left to my own devices, and I had to fight with all my strength to get back up on my feet. That was the only thought that helped me gather the necessary inner energy to not lose heart completely.

He had smashed all my things to pieces. Anything that meant anything to me, he would reduce to shards within fractions of a second, even if it had taken me a lifetime to acquire—in fact, that gave him even more pleasure! What a culture that man had! What manners! All he cared about were the pleasures of the flesh. He was an unbelievable sadist who reveled in destroying anything I admired or made me happy. The immense pleasure was oozing out of his sparkling eyes.

"Here, break them yourself," he would yell at me pointing at my beautiful alabaster lamps and fine porcelain items. "Or else I will break them for you!"

I honestly didn't know what to do! Feeling indignant at the injustice that was been done to me, I wanted to lash out on him, to pounce at him like a lioness and tear him to pieces; still, rationality defeated my passion once again. I did not allow my anger to get the best of me; instead, I made superhuman efforts to suppress my emotions. *No, you must be strong.* That was my inner mantra. And I kept praying to God for some divine intervention. To be accused and defenseless in a country like that was like flipping a coin between life and death. The ultimate sentences in that place—decapitation for men and stoning for women—were carried out with no option for a reprieve or pardon. That was why I kept on trying, stoically and cautiously, to live up to my duties and chose to destroy my personal things, things that I loved, in order to minimize the damage. My heart was aching, but I took the alabaster lamp and tossed it against the wall, some ten feet away, under Sami's sadistic glare.

If I didn't do it, then he would; and he would do it with rabid rage, until nothing would have been left standing. I cannot begin to describe how awful I felt destroying my things against my will! I threw the lamps against the wall, one after the other, as gently as I could. I was living an absurd situation, in which, although rational myself, I was being forced to sacrifice all of things that I loved, at once an immolator and a victim of that irrational man. I could not quite grasp his motives at the time when all this was going down, but deep inside me I was longing to take revenge. He, on the other hand, was taking pleasure and pride in the performance staged before him, as if he was channeling God's will. I wondered—was he truly insane or was this yet another chapter in the "How to Tame your Foreign Wife" manual?

The days were going by, the one more tormenting than the previous one. Time had stood still and I felt as if I was walking down a tunnel searching for the light that would show me out of that hell. I was at my wits' end. It was like I was flowing down a river to the underworld and the gates to hell were right there, amidst the desert. My life had been put on hold, I had absolutely no interests, no goals or hopes for the future, a future that might never come. All I could think about was how to survive and find a way out of that darkness that was growing darker and darker around me.

Without fully realizing it, I had been trapped in a cage, abandoned to the cruel desires of my master-husband, my life a mere toy in his hands. He was toying with me, experimenting with my emotions, as if he had never seen anyone cry, suffer or beg before. And through it all, he would maintain his stance unperturbed, only to drop his mask and lash out on me like a wild beast every now and then.

One Thursday evening, at about eight, our neighbor Mohammed rang our doorbell. Sami opened the door and saw Mohammed holding his telephone in his hands. My mother was calling for me from Athens, so Sami handed me the telephone and stood right above me to monitor my conversation. I dared only say two to three words at a time, such as, "Yes, I'm fine," over and over again. I was extremely hesitant to tell my mother any more of the situation; besides, I could hardly explain to her what was going on over the phone. A mother's instinct made her suspect something was up, so she started to shouting at me in anguish, trying to elicit more information. Sami was straining his ears not to miss one iota of our conversation and then he would grill me about it. "Why did you say the word 'tomorrow'?" he would ask persistently, or "Why did you say the word 'bad'?" And in that excruciating line of questioning, that would go on for hours, I'd eventually wish that telephone call had never taken place.

Sami, on the other hand, had every right to call Enaam whenever he pleased. He was entitled to everything, I was entitled to nothing. At around that time, I recalled something he had confided to me at the beginning of our relationship. "Once a month I cry for my mother," he had said and I had never quite understood what he meant by that. As I never quite understood the meaning of that Oedipus complex going on between them either, or why he would cry for Enaam while at the same time taking pleasure out of making me cry and suffer time and again.

I was inclined to believe that these people might be suffering from an inferiority complex caused by their insecurity in view of the emancipated women from western countries, which prevented them from accepting the latter's free spirit, their opinions and their initiative in making their own decisions. I never intended to offend Sami or underestimate him in any way; he was the husband I had consciously chosen for myself. But it appeared that he wanted to "domesticate" me in accordance to his own habits and views. At the same time, Enaam, although a woman herself, was claiming the indisputable supremacy within her family, but also within the life of Sami, playing the pivotal role of the absolute despot.

Sami kept picking fights with me over reasons made up by him in order to satisfy his fixation. He would go into endless tirades, mercilessly refusing me the chance to contribute my side of the story. We'd end up quarreling very badly, my part restricted to that of defending myself. And the fights would rarely stay at the level of verbal altercations; he was a man of action, too! He'd hurl against me any object readily available, be it the dressing table stool or the lamp on the bedside table. He was fighting me with rage, completely disregarding any damage to our property, until I was completely utterly defeated. During one of those fights, he had inadvertently cut his hand on the broken glass of the lamp and a river of blood painted the white carpet red. The final tally of that fight included the complete destruction of our bedroom; the place looked like a murder scene at the end. And every time after the storm, Sami would admire his accomplishments with a smirk on his face, which implied that the power of money gave him the chance to promptly replace everything and that seeing me defeated was more than worth his trouble! After the incident with his bleeding hand, the next day he had the carpet replaced and a craftsman brought in to repair the damaged furniture. Destroyed by night, rebuilt by day.

At some point our neighbor Mohammed felt like he could no longer keep silent about the screams he heard coming from the apartment across the hall. So, one day when Sami was away, Mohammed risked knocking at my door.

"I can't stand to hear your desperate screams and do nothing anymore," he said to me. "I must do something about it. So I will either call the police or I will call his mother in Riyadh."

"I'd much prefer you call the police than call his mother in Riyadh," I said. "You see, she is complicit in this situation."

Of course, Mohammed did neither. He was all talk and no action. It might be because he was afraid or simply out of Saudi solidarity against the foreign element. Instead, he chose to pay me some more visits and making things even more difficult for me since visits such as these were not allowed according to their conventions.

On one of my lonely but peaceful nights, when Sami was on duty on some short-haul flight, Mohammed employed the following scheme:

It was two thirty in the morning and I was asleep, when the ring of my doorbell woke me. I was petrified.

"Who is it?" I asked trembling.

"It is me, Mohammed," said the voice from the other side of the door.

"Is something wrong?" I asked.

"Open the door, please."

I hesitantly and reluctantly cracked the door open, just about enough to look at him with one eye. Putting on a gooey expression, Mohammed asked me if I wanted to eat pizza. Startled at his strange proposition, I turned him down, thanked him and closed the door.

Why would he, a strange man, knock on my door in the middle of the night, when he knew that he was not to come into any such contact with me under any circumstances? The answer to that question was probably quite a complex one. The epicenter of all these dicey attempts was the fact that I was a foreigner, a non-Arab, and Mohammed thought it would do no harm to test the waters. Perhaps it was Sami himself who had put him up to it. Or perhaps Mohammed was acting on his own initiative, behind his friend's back, out of some competitive feeling towards Sami in case he could take advantage of the situation. Either way, the conventional respect Saudi men showed towards each others' wives appeared not to apply in my case. I was considered vulnerable and an easy prey because I was a foreigner. Sami never mentioned anything to me about that visit and, naturally, I didn't bring it up either to avoid creating problems for myself. I was certain that, once again, he would find a way to turn this against me and make me out to be the culprit, instead of confronting Mohammed and protecting me. Mohammed's action had left me wondering, but I kept my mouth shut to avoid any more trouble.

Perhaps another factor that had played into that whole episode was Mohammed's sister, Ebtisam. The latter appeared to be pursuing Sami and my presence there had thwarted her plans. One way or the other, that whole lot appeared to be made up of vindictive, resentful people who feigned magnanimity but in reality took pleasure in the misfortunes of others.

Sami came back from his journey with replenished energy, ready to resume his "work" at home. It was impossible for him to stay calm or quiet, although I gave him no grounds for attacking me—I was pretty much locked up inside the whole time, for crying out loud—and was being polite and calm, despite my exasperation. I was trying to keep my calm primarily as a favor to myself, but also because I was curious as to the lengths he would go to raise hell and what his ultimate objective was.

I took care of him like an exemplary wife, but without bending over backwards to entertain him—I couldn't be much fun after everything that I had been through. Then, lucky me, Sami took off to visit a friend of his—naturally, he was allowed to go wherever he wanted, whenever he wanted, without having to inform anyone about his whereabouts. That time, too, he left without saying a word to me.

I was exhausted that night and decided to turn in at around eleven, when Sami had just come back. He came into the bedroom, squatted down on the carpet by my side of the bed and—while I was dozing off I felt a strong smell of smoke peering through my nostril. I opened my eyes and saw Sami next to me, ten lit cigarettes between his lips, blowing the smoke into my face. As soon as he realized his goal—of waking me up—had been achieved, he put the cigarettes out, and I had to reward his idiocy with a smile. He had succeeded in his purpose: I was supposed to stay up late into the night, because that was how it was done in Saudi Arabia. He did not even respect my right to sleep. He thought I was his property to do with as he pleased. There was no husband-wife communication, as is the case in the civilized world; the only opinion worth hearing or exchanging was men's opinion. The woman was—and probably still is—merely an object.

Before I relocated to Jeddah, the wife of Salah—a former colleague of Sami's—had been called in to clean the apartment. I met her once; she was a low-profile person, totally subdued to her husband, who kept on repeating the mantra, "Whatever Salah says." He was her God because, if she did anything wrong, she would find herself divorced and sent back to her parents in no time. In that context, she unprotestingly accepted Salah's month-long journey to America, where he proceeded to indulge himself in every possible way while she was back home taking care of their children. She was pleased that he was having fun, for otherwise she would have a hellish time upon his return home. I will never forget that look of immense unhappiness on her face; she was the young mother of small children, but she looked tired and aged. If her husband divorced her, who would care to marry her? Especially if one factored in the fact that a woman's "worth" plummets after she has been married once—much like the Blue Book value of a used car—and her options dwindle—as we all know, beggars can't be choosers. Seeing Salah's wife one fully comprehended the meaning of subjugation and blind obedience.

An additional means of pressure that Saudi men had in their quiver was the option of taking on a second wife. And they would casually bring it up at will as a threat hanging over their first wife's head, in order to ensure maximum compliance. You see, the Saudi man is the absolute lord and master, vested with all the powers and authorities.

Maha, the recent bride of Halil, had expressed her fears about that one day. Halil had announced to her that he was going to get a second wife, a decision strongly supported by his father, who was commending him and encouraging him in that direction. Having two or three wives meant that the husband had to treat all of them equally and ensure the same financial security to all of them. In reality, however, one wife was always more favored than the others and one might even be pushed aside.

As for myself, in addition to my woes as a "foreign" bride, I naturally also had the "pleasure" of experiencing the regular woes of local wives. On one of his usual incidents of picking up a fight with me, Sami had told me among other things: "If you are not obedient, you will make me divorce you three times right this instant." (In order for a Saudi to divorce his wife, he merely has to say "I divorce you" three times and the divorce is deemed final and irreversible before people and God; simple as that!) It was a direct threat and he thought that I was going to panic and lick his boots to prevent it. Instead, I ignored him and, for a while, my apathy caused him to postpone making good on his threat. I was not raised in a way that would make me grasp the solemnity of his threat and, besides, I really didn't care. On another occasion, he had threatened to bring another wife to our household so that I could watch and learn how "good wives" behaved. Thus, with these threats, I had completed the circle of verbal abuse and oral trials.

One evening, at dusk, Sami looked at me solemnly and announced to me that a friend of his was coming over for a visit and that I was not to show my face under any circumstances. His term was non-negotiable and I was to lock myself up in one of the back rooms of the apartment, where there wasn't even a TV set, and quietly stare at the four walls around me for as long as he and his friend were going to have dinner and entertain themselves in the living room.

I did as I was asked. I was bored out of my head and was feeling gloomy and stuffy, tucked away, doing nothing. Plus, at one point, I also felt very thirsty, so I decided to tiptoe to the kitchen and get a drink of water. I silently opened the door and made my way to the kitchen, but alas I was made and, all of a sudden, I found Sami standing before me. I swallowed hard and tried to catch my breath, but his shout—and not only his shout—beat me to it.

"What are you doing here?" he yelled at me and begun to mercilessly slap my face with all his strength. It all happened so fast I didn't even have time to raise an arm in a reflex defense.

I let out a scream of pain and right after he hit me I realized that I could not hear through my left ear. I had gone deaf! In a state of panic, I started to cry inconsolably and call for help at the top of my lungs, saying: "I lost my hearing, please, someone help me!"

Witnessing that sort of incident, his friend got very scared and ran off, because he didn't want to be put in the spot—the punishment for that sort of behavior is quite severe.

I, on the other hand, had passed out for quite some time, only to realize Sami and I were alone again when I came to.

Helpless and defenseless, I spent an agonizing night facing a serious problem: I had lost the sense of hearing in my left ear— just thinking of it was driving me crazy—and, at the same time, the sensation of sound was amplified in my right ear, so much so that the slightest sound echoed like an earthquake! Powerless and alone against that unprecedented, barbaric and cowardly act, I don't know how but I managed to get some shuteye, until I was awaken abruptly by the fall of a hanger on the floor, which resounded in my right ear as if a drill was piercing straight through to my brain. Once awake, I was immediately aware again of my situation and begun to cry in desperation.

The sun was up; a black day was breaking for me. I wasn't strong enough to resist anymore. Sami was gone and would be back in the evening. I felt like a walking dead. I withdrew to the back rooms and, holding a pillow over my right ear to muffle all sounds, I just sat in complete silence. The slightest noise would startle me and give me terrible headaches. I was suffering! Even the sound of my footsteps on the carpet was unbearable! I can hardly put the exact feeling into words. It was as if I was living and walking inside my mind and everything was happening on a scale of one to one thousand. The drop of a pin echoed like a bomb blast! I could not stand it, I sunk in my pain. My ailment was complemented by nausea and dizziness, and yet something inside my soul was pushing me not to give up hope. I had to survive, I had to make it!

One of the following days, when Sami was away on a scheduled flight to London, I hesitantly dared knock on Mohammed's door. I had no one else to turn to for help.

"Mohammed, something terrible has happened to me!" I said and proceeded to explain to him what had happened.

"Please, I need your help. Could you please take me to the hospital? I need to see a doctor. I am in terrible pain! My head feels like it's about to burst and I can't hear."

Mohammed was sad to hear about the incident and, to his credit, he defied the relevant conventions and immediately drove me to the New Jeddah Clinic Hospital. Feeling a little better from an emotional point of view, I explained to the doctor the details of the incident and he didn't seem surprised. He told me that he realized my injury had been caused by a violent husband and that that sort of thing was not uncommon in Saudi Arabia. Then I waited for his diagnosis.

"You have injured your eardrum, but you're lucky, it didn't rupture!" the doctor said to me in a straightforward, yet highfalutin manner.

"Will I get my hearing back?" I asked him anxiously.

"You'll have to be patient, but it will come back with time."

Comforted by the doctor's assurance, I drove back home with Mohammed. I was very lucky I had not completely lost my hearing. But it was also obvious that both Mohammed and the doctor, each one for his own reasons, were afraid I might be filing a police report. Everything operated under a veil of fear and I, having no place else to go, simply returned to the house of my desperation. I was living in a true world of nightmarish illusions, experiencing a living hell. I had no way out—or so it seemed to me—so I would have to patiently wait out that trial, too.

As the time went by, I was feeling much better. After several days had gone by and Sami had noticed my recuperation, he had the audacity to tell me that, "If something had gone wrong, I would have taken you to the best doctors in the United States." Sure, after the worst was over, he was promising me the moon and the stars. And on top of it, he did it as if I was to blame for the damaged he had inflicted upon me. God! What an absurdity!

Getting better was of course a relief, but I could not rely on that. I kept thinking of various ways to escape, keeping my eyes open in all directions. "There must be something I can do," I kept telling myself, trying to convince my soul to follow my mind. But my mind was blurred by the convoluted chaos of ideas and decisions leading to dead ends; and then I would scratch that idea and start all over again, only to be lead to another dead end. And while I was tormented by such thoughts during my intervals of isolation, when I was together with Sami he'd make sure to discipline me back into marching to the beat of his drum.

"What are you doing? What are you thinking of?" he asked me once in his usual bossy way, as if he'd be cursed were he to talk to me in a more humane, caring manner.

"Why? Am I not allowed to do some thinking of my own?" I said to him reluctant to enter another endless discussion with him.

"No!" he replied menacingly. "You need to understand that here you are under my control, and you must forget the way you used to live. You will obey me and only me, no matter what anyone else tells you. You are not to listen to anyone else but me!" Apparently he must have implied my family, seeing as I had no other contact with the outside world, except with the people that I trusted.

"If I find out differently, you will be in a lot of trouble," he kept threatening me and reinforcing his tyrant's position, which suited him perfectly!

"Now go and cook us dinner!" he ordered me, eyes afire like one of the dragons we read about in fairy tales.

"No!" I retorted courageously. It had not been a long time since I had regained my health after my hearing loss incident and that was why I was striving to stand my ground and try to resist. I was ready to go all the way. "I won't put up with this sort of threats anymore," I thought to myself and stood up to him, all alone, against that most barbaric and vicious man.

"Did you just say no to me?" he screamed and then ran like a demon to the kitchen. When he came back, seconds later, he was wielding a broom in his hands and, before I knew what hit me, he grabbed the broomstick and started to beat at me fiercely, blinded by meanness and rage.

With the first strike I felt my fingers almost break. Once again, he was beating me, spinelessly, to my hands. After that, I couldn't move my fingers for a very long time. I was beat at the same hand that he had injured in London, the time when he had given me a wrist fracture as a token of his love and appreciation. As it turned out, Sami was not the only member of his family to… value "practice over theory"; some time later, his father corroborated Sami's stance as he, too, claimed that the woman must get a sound thrashing and that this was stipulated by some verses of the Koran!

The violence and physical pain had forced me to once again give in against my will. Hurt and humiliated, I went into the kitchen and cooked him dinner, as ordered.

In my heart of hearts, I kept hoping for him to leave and go far, far away. But that was just my wishful thinking… The next day he was home again. And somehow, each month, he would manage to stay at home as much as possible and keep an eye on me.

At eleven the next morning I cautiously ventured to get out of bed without his noticing it. But almost immediately I felt his hand brutally pulling me back down to bed.

"Where do you think you're going?" he growled. "Stay here and sleep!"

And just like that, I found myself lying on the bed again, staying absolutely still and waiting for him to wake up in the afternoon for a new round of rout.

"Would you like to call your mother?" he said to me unexpectedly like he was daring me, rather than inviting me, to do so.

On one hand, I was thrilled at the opportunity, but, on the other, I couldn't shake the suspicion that there was an ulterior motive to his offer. Surely he must have been apprehensive on some level that, after all the violence I had been suffering, the day would come when I would manage to find a way to contact my family in Athens, making things rather difficult for him. So, I guess he preferred that I do it in his presence so he could monitor the conversation. He would filter every word out of my mouth, as he had always done before, and at the same time he could pass for the benevolent husband that was allowing me to contact my kin.

So, he went to Mohammed's across the hall and brought the telephone back to our place dragging the long cord behind him.

"Go ahead, make your phone call. But make sure you don't put me on!" he said to me with a solemn look on his face.

I did not answer him anything, but I felt like I utterly disliked him at that moment. All the injustice I was suffering was like a chokehold around my neck; nevertheless, I was there, with no other choice—he had my passport and my belongings—and took advantage of his offer.

I was incredibly happy to talk to my mother, even though I had no way of expressing my true feelings to her. My heinous tyrant was right opposite me, staring at me with his vicious glare. So, I was expected to sound obedient and calm, pretending that I was enjoying a happy life as a devoted wife. Under the circumstances, I could only speak very simply and plainly to my mother. Still, my mother understood that I was in a difficult spot, although she could not fathom the entire insanity of this man's mind.

As soon as I hung up, he started his second round of questioning.

"Why did you say 'tomorrow' again like the last time?" (He only knew a few Greek words and tomorrow was one he understood.) What did you mean by that?"

He kept grilling me, asking the same questions again and again, because his guilt-ridden, evil mind could not accept my simple answers. The telephone call was meant to put me at ease, but instead it had stirred his apprehension.

All through the rest of the evening until late into the night he kept tormenting me to extract explanations about why I had mumbled the word 'tomorrow' on the phone with my mother.

"Spit it out! Why did you say this and what did you mean by it?" he'd ask over and over again.

It was an endless questioning, just like after the last time I had called my mother. My answers were simple and clear, but his twisted mind refused to accept them. Six never-ending hours went by, during which he was drenched in sweat as he was trying to elicit something that would justify his suspicions, satisfy his ego and open the show the way to another vicious circle of torture. I was so worn down by these interrogations, in the course of which I was called upon to answer for inexistent trespasses of mine. These consecutive traumatic experiences will remain indelibly imprinted on my heart and mind forever. *What is the reason for this inhumane behavior?* I kept wondering. I had not done anything to harm him and we hadn't known each other for years on end, so that perhaps he might have been holding a grudge against me for something I had done a long time ago and had forgotten about it. The only mistake for which I faulted myself was that I had trusted him, believed in him and placed my life upon his hands. Everything pointed to the conclusion that he might have been motivated by some verse in the Koran—or his interpretation of it—in relation to how Muslims should treat the *kaafirs*—the infidels—and especially Christians. *That must be it! There is no other explanation!* That was the best plausible explanation I could deduce. I felt like I was the expiatory sacrifice to offset the mistakes of all religions that poisoned people's minds and turned them into fanatics and against each other. And Sami was by nature extremely susceptible to such extremes.

All these thoughts kept running through my mind, preparing me to confront those kinds of behaviors. Perhaps that was the explanation for all the erratic situations and horror-movie-type episodes I was going through, such as the incident that took place in Paris during our honeymoon, when I had escaped death by a miracle, or all those other life-threatening situations. For if it wasn't a matter of religion, what was it that possessed that man and turned him into a monster? I was looking for answers because one thing was for sure: something out of the ordinary was definitely going on! I thank the divine providence for protecting me and saving me at those moments where there was no human intervention, so that I could gradually and timidly each time resurface back to life and see the light of day. That was the man, the Saudi "husband" of the highest caliber, held in great esteem by everyone around, a captain with Saudia airlines, the epitome of a gentleman! And in spite of everything, nothing would urge him to come to his senses. He remained tough, rigid, unyielding, a man fighting for his misplaced beliefs to the death. And after each disaster he would look for ways to save his own neck. It was as if he was a robot programmed to destroy me.

I dare say that, during our trip to Paris, he had behaved as if there had been a contract out on me and he was eager to deliver. He had failed then but the idea seemed to have been stuck in his head. "Man proposes, God disposes," as they say, so my trip to Paris ended up being a roundtrip indeed, although it had come dangerously close to being a one-way trip for me. But the problem was not the venue. It didn't matter if we were in Paris or in Jeddah. My emotional and physical torture was the same everywhere, much like the same theme painted over and over again on a different canvas. And quite a ghastly theme at that—new versions of a *Massacre of the Innocents*, at times painted against a backdrop of hell and, at other times, against a backdrop of heaven, where I'd always be in the forefront, a terrified look on my face as I tried to resist the powers of evil and not get slaughtered. And while I was having all these thoughts, his coarse voice would bring me back to the present time. It was he and I, face to face! My near-death experience in Paris flashed like lightning before my eyes once more, before I was fully aware of the ominous present. I was staring at the horizon through the large window of our living room, sunk in a deep void. Physically I was there, but emotionally I was nowhere. I was devoid of expectations, devoid of hope. I was perishing in my silence!

According to the calendar, it was August; but time for me had stopped five months ago. Nothing was changing. I was pacing back and forth in that immense apartment, oozing of emptiness. I was looking for the impossible. I wanted so badly to go outside, to walk about as a free person, to feel the hot sun on my face, to hear my footsteps, the slightest sound that would awake my senses and remind me that I exist! But I had nowhere to go. I was deserted in the desert—I felt the meaning of that word in my bones.

Prohibition was the predominant feature weighing down on me: I was neither allowed to go out alone nor to be escorted by anyone other than my husband. And even if I broke those rules, I had nowhere to go. I was a stranger among strangers. I was a free to be a prisoner. When he wouldn't want to leave me behind in Jeddah while he was away at work, he would load me like a piece of luggage onto an airplane and fly me like a parcel, airport to airport, to my alternative prison: his parents' house. The only time I could feel like a human being was during the one-hour-and-twenty-minute flight when I was alone in the passengers' cabin and had the chance to exchange a few words with other people and accept a few kind invitations. Of course, there was no following up on these invitations. Everything stopped where it began. Castles in the air…

When I'd get off the plane, I'd be picked up by his brother to be further shipped to my final destination: their impregnable fortress. Enaam, the lockkeeper, would be waiting for me there like the new convict in the block, ready to pick up the baton and place me under her vile and vigilant supervision, confined in the room of the upper floor for the whole duration of my stay there.

"Would you like something to eat?" she'd ask me the self-explanatory.

"Yes, if you please," I'd respond awkwardly.

"How about some eggs?" she'd offer—such were the sumptuous meals I was being served while under her roof.

And for the two or three days I'd spend there, pending Sami's new orders, I had to obey the mandatory house regulations, from food to sleep. After each stay there, I'd leave thinner and weaker, suffering from vitamin deficiency. As of late, Enaam had even forbidden Hari, the maid, to speak to me and the poor woman was so afraid of her that she only dared exchange some furtive signals with me. Actually, we were both afraid; Hari was afraid of the hard work she would be forced to do as punishment and I was afraid of my own future torment, since Enaam would regularly call up Sami to report to him and he would make a point of coming up with the proper series of torture for me.

"Well, did you have a good time in Riyadh?" he'd ask first thing upon my return to Jeddah.

"Very good!" was my compulsory reply.

"Did you talk to anyone?" he'd then ask ironically.

"No, I didn't, I'm sure!" I'd respond in the only way I could.

He wouldn't waste any time. As soon as we'd step into the house, he'd start with the questioning all over again. God, it was like a job to him! And his grilling would go on until he broke me and I "confessed" so that I could suffer the appropriate punishment.

"Would you like to go to sleep?" he once asked me overeagerly. "You may go!"

Physically and emotionally depleted, I took him up on his offer and fell asleep almost immediately, unsuspecting and uncaring of what might happen to me. Suddenly, I woke up with a start, feeling something cold on my face. He had poured water on me water and was standing there, looking at me sarcastically. Repulsed, I looked daggers at him, but kept my mouth shut and armed myself with patience to avoid being put in harm's way. I would have loved to be in his shoes and he in mine, even just for a moment, so that he could feel how much pain he was inflicting on me. Yet I preferred to remain silent and swallow the latest humiliation and debasement that I had suffered. My superficial apathy drove him crazy. He'd rather I was like him—brutal, vindictive, a torturer.

During the night he'd put all his evil powers at work and during the day we'd take count of the damage done: broken treasures, torn clothing, blood spatters—a disaster area! Each night I was subjected to the terror of watching all this mayhem around me and him sleeping the sleep of the just. It was like a horror movie masterfully written and directed in the most nightmarish way possible. Time was slipping through my fingers and I didn't know what to do.

One evening his cold presence near me made me jump. Fear was an integral part of my life now, I was living a nightmare! Whenever I'd looking at his face, I would freeze from shock! The image of him radiated everything negative in this world. The man that had once charmed me and won me over was now repulsing me with horror and terror. Nevertheless, I thought that I had managed to keep my mental health intact.

Although I did my best to keep them concealed, Sami would pick up on those feelings he stirred inside me. But I would remain calm and visibly unconcerned, going about my business. He just stood there, by the door, staring at me. I could feel his glare peering right through me—it was a horrible feeling! In my mind there was no doubt he wanted to provoke me into another confrontation, but my external indifference threw him off. Every moment of peace was a godsend! I couldn't take any more of that constant ruckus; I was by nature a peaceful person!

Luckily, he was about to leave on assignment. I was extremely glad when I saw him pack his stuff. I would be free within my prison; I would at least be able to breathe in my share of air freely.

He was leaving for Paris and, just before he closed the door behind him, he turned around and showed me some of my jewelry, which he was holding in his hands. I ran to our bedroom and saw all my jewelry scattered around the carpet—some of them had been stepped on! I ran out to the balcony and looked down. Before he got into the car, he provocatively showed me a bunch of rings he held in his palm.

"Get out of here and never come back!" I yelled at him furiously.

He was mistreating me, abusing me and torturing me, as if that was what "marriage" and "coexistence" meant to him and in defiance of the Mufti's explicit suggestions. "Take care of her and enlighten her," he had told him at our wedding; instead, Sami had become my executioner on the prowl.

In a blatant display of his phony side, once in Paris, he called up my mother to reassure her that everything was fine and we were having a great time together! Instinctively, my mother called me up on Mohammed's telephone to make sure that was really the case. Instead, she heard me crying at the other end of the line. I couldn't control myself, my pain and sorrow ran so deep. I told her that he had physically abused me on several occasions and that I was being mistreated by both him and his mother.

"This is very far from the picture he painted to me during his phone call from Paris!" said my mother, bewildered.

From that moment on, the ball had been set rolling. My mother initiated the procedure to get herself a visa and come to me in Jeddah. But it would be a while before she could get one, owing to the relevant red tape—in order for her to get a visa, she would have to be formally invited.

Meanwhile, that August seemed endless. It was extremely hot, with sweltering temperatures and a stifling atmosphere; both the pavement and the sand were literally scorching under our feet. Sami was away for work a lot, because it was the typical month of summer vacation, and I would often end up, where else, at Enaam's place.

During one of those stays in Riyadh, Enaam decided to take me along to an all-women dinner party at some relative's house. Although only women were present, when we got there I saw they were fully covered anyway in overstated proof of piety. There were about two or three empty rooms in a row and the women were all seated cross-legged on the carpeted floor, waiting in a row to be served. In front of them were laid out newspapers instead of tablecloths.

Unsmiling and inhospitable, they would stare at me, their looks revealing what they were thinking about me. I was clearly an outsider. Unabashed, they dug into the food, one hand grabbing pieces of meat and grilled lamb's heads from the platters in front of them, the other one shaping a handful of rice into a ball before it ended up in their mouth. That was their way of enjoying their food: no frills, no refined manners...

I couldn't go along with either their way of life or their taste in food, but joining in, one way or another, was a necessary evil. I didn't want to be pegged as the haughty foreigner; they were noticeably hostile as it were, and I was one against many. Their nasty looks were quite telling of what they thought of me—they appeared to have no knowledge of, or interest in, keeping up appearances. One way or another, I managed to get through that occasion unscathed. All is well that ends well!

The next day Enaam had arranged for us to go with her friends to the souk in downtown Riyadh. A chauffeured big Buick picked up Umm Khadija and Umm this and Umm that, and they all frolicked like schoolgirls on a daytrip throughout the ride to the heart of Riyadh.

The commercial center of the city of Riyadh—and any commercial center in any city around Saudi Arabia—was doubling as a clandestine meeting place, an underground monkey parade for matchmaking purposes. Groups of women, allegedly out shopping or window-shopping, would bump into groups of men or individual hopefuls, strutting up and down the market isles, each one in the hopes of releasing his repressed frustration.

Not long after we arrived at the marketplace—actually after only a few minutes—I realized that a bunch of young Saudi men were following us around and Khadija, a mother of married children, was signaling them seductively under her transparent, mystery-enhancing veil. The game was on! There was an entire "philosophy" to the *niqab*, which the most progressive and sensuous of the women had upgraded to an instrument for exciting men's hankering imagination, having them yearn to uncover the mysteries beneath it. That was these women's "Dance of the Seven Veils," aimed at fulfilling their ambitious aspirations—which would hopefully be different than what Salome had in store for John the Baptist!

The "girly" group had been successful at their ritual of seduction, so, on our way back to the house, we were tailed by a limo carrying six Saudi men. Their masterful technique had left me speechless! Everything was forbidden yet everything was happening in the most remarkable way! Unfortunately, I couldn't talk and exchange views with the rest of the women under the watchful supervision of Enaam, who was feigning the utmost innocence and virtuousness at my presence; but I had certainly dipped a toed into the murky waters of how to be a seemingly repressed woman of the Orient.

When we got back to the house, I was surprised to see Sami waiting for us with a jolly smile on his face.

"Did you enjoy your outing?" he asked me, still smiling in contentment.

"Yes," I told him. "It was quite the interesting ride indeed! It was Khadija's day!" I said and proceeded to recount everything I had witnessed.

Sami's face contorted as he feigned a smile. He shrewdly and silently sidestepped the matter, avoiding to confirm (or deny) any part of my narrative, including Enaam's role in that charade.

During one of my trips to Riyadh, Sami left one morning to go to work and I was to join him later on in the afternoon on the flight back to Jeddah that he would pilot himself.

As I was walking up the boarding stairs and before I got onto the aircraft, I was recognized by an old friend and colleague of mine. This sort of thing had happened before at exactly the same spot and I had a bitter experience of it, so this time around I tried to be restrained and cautious. Yet, my colleague was more effusive. She hugged me impulsively and immediately inquired what had happened to me and why I had disappeared for such a long time. Sami was on the lookout right behind me! Before a word came out of my mouth, he suddenly pulled me into the cockpit. Once again, he started to accuse me and ask me how I knew that woman and why I had greeted her.

"If she speaks to you again, I will slap her in the face," he snarled.

Mortified and heartbroken, I silently slipped into my first-class seat and refrained from speaking to anyone until the end of the journey. My only response to my former colleague was a brief glance of sorrow signaling my "goodbye." She and I had been rather close in the past and had shared some good times during our travels and in the compound. She was a woman of impeccable manners, ethics and education, and I thought very highly of her—which was one of the reasons why I had felt so humiliated by Sami's conduct! Memories of the good old times flashed before my eyes, but that was then and now was now—and it was a horrible now to be in! I sank into my seat, closed my eyes, swallowed my sorrow deep inside me and wished that journey would never end… I was well aware of what was to come upon me once we had reached our destination!

"You will wait for me at the arrivals hall," Sami said to me authoritatively after landing the plane.

After I had waited for him for quite a long time, he eventually showed up and signaled me to follow him. He got in the car first and waited for me to get in like a beast of prey waiting to mangle me. It was the second time that I had been prevented from catching up with an old friend who had recognized me and I couldn't help wondering what could be so sinful about old friends displaying their amiable feelings and sharing a chat!

I still recall his frenzied driving on the way back home. He was speeding without even looking so much at the road as at me, demanding answers to his paranoid questions about why I had exchanged a greeting with that fellow air hostess. I was forced to defy my own intellect and agree with his unreasonable obsessions in order for him to leave me alone. That was the only solution! He was a man of a convoluted idiosyncrasy; there were so many different factors playing into the synthesis of his psyche, a psyche that typically reflected the general mindset of the people from the Gulf, the most rigid and intolerant among all the Arabs. They appear to believe that they are infallible, hardly ever regretting their actions and always blaming others for any fault. Sami was a miniature representation of this phallocratic society centered around the nucleus of the predominant male. And those among them that are the most hard-core in their conduct are the men of Riyadh; the people of Jeddah, by contrast, are more or less a mishmash of outsiders left over from caravans of pilgrims to Mecca. At first, I had been puzzled to see Saudis that had oriental or

Mongolian facial features or African black skin, but then with time I realized these were the upshot of many generations of pilgrims originating from Africa, the Far East, Iran, Turkey, etc. The "authentic" swart Saudis also had certain distinct features depending on the particular part of the land they came from. Nevertheless, I had come to be suspicious of all of them; I did not trust them, because I had come to believe that they were all alike under the mask of hypocrisy. I felt that there were traps hidden behind their superficial kindness and manners; they were full of promises but wouldn't do anything for you if you were not a relative or if they had nothing to gain from you! Foreign women were in quite a high demand, but their safety was all but guaranteed; from time to time I would hear of some of them vanishing from the face of the earth without anyone looking for them while, of course, the law was not on their side either. The Saudis were untouchable; and I was experiencing this on a daily basis, as I was being accused and burdened with the responsibility for everything that was happening.

Meanwhile, the intrigues and conspiracies between Jeddah and Riyadh, focusing on me, continued! Worried to see Sami's persecution slightly abate for a while, Enaam sent out her younger son Abdullah to our home. Sami's brother's supposedly innocuous visit served to further muddy the waters. Seeing as her own mobility was rather confined, "Mama" of Riyadh had decided to send over Abdullah to spy on me.

I was quite skeptical about his visit, because I knew there was nothing innocent about it and, besides, it had only been three days since I had come back to Jeddah from their house. He was there to keep an eye on me and report back to her.

On the afternoon that he arrived, I welcomed him amiably but reservedly—I chose to be cautious despite the fact that he was only sixteen years old.

"Would you like some coffee?" I asked Sami.

He nodded to me that he did, so I made my way to the kitchen leaving the two brothers alone in the living room.

"You come back here!" I heard Sami commanding me.

"Yes, sir!" I responded in a condescending manner.

"Why you didn't ask my brother if he'd like some too?" he admonished me.

"Well, he's so young and I wouldn't imagine he drinks coffee at this age—"

"Well, he does! And you'll get him one right now!"

I wanted to scream at the top of my lungs so that everyone could hear me! I was being treated like a worthless servant in the Dark Ages! Instead, I abided.

"Here's your coffee, Your Highness!" I said with a slight bow, as I came back from the kitchen and handed Sami his coffee.

"And here's yours, Your Excellency!" I said to Abdullah and then withdrew to the back rooms, leaving the blue-blooded Arabs alone to enjoy their hot beverages!

Five minutes later I heard Sami yell out to me; he was calling me back to apologize to his brother who had taken offence upon figuring out my sarcasm.

I went back into the living room and answered to them that my words had been innocent and impulsive and that there was no pun intended. Then I walked out to the veranda to avoid a head-on confrontation, which, however, seemed inevitable. I usually avoid giving any answer at all, knowing full well that nothing I said to defend myself made any difference to Sami.

"Come back inside!" he yelled at me ferociously.

I purposefully ignored him, because I knew what he was looking to accomplish: he wanted to humiliate me in front of his brother.

His screams escalated with more and more fury. Then he came out to the veranda himself and tugged violently on my arm. I had been leaning against the wall so, as he yanked me forcefully, my skin was scuffed by the rough surface of the wall and blood started to drip and stain all over the floor.

I was feeling powerless; I couldn't yell, cry or say nothing. But I resisted in my own way: by ignoring him...

He dragged me along the carpet like a slayer dragging a helpless animal to its slaughter. He pinned me down to the floor, straddled on top of me pressing his knees down on my wrists and keeping me still with his entire body weight. I felt his sweat trickling down onto my face as I kept mine turned away from his gaze, waiting for yet another torture to be over... As he kept on talking to me but I remained inexpressive, silently praying to God for protection.

For over thirty minutes of agony I endured the full pressure of his body on top of me without any complain or protest, so eventually he gave up the futile fight—his opponent wasn't reacting.

"You're strong!" he said as he released my arms in an indirect but clear acknowledgement of my great reserves of strength. After half an hour of immobility and pressure, all I could feel in my limb arms an excruciating pain in my joints. God knows how I made it through that!

After yet another battle in that ongoing war of attrition, I had once again made it out alive, reaffirming—to myself more than to anyone else—my strong will to survive.

The enchanting sunset was the most comforting, albeit temporary, remedy for my deeply wounded soul. No one around the neighborhood knew the daily drama that was going on at 38 Knuz Al Elm Street. I was living a life on the edge, walking on a tightrope of delicate balance. To make things worse, I now had to face a brother as well, who was acting upon orders from the headquarters in Riyadh. The following day was to be one of the toughest ever for me, as I now had to face two opponents.

Around noon of the next day, a cruel battle broke out. Sami's screams and insults electrified the atmosphere. His continuous verbal abuse made for a never-ending altercation. Still, I was trying to get a word in edgewise and explain to his brother what was happening to me. I had nothing to hide, and yet I couldn't stop crying disconsolately.

Suddenly, I felt an overwhelming force push me against the wall, my head wobbling like a bobblehead doll on a dashboard. He started to beat my head against the wall mercilessly. I passed out, so he left me alone. I could not remember much afterwards…

When I woke up the next day, it was almost noon. Abdul Aziz rang our doorbell; he had come to pick up Abdullah and take him back home. Before he left, I asked him what time it was. It was exactly twelve o'clock! As soon as he was out the door, I was all alone at home. Sami had left to attend his annual retraining session at the training center in Jeddah.

As I got up from my bed to go to the bathroom, I felt my body double up in a ninety-degree angle. I was terrified, I panicked! I could not understand what was happening to me; my best guess was that this was due to the beatings on my head of the previous day. I was so frightened that something even worse was going to happen to me. I was unable to react and that was killing me.

I tried to move, but it was impossible! The room was spinning, I saw everything upside down. Not long ago, I had lived through that other horror when I almost lost my hearing, and now this! I was all by myself but, as usual, I relied on my self-preservation instinct. I had to find a solution right away. My first thought was to sit down on the floor and slither back to the bedroom moving backwards on my behinds, since I could not balance my body. So I did and managed to haul myself back to bed. I lay still for many hours; even the slightest move of my eyes made me dizzy. In my mind I kept asking God desperately to give me mercy and to help me, because only He was there for me to give me strength during those cruel tests. That day was a gloomy day that has marked my mind and soul in the darkest of colors, forever. I felt so alone, so powerless, so helpless...

Late in the afternoon, my bedroom door opened. It was Sami who had come back from his training session. I saw him standing over me in his uniform, pondering concerned—and with good reason. The terrible condition I was in was his doing, the outcome of his fury, hate and beatings.

Using the fewest words necessary, I explained to him how I was feeling. Albeit alarmed, he kept his cool and said that it was probably something temporary and that I was going to recover soon.

I don't know exactly how I pulled through but I did. Meanwhile, Abdullah had returned to Riyadh and presumably reported back to the woman who had sent him to Jeddah in the first place and was solely responsible for all my troubles.

It was around that time that a peculiar commotion in telephone communications between Riyadh and Jeddah began to take place. Enaam was calling on Mohammed's phone almost nonstop. Apparently, they wanted to get me out of the way once and for all; but they didn't know what to do with me, so they were looking for a solution to their impasse. On one hand, Enaam was probably quite content that her devious plan of getting rid of me was moving forward, but, on the other, she hadn't quite factored in my reactions. Something was thwarting their plans!

"Samia," Mohammed said to me one day, "I'm afraid that they're up to something. Sami's mother called and—"

"And what, Mohammed?" said I. "Please, tell me what you know!"

"Well, don't you understand? They believe that Sami is too good for you. You are a foreigner, a stranger, and it is you who brings these misfortunes upon yourself."

What a Dark-Ages way of thinking! Apparently, I was to be burned at the stake because I was a foreigner, a miasma!

"I see, Mohammed. So, I'm a foreigner. And for this reason they have to torture me? Kill me even?"

"Listen, I cannot tolerate all the shouting and screaming anymore," Mohammed said. "I'd like to call the police."

"So why don't you?" I asked.

I received my answer merely by the look in his eyes. He was terrified of the consequences if he were to go on police record about this. Sami and his family would go after him until they did him in. Mohammed was not a Saudi; he was of Palestinian descent and, although he had lived in Saudi

Arabia his whole life, his non-native status placed him in a position of disadvantage.

"You need to call your family and tell them," he kept on advising me.

"Please, show me the way I can deal with this," I said to him. "I don't know what I am supposed to do because they are keeping the truth from me!"

"I know. Unfortunately, though, I can't do anything for you or I'll get into trouble myself."

And with that, our conversation came to an end, leaving me rife with questions about the void of my presence in Saudi Arabia. I had received clear and explicit guidelines that, even if I were at the edge of death, I would not ask for help. And that implication was also clear to Mohammed who had nevertheless offered me his precious assistance some time ago, when he had taken me to the hospital after that other incident. Of course, we had kept that occurrence to ourselves; only he and I knew that he had helped me. In fact, Mohammed had been quite discreet, when everyone and everything else around was colluding against me. Under the circumstances, even a "friendly visit" or a courtesy call could backfire. I had no support and could not be heard by anyone, even for a moment: that was the law. As for the women, who hypocritically pretended to empathize with me, all they'd do was listen and learn and then relay everything they had heard or saw to their husbands who would in turn report everything back to Sami. The word "trust" had been deleted from my vocabulary. The prevailing atmosphere was inspiring secrecy, fraudulence, conspiracy, and every word and move of mine was being scrutinized and filtered by their weights and measures, without their ever taking into account the fact that I was a newcomer to their country and I needed help to understand their religious and social customs. Instead, like severe judges, they imputed my faults and watched over my every move with only one goal in mind: to elicit my opinions about Sami, his family and Enaam who would then punish me accordingly. I was always the one who had to be understanding of their ways, be patient and accept every aspect of their perfectly made angelic world...

After the incident of the blow to my head and upon numerous consultations between Jeddah and the queen bee's hive in Riyadh, it was decided that things should be allowed to cool down for a while. So, "good boy" Sami very willingly took me along with him on a journey to Paris.

The trip was meant to soften my pain and make me forget the things that, to this day, are indelibly imprinted into my mind and heart. To reinforce the fallacy of normalcy, we spent three days with a couple of Saudis, who were nice, ordinary people. There I was, back in my beloved city of light, but I could not let go of the recent past and enjoy myself even for a moment. My sorrow ran very deep! I knew full well that Sami was pretending throughout that trip, giving me a morsel of fleeting pleasure in the hopes that that could make all of my pain go away—as if he could buy my pain out. His intentions were almost well-meant; he didn't know any better. That was how he had been taught to act, in a superficial and materialistic manner. "Money buys everything," he used to say to me, while he had forbidden me to think, read, function like a normal human being.

In our hotel suite, he delivered a long catechism about how many times a man can divorce in Islam by saying the phrase: "I divorce you." Special emphasis was placed on the third and final time: once he's said it a third time, he can never take it back, unless certain conditions are met, under which a couple is allowed to get remarried. A glaring example of such a divorce case was that of Mona and Ahmed, Sami's brother. Ahmed divorced her within a matter of seconds and, once released from her bounds, Mona left, leaving their two children behind with Ahmed, as a form of revenge to which Saudi women often resort. Children are treated almost like inanimate objects in this process, left to grow up on their own or under the supervision of some nanny from Sri Lanka or the Philippines who teaches them her native language as their mother tongue. That was precisely what had happened to Fahd, Mona's son, who could understand Sinhala better than Arabic. Their children's education appeared to be of lesser importance, since Saudi women were hardly educated themselves: the first school for women was only established as recently as 1965.

I gathered the impression that education was not considered a plus for a Saudi woman; instead, it was considered to reduce her femininity and bestow her with manly traits. Women and emancipation were contradictory concepts. As if knowledge was a sin, probably because education broadens one's horizons and that might allow women to see the bigger picture and the myth of subjugation to be debunked. Therefore, instead of learning, I too had to forget what knowledge meant, by not reading or hearing anything else but Sami's brainwashing that would lead to the subjugation of my conscience. It was too cruel for a thinking, intelligent human being to accept this sort of downgrading, to go from a mind full of thoughts to emptiness, from everything to nothing. I had already made plenty of compromises, but I could not compromise who I was and where I hailed from like he was asking me to. In fact, he was even planning to have an Arabic identity card issued for me at the most opportune moment in the foreseeable future; that would mean giving up my Greek identity card and finally becoming a true "woman of Saudi Arabia" with a Muslim name. Once more, nonetheless, time would overturn his plans for my full subjugation...

It was a sizzling hot summer day when I went back to the house in Riyadh. When I didn't see Mona there, like I had every other time before, I thought that she had gone to visit her family in Dhahran. Around noon of the scorching hot day, Hari knocked gently on my door and came into my room.

"Mona is gone," she said.

"Gone, how?" I asked rather alarmed.

"She broke up again! Ahmed beat her severely and sent her back to her parents. 'Mama' told him to beat her up because she was not a good wife. She said she would get him another wife and a Filipino maid to raise his children."

I was very disconcerted as my situation was not all that different from Mona's. On one occasion when she had seen the fresh bruises Sami's beatings had incurred on me, she had appeared quite understanding towards me and had even freely expressed her objections to Enaam about those acts of violence. Enaam didn't like that at all; she didn't like Mona knowing and she didn't like Mona interfering. She was the only one entitled to know everything and pull all the strings, under the wraps of secrecy and cunning that best served her own desires and passions. That stumpy woman with the lustful gaze and the hearty laughter gave the impression of a kindly person but in fact was tormented by a great demon inside. She had pride of place among her six sons and her husband and demanded special attention in the fulfillment of her ambitions. Being the archetypal Mother,

her prestige soared on the grounds of the relevant verses of the Koran, making her feel like an almighty goddess who was revered and worshiped by seven men. She was conceited, unyielding, shrewd, insidious and unfeeling. Yet, to her friends and relatives she was a charming, nice person. How ironic! Her only occupation was her endless phone calls, in the course of which she would criticize and gossip all the goings-on in various Saudi homes.

Weddings and wedding receptions were the featured weekly entertainment—in fact, weddings were the only *entertainment* they had. Quite frequently they would travel from one town to the other in order to attend a wedding. Each one of those parties would often fill about half an airplane, as these ladies were travelling along with their maids and servants to make sure everyone knew they were high society. On one of these occasions I went along with them; and very soon I began to feel annoyed and bored.

The wedding reception was taking place in a big garden of a house in Riyadh. A cousin of Sami's was getting married. In the area that was strictly reserved for the women, they had set up a platform and the seats were arranged in an auditorium layout. Dressed lightly, European-style, I took my seat among the rest of the guests, who were all dressed in heavy gold-stitched gowns and laden with tons of gold in jewelry all over. It was like an informal beauty contest among them; for every wedding reception, they would buy a brand new set of jewelry to match their outfit. They appeared to have no financial concerns at all, not a care in the world about matters of everyday life, and in that phony world of ephemeral blissfulness they reveled in material pleasures. The whole world was tailor-made for them! The dizzying blend of their heady fragrances filling the warm, humid air was complemented by the ritualistic, quite expensive and imported from India, incense that was creating an atmosphere of sacramental ceremony.

I felt so lightheaded I almost fainted, but their ululations of joy appeared to have a regenerative effect on me and the unpleasant incident was avoided. It was night and the outdoors lighting wouldn't allow me to make out clearly the newlyweds that were dancing on the floor, although I could see that the bride was flinging her hair in circles for quite some time—it was a Saudi dance. The burning candles, the incense, the heavy perfumes and the aroma of the Arabic coffee brewed and served after midnight made for an almost hallucinatory mixture of scents and flavors, yet to them this was a glamorous event, vested with all the grandeur it deserved!

Food was served after two or three in the morning, their most famous delicacy, *kabsa*, featured at center stage. The celebrations lasted until dawn and my strength began to wane after some time. I did not find anything remotely interesting and it was impossible for me to participate in an event that was physically and mentally straining. Ahmed showed up to pick up Mona—they had reunited again after their second breakup—so I asked "Mama" if I could leave with them and was granted "permission." Stepping out of that place felt liberating, a deep relief, albeit temporary…

I went to bed absolutely exhausted from all the heavy scents and the heat. The following day was Sunday, the day of the Lord. Just another ordinary day for the Arabic people, but a very meaningful day to me: my wistful thoughts about who I was and where I was coming from had flared up again inside me. I so wanted to be in a place of worship of my own denomination, share into the serenity and love that I had missed so much. The nostalgia and melancholy overwhelmed me…

Later on that same afternoon, when the sun had reached its nadir and the sky was painted in rose-colored sheens and the muezzin's voice resounded in our ears, Mona and I went out for a walk around the stores under the supervision of Sami's brother Waleed. She was very happy about our outing, so she put on colorful clothes and bright makeup, which she then covered up with the abaya and niqab, just as I did too.

"*Emshi*? Shall we?" Mona asked me.

"Sure!" I said and we were on our way.

Waleed drove us to an architectural jewel that was housing a colossal shopping mall and our first stop was—what else—the cosmetics department.

We really enjoyed that day out; there was a touch of insouciance to it, far from the control and pressure exercised upon us by the "watchdog" called Enaam. Even that little precious time that we spent outside the house acted like an elixir upon my soul; I felt like I was reborn. It was such a magnificent feeling to feel free from that burden, even for just a short while, that I felt like I was soaring in euphoria. And at that moment I had an epiphany: at that moment I realized truly what freedom is and that human beings are born to be free.

The intense gaze of a shopkeeper brought me back from my reverie. He was eating me up with his eyes, which made me feel quite uncomfortable. You see, at the shopping mall we were free to have our faces uncovered—that was one of the small pleasures shopping afforded us. Pretty soon, our time out had come to an end and we had to return to the cruel reality.

The temperature was well over 110, the tarmac of the pavement was steaming as if it was melting under the car's wheels. The entire city was shrouded in vapors like an oversized steam room, but I would not dare break the dress code. Even under those unbearable weather conditions, I was expected to be covered in black clothes from head to toe, as if I were some masochistic fan of some underground cult. And even in that respect, Saudi men were once again enjoying the privileges afforded to them by the blatant double standard. They basked in their airy, snow-white silk thobes, their heads covered in snow-white or white-and-red checkered *shemaghs*, which they wore either casually and saucily thrown over their heads or majestically and elaborately folded and tucked under the *igal*, clearly standing out as lords and masters compared to the women around them, those dark-cloaked creatures of a lesser god.

In that general ambience, it was not only the local men who coveted foreign women, but local women as well shared similar considerations and were acting upon them in their own covert ways. Quite often they would set their eyes on some male store employee that was obviously "imported" from some other Arabic country and would use shopping as a pretense to put the moves on him in their own underhanded way. The foreign store clerk was quite the easy prey; as risky as it was to give in to their lure, it was nearly unthought-of to refuse or resist them in any way, as any given situation could so easily be turned around to lay the blame on the foreigner instead of the local. Such an odd society filled with contradictions in its convictions and marked by intense feelings of guilt and fear! And all that made people suspicious and dishonest. I had experienced that first hand from Enaam when she'd take me to the stores around her house and watch over my shoulder under her niqab, prowling to identify any suspicious move. She would scrutinize the gazes of the men around and then stare at me to inspect my reactions.

At other times she would look me in the eyes as if striving to see in them the reflection of her financial superiority—that was about all she could hold over me. It was blatantly obvious she did not like me at all and was trying to drown me in a glass of water. More often than not, she and her friends would badmouth me, both behind my back and in my face, to make me feel uncomfortable because I did not belong. I was an outsider, a pariah, and they made sure to take all their frustration of deprivation and all their meanness out on me, as if I were the one responsible for their predicament.

Time and again, I would be handed the apple of discord for the additional reason that many women were hoping to claim Sami for themselves. He, on the other hand, would systematically avoid being in Riyadh while I was there and when he'd come, he'd put up a disdainful attitude towards me by ignoring me, especially in the presence of his mother Enaam, his allegiance to whom was proverbial. He adored her, he had an inexhaustible admiration for her as if he were living and breathing just for her! When, in the beginning of our acquaintance, he had made a point to me about how he cried for his mother once a month, I had felt deeply moved by his sensitivity and devotion. Alas, I didn't know he reserved that sort of loyalty only for her.

"I would have married her if I could," he'd mumbled one day in Jeddah, during one of our altercations.

I was dumbfounded! It seemed that what I was trying so hard not to admit was actually true. I couldn't deny it to myself anymore. The confirmation shocked me, but it was finally out in the open: my suspicions about the nature of their relationship were well grounded.

Sami was a torn man, struggling to love and to be loved in his own misled way, a way which would turn him into a monster at times. He yearned to break free from all the things that trapped his mind and soul, but he attempted to do it by becoming an oppressor himself. You see, these are the inherent risks of such closed societies.

I had heard enough. Vexed by the oddity of it all, I had started to realize that I was in a place where fantasy merges into a blur with reality and space merges with time. And I was entangled in that black hole, body and soul, the victim and sufferer of all kinds of misfortunes, feeling defeated and deprived of the dreams and ambitions I once knew to have…

One day in the beginning of September, when Sami and I were at his parents' house in Riyadh, we retreated to our room to get some rest. Not long after we climbed up the stars and lay down, the monster inside him woke up with a start to gift me some more nightmarish moments. I don't know exactly what it was that upset him so, especially when we were at that house, but yet again, for no good reason at all, he snapped at me big time. He opened the window and started to throw out all my personal belongings—clothes, cosmetics, anything he could get his hands on. I was pleading with him to calm down, but he kept on acting like a lunatic and shouted even louder. Abruptly woken up, his father and brothers jumped out of their beds and hurried to our room to see what was going on. I felt so humiliated and ridiculed; I wished I had never been born. They had barged into our room while I was trying to cover myself and hide. He had given them the reason and right to barge into our room and invade my privacy. I just stood there absolutely mortified, trying to cover my nightdress with my hands. I was in Saudi Arabia in my private dressed in a negligee amidst four men. I felt so emotionally violated I wished the earth would open up and swallow me. As low-key and discreet as I was personally, Sami strived to disgrace me. Well, his theatrics got him what he wanted: once again, he had made me a wreck.

"I want to sleep. Take her out of here," he shouted hysterically while his father and brothers were trying to calm him down. As for me, overwhelmed by my feelings of injustice and shame over his degrading and sordid histrionics, I could not utter a word...

"Mama" was auditing the show from downstairs. He had succeeded in showing her how he felt about me beyond any doubt. And I did not like that at all! I hated him with all my heart because he was a coward! Once again, he had taken advantage of my position of weakness to annihilate me.

Devastated by that episode of extreme behavior and feeling terribly alone, I waited for the night to be over. My clenched heart and dark soul blurred the thoughts in my mind. I felt the nightmare sleeping and breathing right beside me as if nothing had happened! My emotional response was deep desire to avenge myself, to make him hurt, make him feel like a powerless nothing; but my good sense was holding me back. I was not about to become a victim turned torturer, a civilized person turned crude.

Eventually I got some sleep. When I woke up he was gone and I was able to spend some time temporarily free from my tyrant. My short stay in Riyadh was almost over and pretty soon I would be flying back to Jeddah, making that same useless trip from one city to another, from one house to another, back and forth between different sides of the same coin. And yet, that particular time I was about to say my last good-bye to the house in Riyadh—only I didn't know it yet…

Politely and discreetly, I said my good-byes to everyone. Waleed was waiting for me in the car to take me to the airport. When we got there, he spent another five minutes chatting with me and then left, after pointing me to the waiting area for the women. After a short while, I boarded the plane. I was miserable, knowing I was only leaving one prison to go to another. All alone on the plane again, I was tormented by harrying thoughts. The memories and wounds were still too fresh and deep to be healed.

Just three days before I left Riyadh, on a night when the temperature tallied 115 degrees, I had gone to my room to sleep to find out that the air conditioner was not working. I was certain the family knew about it, but they let me suffer until the end of that unforgettable night. It was madness! The sheets, the mattress, the carpet, everything was sizzling hot. I would open the window and the air coming in was like a gust of volcanic lava. I would shut it again before I'd burn to death. Everyone else was sleeping quietly in their rooms, but I was up, crying, not knowing what to do. I was on fire!

Finally, I mustered all my courage, came out of the room and started to pace up and down the house like a ghost in my long nightdress, ignoring the rules and risks, until I ended up in an air-conditioned dining room and crashed on a couch. That was where they found me the next morning, Enaam putting on a sardonic smile feigning sympathy…

Those memories would come crashing back and make me relive those nightmares even during the most relaxing moments of my trip. By then I had no more dreams or visions except one: my salvation. I needed to find a way out of there.

After a short while, the air hostess announced that we would be arriving in Jeddah shortly, an announcement that made me jump, not for joy, but for fear of what was about to follow.

My "knight in shining armor" was there to pick me up; only he was a black knight on a black horse, the dire reminder of my predicament. He was waiting at the airport to pick me up like a piece of luggage and bombard me with his endless grilling all the way back to our home. This time the questioning was about my shopping outing with Mona. It was clear that Enaam had, as usual, briefed him thoroughly before I had gotten back to Jeddah. She was taking no chances with losing her absolute power, still asserting her complete control with her "divide-and-rule" tactics.

The situation kept deteriorating. There was nothing bonding me with that man anymore; we had lost all contact and it was only through violence that he would try to impose himself upon me. Yet, inside me I was still tormented by a great big "Why?" Why was all this happening? Why was our marriage leading nowhere? Why did he cut my career short if he wasn't absolutely sure about what he wanted from me? Why should I be treated like that? What wrong had I done to suffer such tests that would mark my entire life? Countless "whys" that remain unanswered to this day.

Sami would exhibit an unprecedented rivalry towards me, as if that man hated all women on the face of the earth and I was the chosen one to suffer this torture in order to purge the entire womankind—especially that of another creed—of its sins. Our relationship had devolved into a never-ending fight for dominance of the strongest, in all the forms and manifestations that such a fight can take. Even the most trivial, the most insignificant of matters, would spark a confrontation and I would be called upon to pay the price. Nothing was nice or pleasant anymore. Even every leisure trip he initiated after everything he had put me through came to me as nothing more than yet another manifestation of that man's squalor.

Our safari to Kenya turned out to be my personal hunt, me being the prey and Sami the hunter. I would run in a state of panic from floor to floor of the Hilton hotel, Sami chasing me and eventually trapping me in our suite, made entirely of bamboo—an incredible environment for a human cage!

When he announced to me that we would go on a trip to Cairo, I was quite delighted, thinking that this might be a way to my freedom. I made plans to visit some archaeological sites, but they proved utopian. I would never get there! I so wanted to see the pyramids up close and take a trip back in time to humanity's distant past, but when we arrived at the passport control, I was astounded to hear the Egyptian policeman say:

"You, Sir, may proceed, but not the lady."

"Why?" I asked the Egyptian utterly dismayed.

"Well, madam, it appears that your husband has not issued the proper visa for you. But he can go ahead."

The sarcastic and contemptuous attitude of the Egyptian policeman irritated me terribly. Once again, I was faced with racism and discrimination in all their splendor!

Sami smirked rather amused, but he did not abandon me in view of that impasse. Besides, he was responsible for me and I had to be immediately removed from Egyptian territory. We took the next flight out on the same plane that had brought us there and found ourselves back to where we had begun our trip.

I could not understand his way of thinking for the life of me! He knew full well that I needed a visa to get into Egypt and yet he'd rather put me through the humiliating experience of being taunted by the Egyptians, who shared the same attitude and mentality with him. I didn't know it at the time, but later on he would be using Cairo as his headquarters of operations in putting his devious plans into action. You see, that place shared the same dominant culture as his home country, but it allowed him more room to move about freely. Unbeknownst to me, I had been baptized with fire.

Cairo was meant to become a turning point. Trapped and naïve then, I was meant to come back one day, only this time I would not be a prey to his noxious plans. For the time being, I was once again coming out unharmed from the fateful games he was setting up for me in various Arabic territories. Every city we would visit was another page in the long saga of his persecution of me and unparalleled rivalry against me, as if he had set out to eliminate me from the face of the earth. But who was behind all this? Who was the mastermind that had led that man, who used to love me, to develop such hatred for me, turning his initial feelings of affection into my relentless persecution?

During our flight back to Jeddah, I was sunk in an abysmal void of sadness and disappointment, no pleasure or excitement anywhere in the horizon. As for Sami, he appeared completely unaffected by that whole episode. Distant and composed, he was simply on another routine flight.

The only thing that caught my eye on that plane was a young woman dressed as a bride. She was travelling alone, dressed in her wedding gown and all her gold jewelry, apparently on her way to meet with her groom-to-be who would be waiting for her in Jeddah. Yes, brides travelling alone was another sight one was likely to come across in domestic flights. That strange world of theirs was rife with contradictions and inconsistencies in their way of life.

We had only been away from Saudi Arabia for roughly four hours, but as soon as our car came to a stop, brakes screeching before our home's front entrance, Abdulrahman hurriedly snapped to attention like a soldier to let Sami pass through. Abdulrahman was a taciturn and gentle little man, who had come to Saudi Arabia from his poverty-ridden home country in search of a better life. His makeshift cabin by the entrance of our building was his own little palace. And from that post he performed his one and only duty: guarding the house. One day, I had asked him reservedly if he could buy me some celery from the market—I even took him into the kitchen to show him what I meant because he did not speak a word of English—but he just looked at me puzzled and stood at the door opening waiting for his orders. At that moment Sami came back unexpectedly. Abdulrahman started to tremble in fear before he took to his heels and scurried away.

"Why don't you invite him in for some tea the next time?" Sami said to me with palpable sarcasm.

"Why not? He has the right to have some tea too!" I replied unabashed.

"But he is the help!"

"So what? Those days are long gone. It's about time you get with the program!" I went on feeling indignant at the discrimination and segregation.

That brief incident became the cause of numerous brawls between us. I simply had to learn my lesson. "You don't get it" or "why won't you listen?" he would say to me and then proceed to make me "get it" and "listen" to the correct opinion that was his.

My immediate punishment was that he seized my jewelry, my passport, my residence permit and my money. In keeping, among other things, with his typical theory that women were incapable of managing their money and should therefore refrain from coming into any contact with it, he callously opened up my wallet, took out the four hundred dollars that were in it and furiously tore them to pieces. Flabbergasted, I just watched him sweep everything clean. He was totally uninhibited and unstoppable. He was capable of anything!

In one more display of that same combative attitude, he threw a similar destructive fit one evening, tossing and scattering my dresses all around the apartment. His goal was to destroy and eradicate anything that belonged to me, anything I loved and held dear, anything I had invested, emotionally or materially, in him and in that home. He wanted to break me and turn me into a gutless creature without choices or opinions. Enslaving my spirit was the hardest task for him, but he thought he could accomplish it by destroying my possessions. This was, among other things, a clash of civilizations...

The place was a mess. By the time I could pick up my trampled dresses, I could see my silk blouses smoldering on top of the lit up light bulbs of the chandelier. Huge burn holes, like volcano craters, gaped on my muslins too. Taking stock of the damage sustained by my wardrobe that afternoon was quite the disheartening task. I cried a lot because these were all pieces of my life that I had carefully selected and lovingly bought on my hard-earned salary. They were my things and it pained me to see them ruined. It only took a few moments for my beautiful French creations to turn into ashes. My grief was so great that I snapped. It was the straw that broke the camel's back. I started to scream and chase him around the apartment. I pounced at him with my nails. I wanted to cause him as much pain as possible... Still, in the end I lost that battle because he was physically stronger than I was.

"It doesn't matter," he smugly said to me the following day. "I will buy you stuff, better stuff, by any designer you like!"

I had heard those words many times before. My defiant silence attested to my disbelief. I was in no mood to pick up a conversation with a person that would destroy me to pieces one day and try to glue me back together the next, only to play his destructive games on me again and repeat the process all over again. I wasn't used to dying so many deaths...

In an attempt to redeem himself, I saw him showcasing to me a number of expensive gowns he had bought for me while on assignment in Paris to replace those he had destroyed. But none of it meant anything to me. The display of some material objects could not mend my broken heart while he was still crushing me every single day. Nevertheless, his gesture had showed me that, in his way, he was attempting to provide even some temporary relief to the wounds he was causing...

With time, he had gradually forbidden me to use the word "mine," thus denying me of the right to ownership of my belongings. So I had to be very cautious in the wording of my phrases. Every mistake, every slip of my tongue, was paid for dearly with more "lessons" in non-entitlement and enfeeblement.

One day, around noon, he hurled out from the balcony onto the garden all my plants, along with their expensive porcelain pots, which I had acquired at an antique shop in Thailand. In only a few seconds, a small fortune was smashed to pieces. What a cruelty! What vandalism against art! Everything was completely destroyed. And my stamina was being put to multiple tests by that barbaric assault.

Then, one afternoon, Sami appeared changed. He had just come back from Casablanca, where he had stayed for three days. For the first time he looked downcast, pensive, and guilt-ridden. He even said he needed to speak to me! Very calm—so calm as never before—and soft-spoken, he approached me in a very humane and emotional way.

"I want to tell you something," he said in a low, slurred voice, "but you shall not tell anyone, not even your mother."

I nodded my head in agreement and waited eagerly to hear what it was that, even for a fleeting moment, had softened that man's heart.

"I was in Morocco, you know, and while I was there I was introduced to a woman. That woman was a fortuneteller using plumbomancy in her divination…"

I had no idea what he was talking about, but I found out later that this was one method—out of many employed in those countries—of divination, a magic of sorts, in which the seer observed the shapes molten lead took when poured into water.

"In her own way," Sami continued, "that woman explained to me that there is some abnormal energy stemming from a woman who is bent on destroying our relationship. I asked her to elaborate and the seer told me, 'There is a Saudi woman in your inner circle who has done something to break you apart. Your wife is a very good, devoted wife.' Then she told me that, unless we take appropriate measures, our marriage is doomed to end badly."

Just as I was about to feel hopeful that Sami might finally see the light, he continued:

"'Could it be that a mother is intervening to ruin our marriage?' I asked the seer. And do you know what she said to me? She said, 'No mother would ever harm her own child!'"

And with those last words of wisdom Sami had once and for all exonerated his mother, in my opinion the number one culprit responsible for the bane that had wrecked our marriage and my life. I, for one, was reluctant to even ponder the validity of such practices as magic and divination, and was utterly uninformed about them; but I had to admit that clairvoyant had really hit the bull's eye—even though Sami doggedly refused to acknowledge the elephant in the room.

Still, his harshness and intolerance seemed to have given way to remorse and penitence for his hitherto behavior. I imagined that, having resorted to such methods as the lead lady, perhaps he had started to seek some help or redemption from past deeds.

"Unless you break the spell, you will be divorced." That was the Moroccan augur's verdict, and it was a straightforward one.

Unfortunately, that moment of Sami's halfhearted apology was a brief parenthesis in the overall course of events. His rage had only subsided temporarily, long enough to downgrade the severity of his past actions. But perhaps the most interesting aspect of that episode was that it had brought magic to the forefront.

I had heard a lot about magic practices in that country. In fact, it would be no exaggeration to claim that it was an integral part of the Saudis' daily lives. One day, Fauziah, the wife of Abdul Aziz, one of Sami's friends, was trying to convince me that a spell had been cast upon her and that was why she had suffered so much at the beginning of her marriage.

"I was really suffering, I didn't want my husband anywhere near me, something very strange would overcome me during our private moments..." she'd say and proceed to tell me things that I could only attribute to her wild imagination. The things she said were unbelievable!

"Then came a magician," she said meaning Sami's uncle, Enaam's brother from Lebanon, "and he healed me!"

As Fauziah continued her mind-boggling confession, Ariadne's thread began to unravel and I started putting two and two together. Suddenly the words "magic" and "Enaam" appeared to be closely associated and some pieces of the puzzle were finally falling into place. Sami's family had a long-standing tradition in such activities. His uncle Hussein was known to be a famous magician in his hometown. So I couldn't help but wonder whether those strange pains that had doubled me up once in Riyadh and once in Jeddah, so much so that I had to be taken to the hospital—even though my mother never found out about either occasion—were related to some magic spell cast by Enaam. Sami had kept that aspect of his mother's family activities under wraps for a long time, but now someone very close to them had come to put things straight and open my eyes. Fauziah's revelation to me had rattled Sami, but he did not have the means to rebut the "slander." The "primary witness" was the wife of a friend of his. He could not discredit or challenge her and this was driving him crazy.

I began to connect the dots between everything that he had told me from time to time about various situations, at a time when I simply considered all such talk about magic to be pure hocus-pocus and Sami to be naïve. *How could he believe such nonsense?* That was what I thought of the things he was telling me, completely oblivious to the fact that I might soon be falling prey to those mindless people and methods in their effort to get rid of me. Besides, the daily abuse and various means of exercising control over my will were meant to "train" me into forgetting who I was and where I came from and ingrain me with the conviction that I now belonged in another world, one where a woman's place is not simply degraded but virtually nonexistent. Still, I couldn't nullify myself and become an object that could be tossed away at any given moment, nor accept all that violence aiming to subordinate my personality to his. Nevertheless, the repeated episodes of violence and terror were intended to influence my consciousness and cause me injuries that would lead me to total and blind obedience.

"Just you wait and see what's coming to you," was Sami's immediate reaction every time I would disagree with one of his absurd orders, followed by his rushing to the kitchen and coming back wielding a huge knife in his hand before he pressed it against my neck or my stomach and said:

"Now tell me, will you be doing that again?"

Blade against my neck, I would hold my breath and stand there astoundingly collected to bravely confront the horror. I was being guided by my instinct telling me that I should not falter or collapse before that tyrant because, trembling in his fit of insanity, he might not hesitate to deal me the final blow. There, in the hallways of my house, cornered against a wall hung with gold-embroidered thobes,

I could feel his vitriolic breath on my face, knowing full well that the slightest movement could lead me to my death. My life was hanging on by a thread dangling at the edge of a cold knife blade. I was giving the greatest fight of my life for my survival. To this day, I still don't know who or what was giving me that courage and composure that literally saved my neck. The torturer would be disarmed, but the marks on my neck and stomach are permanent reminders of his atrocities and proof of his decadence. It was as if I was living inside a horror flick starring him and me, only there were no cameras or lights or crew around; the film reels were my body and mind and those horrific scenes have been impressed on them forever.

That type of criminal violence against me was not a once-off occurrence. On another occasion, I was striving to get away from him and hide somewhere in the house, but he caught up with me, pushed me into the hallway and immobilized me. He wouldn't let go. A menacing look in his eyes and his one hand clenched around my neck, he unhung a painting from the wall with his other hand, broke the frame against his knee and brought a piece of broken glass against my throat.

I froze, trying not to move at all. In that horror I was living, I didn't want to make some fatal mistake of my own. I held my breath and swallowed my tongue. It was a tragic moment. I was trapped in the hands of a ruthless wannabe killer, who'd bring me to my sacrificial altar on a daily basis for no apparent reason. His gaze and actions at that moment were etched in my memory forever to remind me that Sami, who had first appeared in my life as a loving angel, was now nothing more than an evil demon seeking to destroy me. And, from what I had experienced thus far, it appeared that that sort of self-serving, domineering and aggressive behavior was shared by many of his fellow countrymen as well.

Another incident that had made me shiver in horror and despair took place one day when our home was transformed into a battlefield after a long chase. Flower pots were hurled around, soil spilling on the beige carpet, and I was running to find a way to escape. Once again, I found refuge in our guest room. I managed to lock myself in and find a moment's peace, hoping to wait out the storm in there. But my relief was short-lived. Sami came banging on the door. His thunderous blows painted my face with horror. In his frenzied desire to come in, he was knocking down the door! Petrified and powerless, I felt my adrenaline drop to zero, my hands freeze. I was trapped!

Sami kept pounding his fists against the door until the wood cracked. Before long, he had opened a hole in the door panel and I saw his hand slipping through to unlock the door. I cannot even begin to describe my revulsion and horror! I felt like the end was near! I was praying and screaming at the sight of the oncoming evil, knowing that this fight would be a lot fiercer than any other I had ever had with him before. Sami was charging like a wild beast, guided by otherworldly forces, and I was stuck in the corner of the room, holding on to the wall as a lifeline. The agony was so intense that I passed out and collapsed to the floor. I had surrendered!

When I came to and opened my eyes it was dark. I was lying on the floor, the light from the hallway blinding me. The eerie silence made me wary. All I could hear was that sound of my heart beating, the sole proof that I was still alive.

Frightened and hesitant, I began to inspect my surroundings. I was alone.

For the sake of my own survival, I convinced myself that everything was going to be alright. Aided by my two trusted companions, fear and loneliness, I got up, walked to the kitchen and opened the fridge. I wasn't hungry; it was just a mechanical move. Then I turned on the faucet and washed some glasses. My mind empty of thoughts, I merely listened to the sound of the running water. I was ascertaining my existence, one sense at a time. Suddenly, I jumped. My heart skipped a beat and then accelerated as the impregnable fear that had settled inside me took over me. I saw Sami standing at the door opening, looking at me! I had not heard him approach due to the plush carpet. It was only by instinct that I felt the dark shadow of his presence. I was silently distraught and he knew it. He had become my living nightmare! I could not get over my fear even for a second. His aura was exuding something so negative, so evil; it was as if the entire world's malice and hatred were reflected into his eyes. How could I possibly feel differently since he had threatened me with a lit cigarette in front of my eyes or with a knife against my stomach or a shard of glass against my neck... Those images had been etched in my memory forever and my being at his mercy made me sick at heart...

"What's wrong?" he said. "Are you scared?" he continued cynically.

"No!" I responded without turning to look at him. But the truth was I could barely speak.

I didn't want him to realize my defeatism. I had to muster all my inner powers in order to protect myself. Our home looked so different already it felt like it was haunted. The recently broken door, the closet, the dressing table stool, my destroyed clothes... Everything around us bore testimony to the fact that something extraordinarily bad was happening inside that home. And I was stuck in the midst of all that catastrophe, unwittingly walking down the road to perdition. Where would it get me? Who had condemned me to be destroyed by love? How would I escape the trap fate had set up for me? There was still a cinder of hope in me and that was what kept me going!

My thoughts were keeping me alive, secretly legitimizing my right to life. I had not lost that fatal game yet. The sun was rising for all of us, and I so yearned to hold on to the divine gift of life! I refused to curse my fate for all the harm it had brought my way; besides, it had been quite generous to me before that nightmare started. This, too, was a test that I had to withstand with all my strength. I had to overcome it and come out of it a better person, walking along my spiritual path.

Once again, the sound of Sami's voice interrupted my thoughts and brought me back to the rough reality.

"Do you want to go to the Chinese restaurant?" was the uncanny question that came out of the lips of that erratic man.

"Yes, I'd love to," I said composedly. As surprising as his proposition was, it would certainly be an escape from the sad situation at home and would give us a chance to be among other people.

We drove for quite a long time, from one side of Jeddah to the other. Everything around seemed unfamiliar to me because, if you don't go out and walk a city, it is quite hard to know your way around. And being a woman, I was confined by numerous restrictions: driving was prohibited, taxis were dangerous and buses had special seats for the "woman" miasma.

Throughout the ride, Sami was grilling me with countless senseless questions. And I was forced to respond to his outrageous inquiries, which frayed my nerves long before we reached our destination. The main theme of his line of questioning was an old picture of mine that had gone missing and he wanted to know why that picture was not among my belongings anymore. I could no longer endure all that madness. At some point, I felt my reserves of energy and patience so utterly depleted that I thought about opening the car door and jumping out. I wanted out…

That was the first time I had ever turned my back on life. It was the first time that my thoughts were derailed far from courage and hope. The first time I did not care about the consequences. I was ready for the journey with no return. At that moment life and death had become one. My ideals and values were razed to the ground and trampled all over, there, in Saudi Arabia, by a man who had come into this world equally entitled to the right to life as myself, but who was now brutally trying to deprive me of it.

Sami sensed my 'bad' intentions, realizing that I had reached my limits… Swiftly maneuvering the car, he pulled over and told me that we had arrived.

I opened the door and surged out into the two-way highway. All covered in black, except my face, I stood in the middle of the sidewalk and burst into tears. I had covered my face with my hands in despair. A strange man, who was standing on the sidewalk across the street, ran over to offer his help. I was quite the unusual spectacle.

"What's wrong, sister?" he asked me in English, apparently figuring out at once that I was a foreigner. "What can I do for you? Tell me!"

"Thank you," I said. "Just, please, go away because he is coming!"

The man looked up and, when he saw Sami approaching, he left silently lowering his head. There was nothing he could do for me. The law wouldn't allow it. I "belonged" to someone else.

Sami came near me and didn't say a word. He was trying to protect himself from being exposed.

We never got to the Chinese restaurant. He took me back to the car and drove off in the opposite direction. His mood had changed, so he drove towards the beach, which was full of crowds every night.

The shore of the black Red Sea was lined with Saudi families sitting on multicolored carpets, enjoying their hot tea—and the men smoking their hookahs. Word on the street was that the residents of western Saudi Arabia knew how to enjoy their lives better than the arrogant, tough people of Riyadh. Well, Sami was from Riyadh and, despite all his travels, his horizons hadn't open up the least bit. Yet he knew how to appear urbane, more Western-like than the true Westerner, whenever and wherever necessary. In actuality, he was a hard-core Saudi, unbending in his positions and beliefs. When we walked in public he would walk ahead of me and leave me lagging behind, just like all his compatriots did to assert their status as masters. Not used to being treated like a dog trailing his master, I had once stopped mid-walk and shouted at him, "Hey, come over here!" Sami had turned around and looked at me curiously. "Won't you ever learn to walk *with* me like all normal people do?" I proposed. Sami grinned to save face, but he nevertheless slowed down and walked by my side.

It was difficult to "retrain" someone who was used to such a different way of thinking and behaving. Yet, I was reluctant to place myself in his hands or to put up with such barbaric, objectifying habits, at a time when the fight for equality was taking the entire rest of the world by storm. I couldn't bear to watch my life go down the drain, being forced to take steps backwards instead of forwards as a human being with principles and values.

Something had to be done…

One evening, when he had just come back from a flight, he appeared quite happy and eager to please.

"Get ready, I will take you to Maha's!" he said to me.

Maha was his friend Halil's wife and we had paid another visit to her when Enaam was in Jeddah and they had dragged me, a human wreck, to her place after yet another incident. The memories were still fresh!

I assumed that Sami had spoken with Halil on the phone and that the latter's wife was expecting me. I got ready very quickly and, after we drove for quite some time through areas that looked deserted, Sami dropped me off at their front door and drove off quickly. He had not even bothered to get out of the car to make sure someone was inside the house and would open the door for me. The surrounding area appeared deserted; there were only a few closed houses around and, somewhere in the horizon, the edge of the town and the desert beyond it! The fine sand sprawled everywhere, even covering the entrances to the three-story houses with the small yards. Sand all over.

I took a few steps closer to the entrance of the house and rang the doorbell. There was no answer. I knocked on the door and rang the bell again, but to no avail. Apparently there was no one home! And it was half past eight in the evening!

There were only a few detached houses down the street. I had no other choice except to wait and see if Maha and her husband would show up. I was faced with yet another unprecedented situation. I didn't know what to do or where to go. I sat down on the stoop of the entrance, desperately gazing at the desert. For a moment, I thought I should walk back, using my instinct as a compass, although it was quite dangerous for a woman to be walking the streets alone.

Armed with patience and determination, I took off. I was completely unfamiliar with that area, which looked like an endless desert to me, and it was already very dark! When I reached the end of the deserted road, I came to a sudden stop. There was no way out! Nothing but desert before my eyes and zero visibility in the dark. All I could see in front of me was deep, abysmal darkness. The earth blended with the sky and both blended with the vast, dark universe. Awestruck, I felt like a tiny, helpless creature. I dared not take another step forward. I turned around and went back to Halil and Maha's house. Immensely troubled, I sat back down on the stoop, my only company, once again, my loneliness. I had nowhere to go, there was nothing I could do. I felt my destiny weep, weep for me, as I sat there, alone, out on the stoop, in the dark…

Suddenly I was startled by a shadow. I saw a man coming out of nowhere and standing over me. I was terrified! As it turned out, he was a neighbor from across the street.

"What are you doing out here in the dark?" he asked me curiously.

"I came to visit a friend of mine but she's not at home," I responded.

"Would you like to come over to my house?" the man offered politely.

I thanked him but refused to go. I didn't know who he was and whether it was safe for me to go over to his place, especially since he now knew that I was a foreigner. I was very frightened of the unknown! Plus I couldn't help wondering how these people knew what was going on outside, given that they were all locked inside their shuttered houses. Perhaps he had been watching me for some time before he decided to come talk to me at that moment…

I kept on waiting and it got really late. Various disturbing thoughts were going through my mind and the only conclusion I could draw was that Sami had planned this as a means to get rid of me. There was no doubt he knew that his friends were not at home and that was why he wouldn't come out of the car when he dropped me off and hurried away. He also knew that I was bold and I would probably attempt to walk back to our place. He could read me quite well after all this time; he was aware of my strength and endurance. He had left me there on purpose, in the hopes that I would perish and that he could then move on, free from any relevant responsibility…

There were quite a few known cases of people having disappeared in the desert. Apparently he was hoping that I would be the next such case. But Divine Providence did not abandon me even for a minute. Once more, the power of the loving God would not let me perish.

At half past eleven at night, Sami drove up in front of the house. He feigned surprise seeing me sitting on the stoop, but didn't ask me that many questions—apparently he knew. Perhaps this was just a reconnaissance drive-by meant to establish whether I was still alive or not. Or perhaps this had been yet another sadistic game he had wanted to play on me. Either way, he took me back with him. At that point, that seemed like the lesser of all evils available to me, so I got into the car. Once more, his plan had failed.

I kept on fighting for my life. I had been living in limbo in Saudi Arabia for several months, but come September I received the first hopeful message for my future. I had a strong sense that something was very different and a constant feeling of nausea led me to conclude that I might be pregnant.

When I told Sami about my symptoms of queasiness, he decided to take me to the doctor. Refraining from helping me in any way, he let me climb down the staircase all by myself, even though he knew I was feeling dizzy. He seemed to be wishing ill upon me, but I held on tight to the railing and got down in one piece.

"Congratulations!" said the gynecologist as he confirmed my pregnancy.

Sami smirked and thanked him. Then he sank in deep thoughts under a veil of mystery.

The disclosure of the pregnancy to the family appeared to displease and trouble them, although they claimed that they were all hoping for it. Their concern was palpable and Sami appeared particularly worried, even though that would be his first child and that should make him happy and proud. The first-born, especially if it was a boy, was of great importance in their society, as he would be the heir and successor of the family. At that point, I didn't know the gender of the child, but I was secretly rejoicing anyway, in spite of all the hardships and adversities I was faced with. I stopped feeling alone. The life growing inside me day after day was strengthening my resolve and reinforcing my will to live.

Sami was clearly concerned about that unexpected development that had come to overturn his expectations and plans. He kept pacing around the house as if searching for solutions. His aversion towards me and the child in my belly was patent. The countdown had obviously just begun.

In light of my situation and upon giving it plenty of thought, one day at noon, in a moment of weakness, Sami announced to me that he was "not that bad of a person" and that he was going to allow my mother to come to Saudi Arabia, as he was the only one able to have her special entry permit issued. Pleasantly surprised, I thanked him for that piece of good news, which truly made me feel more hopeful and optimistic. I would have never expected such a decision from him, especially since only some time ago he had made it absolutely clear to me that any visits from members of my family would have to be extremely few and far between. Up until that point, Sami wouldn't even want to hear the names of my mother and other relatives spoken out loud, so his decision was quite startling. I didn't know what had brought about that change of heart and decided not to comment on it at all, seeing as the slightest thing might make him change his mind again. So, I kept quiet and celebrated inside of me. That was an unhoped-for victory and I didn't want to risk forfeiting it because of some "wrong" word or action of mine. His decision was so major that I'd rather walk on eggshells than risk even thinking of something that might overturn it. Nothing in the world should jeopardize the prospect of that visit, which might just prove to be the greatest opportunity of my life.

In the wake of the news, his family in Riyadh kept a low profile, although that didn't mean that they had accepted it.

Enaam seemed depressed, but was most likely scheming in silence. My doctor-confirmed pregnancy had forced them to a deadlock. It must have pained her to say it, but even through clenched teeth, I did hear the word "mabrouk" (congratulations) spoken to me over the phone by Enaam, the woman who had fought tooth and nail not only to prevent such an outcome as a pregnancy, but to get me out of their messed up lives.

One day, our doorbell rang and, when I opened the door, I was surprised to see Mohammed, Sami's fourth brother, who had been studying in Ohio, USA. I knew that he was on vacation in Riyadh at the time and that he would be on a direct flight back to the States in a week's time, but I didn't expect him to be visiting us in Jeddah.

But there he was, at our doorstep, suitcase in hand, greeting me with a sad look on his face. As I gathered from his conversation with Sami, he had had a bad quarrel with his mother Enaam and so had packed up and left to return to America earlier than initially planned. He stayed for three days in Jeddah, waiting to catch the next available flight out to the USA, all the while looking glum, as if he couldn't get over what had happened.

"She didn't even say good-bye to me before I left. She turned her back and went into her room," I overheard him saying to Sami at some point. So, I guess I was not the only one to be treated horridly by that woman; apparently she'd give the cold shoulder even to her own flesh and blood. A ruthless woman, even to her own children, she would always put herself above everyone else, motivated out of selfishness instead of motherly love.

"When I was in the States," I had heard her telling one friend of hers one day, "Mohammed got so mad at his American girlfriend that he started to give her a good thrashing!" Upon finishing her sentence, Enaam had burst into a roaring laughter, as if she reveled in the fact that her "knightly" sons were being abusive of other women in her name, wherever in the world they might happen to be! It was a world made exclusively for her sake! The American woman she was talking about was the third victim of violence and abuse inflicted by her sons that I had heard Enaam boast about.

But this time around, her vile was targeted against her own son Mohammed. That woman had built her empire around herself and anyone who did not agree with her was to be "beheaded."

Sami tried to calm Mohammed down and soften his feelings for their mother, but he didn't seem to succeed. Still steaming in fury, Mohammed got on the plane back to the United States. And it would be a long, long time before he'd return to Saudi Arabia.

That incident was another episode of internal conflict attesting to the dark side of that woman otherwise known as "Mama"—in name only.

The time was nearing when my mother would make the much-desired trip to Jeddah, not because she longed to visit the city, but because she was worried sick about my problems. Besides, the news about my pregnancy gave her one more reason to want to be by my side as soon as possible. She knew just a few things, but could imagine a lot more, about the stance these people were keeping, despite the assurances she had been given time and again.

Acting on the basis of her maternal instincts and with the greatness of her love for me, which had made her accept that direful decision of mine to give everything up and follow that man, she had always been there for me and now she was once again stepping up and doing everything in her powers to be close to me as soon as possible. Being my mother she could sense how much I needed her!

The procedures for the issuance of her visa were well underway. By some divine intervention, Sami had tackled all the necessary red tape so that my mother could get permission to enter the country.

It was October. The temperature was ideal so we could finally be rid of the deafening noise of the air conditioners running 24/7. It was a breath of fresh air and relaxation after so, so many hardships…

CHAPTER SIX

MOTHER'S ARRIVAL

The Saudia aircraft from Athens to Jeddah was about to touch down on Saudi soil any minute, carrying with it the most precious of passengers: my mother. It was the 16th of October, nine o'clock in the evening. My heart was racing as I waited to see her beloved face. Dressed in the usual— by now—way that abided by local customs, I was standing in the arrivals hall, filled with emotions of love and anxiety. It was as if I couldn't believe until I actually saw her before me. I had put all my hopes on her arrival…

Sami was standing at a distance from me. Frowning and sulking, he had his arms crossed before his chest, occasionally bringing his one hand up to his chin in a gesture of concern. He wasn't happy at all about that imminent arrival and was apparently regretting his initiative to invite her. Watching him through my transparent black veil I got even more worried than he was. I could never know what he would do and how he would react, right from the start. He was capable of anything!

As soon as I saw my mother's sweet face as she was queuing patiently at the passport control, my face lit up with joy. We smiled at each other and I waved my hand to welcome her. Sami kept glancing back and forth between my mother and me, in a manner that portended what was going to follow... I started to feel unsafe; I did not like his ominous stance one bit. He was paving the way with thorns even before my mother had stepped foot in Jeddah.

I rushed to welcome her, while Sami distanced himself even further. Somehow our eyes met his and I felt his malicious look darting us like a poisoned arrow. My mother felt it too; that was his "welcome" to her.

Complacently he took us to his Land Rover, expecting my mother to compliment him on the car, to boost his ego. He was so hungered for flattery! He was very insecure, expressing his feelings of inadequacy either by being brutal or by flaunting his wealth to assert his ego in that world made of glass he lived in. He hankered for flattery and praise but would never say anything nice to anyone himself. As if his style stock price would plummet if he behaved kindly and politely. The unspoken rule for continuous coaxing and cajoling was applicable only one way: from us to him.

My mother's welcome at our home was quite humble as it merely featured an ordinary dinner. Sami did not pay her the proper attention, treating her in the same disdainful manner he would treat me, as if he thought of her as an extension of me. He was a petty man, processing his thoughts and emotions in the most unrefined way.

"Take off your shoes and change into something more comfortable," he told my mother in a display of his hospitality. It was one of their habits to take off their sandals before entering the house and putting on a light thobe.

"Sure," said my mother following his instructions.

Displeased with his attitude, I went ahead and served the unfussy dinner. The tension in the atmosphere began to grow almost immediately. He did not like my mother being there. And although he was the one who had invited her over, he made no effort to hide his aversion towards her—and neither did Enaam.

She called on the phone to get a feel of the situation and my mother and I were astounded to hear Sami tell her that my mother would be returning to Athens in a few days' time and he and I would be going to New York! That was the first I heard of that!

After only three days of her arrival, he had the audacity—or madness—to tell her that, "There is a flight to Athens tomorrow."

"Sami, I didn't come to Jeddah for a picnic to be leaving so soon," my mother told him vigorously. Apparently she was not only undaunted by his scheming, but also built up more strength and courage to face the even more demanding circumstances ahead.

The masks had come off, everything was out in the open, the balancing act was over!

Very soon, Sami's erratic behavior stirred up trouble. Impulsive by nature, vibrant and with a strong

Mediterranean flare to her straightforward and honest personality, my mother could not tolerate his insults. Her intense, determined gaze would put him in his place every single time—until his next affront, that is.

Sami had erroneously assumed that my mother's presence in Jeddah would be a situation he could easily manipulate. Either she would get on the next plane out or she, too, would have to submit to the local customs. Besides, my mother had been to Saudi Arabia before on the occasion of our wedding; she had understood quite a few things and that was one more reason in his mind to want her out of there. He tried to stop her in her tracks and disarm her, employing his usual methods, so she would be forced to yield and would leave much earlier than initially intended.

This time, however, he was way off the mark. He was completely ignorant of the incredible reserves of alternatives a mother has in order to protect her child and the incredible reserves of strength she has not to be intimidated by the coercion exercised by a man who, just months ago, at our wedding, had put on his façade of kindness, managing to deceive even the most experienced and acute observer.

Things were getting more and more terrible with every passing day. Our mornings were devoid of any activities or interests, spent by my mother and me behind closed curtains. Halfway between despair and determination, all we could do was try to create our own world. My mother was clearly upset about all that was happening around her, utterly appalled by Sami's savage behavior towards me. Nevertheless, his injustice, intransigence and conspiratorial behavior made her all the more determined not to give in. As for me, I was at my wits' end; the constant confinement and the deranged emotional situation surrounding us made me sink into despair. Sami, on the other hand, was quite content with keeping us locked up. My mother's presence there made absolutely no difference to him; all the rules applicable to me were also applicable to my mother.

One afternoon, I decided to abandon my Arabic-style cowls and put on some "normal" clothes to feel like myself again. So, I dressed up and preened myself as if I was waiting for my prince in shining armor, and started to pace up and down the carpeted apartment floors, from one end of the apartment to the other. My heels were sinking into the plush carpets, so only the mirrors betrayed my presence there. I so yearned to go out, to get away from that house where he had caged me. It was the first time I was feeling the need to escape so passionately. The situation had started to weigh down on me so much so that I couldn't take it anymore. The overall circumstances and the protracted confinement were getting to me. I wanted out! I'd give anything for a walk out in the open!

Sami, who was there, simply sat there and let me stew in his juice. He didn't give a dime about how I was feeling, even though my mother kept pleading with him to show some kind of understanding.

"Please, Sami. Can't you see she's going out of her mind? Please, take her out for a walk!" she'd say to him.

I was restless. I couldn't bear being inside that place for another moment.

"Let's go," I'd tell my mother. "Let's go out and walk until the end of the block!"

"Don't mind her," he'd say. "Just ignore her."

Possibly due to the hormonal changes brought about by my pregnancy, I then felt overcome by a strong but indefinable feeling of hunger. I was starving! Distressed and exhausted by the daily fights, I went into a hysterical fit.

"I'm hungry!" I said to my mother, "I want something to eat!"

My nerves were already frayed by the consecutive, daily and daylong, episodes, so I was even more vulnerable to the hormonal changes of pregnancy.

The fridge was empty; Sami would usually eat out, so he would not bother to replenish the food supplies at home. All there was around to eat were dates and the mere sight of them made me sick to my stomach. Of course, I protested about the shortage of food as an essential means of subsistence, but I knew very well that even that was being done on purpose. We were not allowed to go out shopping ourselves and Sami appeared to be enjoying our misery. We were completely dependent on him; it was up to him to decide if and when he, and only he, would go to the grocery store to get us food.

"Sami, you've got to get her food," my mother kept saying to him. "You cannot let her suffer like that!"

"Just leave her be, she's fine!" he said to her in pidgin Greek.

It was the first time in my life that I was experiencing such depravity. I so wanted to open the door and run out of that cage imprisoning my body and mind. I cried, I yelled, I protested, but none of it was heeded. Exhausted and humiliated I turned in hoping to find a way out in my sleep and forget my hunger.

My mother was immensely troubled by his inhuman behavior, but she was unable to find a way to help me being a foreigner in that country herself.

The visit of Fauziah, Abdul Aziz's wife, a few days later came as a godsend! It was a wonderful opportunity for us to exchange viewpoints, bare our hearts and blow off some steam.

She came alone; her husband dropped her off and Sami left the house as well, leaving us some room primarily out of respect for his friend's wife.

The broken door right by the entrance of our apartment featured prominently like a wicked centerpiece, a perverse artwork, a monument in tribute to Sami's acts of the recent past, when that maniac had knocked a hole into the door with his fists so that he could come into the room where I was hiding and attack me.

"What is that?" Fauziah asked quizzically.

I told her everything Sami had done, right in front of my mother. The strange woman started to beat at herself in indignation; she could hardly believe her ears! She began to come up with various possible explanations to Sami's behavior, trying to attribute it to completely unrealistic factors. Then she vowed to me that she was to be trusted and that everything I had said would remain between us to avoid exacerbating the situation. She was so convincing! She swore and I believed her pledge of confidentiality. Regrettably, that same night, she recounted everything, chapter and verse, to her husband, who in turn rushed to relate it all back to Sami. The two of them were thick as thieves, so Abdul Aziz felt he had to protect his friend, regardless of the possible repercussions on me.

Once again, I had been betrayed! The next day was a tremendous one. With no further explanation, other than that we were going on a visit, Sami stowed my mother and me into the car and took us to Fauziah and Abdul Aziz's house, all the while driving in a jumpy, fidgety manner.

The air was already charged but, feeling confident thanks to my mother's presence there, I proceeded to ring the doorbell. Strangely enough, it was Abdul Aziz that opened the door—apparently, there was no time or reason to uphold the formality of keeping the women separated from the men. That struck me as extremely odd indeed, given that these people had been strictly following these rules concerning men and women in an uncompromising manner in the past. For a moment I thought that they might be attempting to appear more liberal on account of my mother—when it came to polishing up their image, all rules could be temporarily suspended.

We exchanged some niceties and, after a long awkward moment, Fauziah finally showed up. She was hiding inside the house, pretending to be at a friend's who lived in the same apartment building as they did. She was reluctant to show her face, knowing full well she had betrayed me. Still, her guilty conscience showed, even under the chador that was unable to disguise her deplorable act. Shrunk back, her whole posture and body language gave away her treacherous deed.

"Hello," she mumbled miserably in an almost inaudible voice.

My mother and I immediately figured out what was going on. I felt repulsed by that woman. She was the epitome of hypocrisy. Twenty-four hours ago she had played the part of the trustworthy friend so well she deserved an academy award! She had sworn in the name of Allah to keep my ordeal to herself, knowing full well how brutal husbands could get! And I had opened up my heart to her and confided my sufferings, because I thought that, as a woman, she would understand me. Besides, it had been such a long time since I had last come into contact with anyone from the outside world, apart from Sami's family, that I felt a burgeoning need to share my thoughts with another human being. Moreover, I believed that she, as a local woman, could perhaps advise me as to their way of thinking. And my mother had felt the same way, asking Fauziah for understanding and help in regard to my case.

Saudi women never opened up about their private matters; they kept them secret, "sealed with seven seals," in fear of the husband-tyrant. Their instructions regarding their marital life were clear and strict: they were to never be the topic of any rumor or anyone's gossip; otherwise things might be dire for them… Growing up in that environment they were wired to relay everything they heard to their master-husband, the ultimate sieve, who would filter the information and act accordingly. That was exactly what had happened in my case as well. I was deemed to be undermining Sami's interests and misrepresenting his name, so Abdul Aziz took it upon himself, as judge and jury, to put things in their right order.

Fauziah was standing up, her arms crossed before her chest and her head bowed, looking like a miserable but obedient "good wife." She did not have the gumption to look us in the eye, so she just waited for her husband to order her to speak. Although fully covered, head to toenail, like the embodiment of virtue, she had inadvertently and irreversibly revealed her sullied soul.

I stood there, too, with mixed feelings. I didn't belong there; and yet, there I was!

Heartened by Sami's yelling at me and plying me with his unsubstantiated accusations, Fauziah finally spoke.

"If you want Sami, you need to conform! Otherwise there are plenty of other women who want him and are waiting for him," she said.

The nerve of that woman! First she vilified me and now she was lecturing me! She was giving a live show of the good, exemplary wife in front of the two men, striving to appear as the better woman. Oh, I couldn't stand her! I felt my blood rush to my head in light of that double offense I was sustaining, by Sami and by his friend's wife, in that unfamiliar place. My manners and culture did not allow me to behave in a similar way—plus it's not like I could open the door and leave. I was in Saudi Arabia!

They started to fire at me from all sides.

"Why did you tell her that I broke the door?" Sami was yelling madly. "And what did you mean by that? Speak up!"

The situation was getting out of hand. I couldn't believe what I was going through.

"I have nothing else to add," I said. "The picture spoke for itself. Fauziah saw the door broken and asked me what happened. What is wrong with that?"

Before I had finished my phrase, Sami attacked me. He hurled my purse against my head; he missed his target but knocked over a cup of tea instead. I flushed. I was mortified and terribly offended! Now I was being brutally mistreated and abused like a slave in front of everyone to see, including two strangers and my mother.

"You will lose Sami, they will take him from you," Fauziah kept saying in the background.

"They can be my guest!" I answered lividly. It's not as if I were one of them, having no other options or aspirations for my life.

"Don't say that," Fauziah went on.

I was so humiliated, I was desolate. I wished I didn't exist. I couldn't tolerate all those attacks on my dignity. Still reason prevailed over my emotions. I kept my calm. I refrained from talking any more, avoiding any further confrontation in that horrid setting. As well I was worried about my mother's health. She was very sensitive and not used to reacting in view of that sort of situations. Besides, she could neither speak nor understand the language. She kept asking me what everyone was saying so that she might try to intervene.

After that incident, my mother and I could no longer see Sami in a different, more positive, light. Particularly my mother started trying to figure out another way to deal with him. On the ride back, none of us spoke. We opted for silence.

The following day, I "congratulated" Sami on his friends—those snakes, those vipers, especially that double-crosser Fauziah.

"Unlike you, *she* is a good wife, loyal and obedient to her husband," said Sami and I just smiled a bitter smile.

That incident had reminded me once again that I should never trust anybody in that ring of two-timing conspirators. Before long, "Mama" of Riyadh became privy to the episode. Their secret contacts had reached new peaks and their scheming continued unabated.

"My mother is fiery red in the face," Sami told my mother and me as soon as he came back home one evening.

"Really? And why is that?" I asked. My question was left unanswered but I knew that Enaam was enraged because I was still there, because Sami had not kicked me out of the house yet. Sami had to travel a lot during that time and that posed some obstacles to the smooth execution of his plans.

On one occasion, he was assigned on a flight to London with a short layover in Riyadh, long enough for him to get together with Enaam and move their scheme forward—God only knows what they were up to.

I was at home with my mother when the doorbell rang. It was our neighbor Mohammed.

"I've got Sami on the phone for you," he said.

"You are never to bother Mohammed again," Sami told me as soon as Mohammed handed me the phone. "Now put Mohammed back on," he ordered.

Mohammed was explicitly instructed not to pay any attention to whatever we might ask of him. Sami was exercising his intimidation tactics even from afar. Only we were not used to succumbing easily, especially not when we were accused for things we had not done. That sort of male-dominance tyranny might work in his world, but it didn't work in ours.

When he arrived in London, he called to threaten us once again. Yet my responses to him indicated that I would not be intimidated by anything and that I wouldn't put myself up for negotiations.

Everything was dark and gloomy. We were living in a controversial, intolerant and hostile environment. Every time Sami would return from a flight assignment, the atmosphere in the house would turn heavy; his presence was unpleasant and it made us uncomfortable. His surly, unsmiling face clouded the air. Still, we had to survive it all.

About thirty yards from our place, at the corner across the street, there was a phone booth. I had no permission or freedom to dare go out of the house myself, as I was subject to the laws of that country and the rules imposed upon me by Sami. But my mother was under no obligation to obey any such rules; she could go out to the phone booth and use the phone. And that is precisely what she did one morning.

"Where have you been?" an astonished Sami asked her when she got back home.

"Out! Is that a problem?" my mother responded firmly. "I went across the street to call my children back in Athens. And then I called Mr. Takis who works here. I asked him to help me out with something and he said he'll stop by later on."

"No men are allowed at my home!" Sami told her solemnly.

My mother had played her part very well. Indeed, she had gone to the phone booth across the street, but the phone was out of order so she hadn't made any calls. Still, she wanted to give him the message that she wouldn't give in to his intimidations and that, even though we were in Saudi Arabia, the two of us were not alone; there were people who cared about us and were willing to protect us, even though we were so far from our home country. Besides, all the neighbors behind their locked doors knew that lady was my mother and had now seen that she had made her first visit to the phone booth. They way these people operated was hard to fathom; everything was done in secret, even if it concerned the most trivial matter. Even the barber who kept a shop down the street had come out to make sure that she was Mr. Sami's mother-in-law from Greece.

"Are you madam from Greece?" the barber had asked her full of curiosity, as if her arrival in the neighborhood had been highlight of the year. "Where are you going?" he continued his prying, which only went to prove that they were all in on safeguarding the "integrity" of that closed system they had going. For, although a Syrian himself, the barber was obviously siding with his fellow Arabs. What an admirable quality that was: there was no one in sight anywhere around the neighborhood, yet everyone knew all about us! Theirs was the prize of secretiveness; the word "transparency" had no place there. Such were the rules by which my mother and I were called upon to play. And play we did: we became fully aware we were living in a fairy tale where the big bad wolf was lurking at every corner.

From that day onwards, Sami began to keep tabs on my mother's movements. He was alarmed, considering her "dangerous"; he wasn't used to such defiance, because women of his country were completely submissive. Pinning down his weak spots, my mother and I made the proper moves in order to put a stop to his frantic behavior.

My mother's visit to the corner phone booth was repeated a few days later. This time around, Sami was watching her from Mohammed's place, hidden on his veranda from where he had a better view. There was no doubt that he was spying on her, seeing as he had no right to restrain her according to the law. My mother had spotted him and did her best to appear natural as she kept on dialing numbers on the broken phone. She only meant to give him a scare and she partially succeeded. When she came back home, she told me all about it. And I was happy to see that something was finally getting to that almighty tyrant—or so I thought at the time…

Albeit concerned, Sami not only continued but escalated his hateful attacks against me, abusing and torturing me in front of my mother's eyes. Instead of taking it down a notch, he would raise hell about anything that bothered or upset him even in the least bit. Instead of respecting my pregnancy, he saw it as one more negative thing he could pin on me, one more reason to attack me brutally, accusing me for all the bad that was happening in my life and his. And yet, he was so paranoid that he had hidden away my mother's and my documents, passports and permits, constantly holding a shadow of fear over our heads, for he knew perfectly well he had never been honest and straightforward.

When my mother realized that her passport was no longer inside her purse, she looked for it for days. And whenever Sami was out of the house we would search every nook and cranny to locate our documents. One day we found them stashed inside a crack on the closet incurred by a punch of his. We didn't take them; rather than alerting him to the fact that we had found them, we chose to leave them there so that we knew where they were if and when we'd need them.

As for Sami, everything he did had an ulterior motive. One day he took us to the supermarket only to show me a large knife for "special uses." He stood and looked at it for several minutes in order to draw my attention to it.

"Are you buying that knife?" I asked him casually.

"I'll need it!" he said looking me intensely in the eye.

I realized what he meant, but I didn't let my fear show, and Sami picked up the knife and proceeded to the checkout. It wouldn't be the first time he'd come after me with a knife, but that didn't mean I had to accommodate his criminal intentions. Cautiously, I told my mother all about it when we got back home. I even showed her the knife, and she was so shocked at the sight of it that she took it and hid it.

His intention was to see me crawl out of fear. He also knew that I would tell my mother and that served his purpose of instilling fear into both of us. Since he couldn't get rid of my mother, he took it upon himself to make both our lives a living hell. He hated us indescribably. And every day he'd call up Enaam to receive his instructions as to his next steps.

One afternoon, my mother asked him to take us to one of the city malls. For the first time, he accepted to do it without asking any questions. But we weren't meant to make it there. After he parked the car at the parking deck on the mall's roof, we took the elevator to the ground floor. Six pairs of eyes starved for women were staring at me. I had not covered my face, something not unusual in Jeddah, and these men were devouring me with their eyes. They were probably Lebanese immigrants working at the mall.

I bowed my head to avert them from their indiscretion that was making me very uncomfortable. Next to me, Sami kept darting his glance between them and me, while I kept my eyes lowered to the floor, to avoid trouble. But trouble was unavoidable. As soon as the elevator stopped at the ground floor, Sami instructed me to stay put and we all took that same elevator back to the parking deck and the car back to our home. He reproached me as if I were responsible for their behavior and he grounded me at home in punishment.

"You will make dinner," he commanded my mother. "And you will make tea," he ordered me.

His behavior had started to take its toll on my mother who was remaining in Jeddah for the sole purpose of protecting me as much as she could until we could figure out what would happen next. She found both the general setting and Sami's conduct towards me and herself utterly deplorable; she hated to see me suffer like that.

"I want to leave," she told me one day clearly upset.

"Please, don't do this to me," I said to her. "I'm begging you, don't leave me alone here. I'm very scared!"

So, she swore that she wouldn't leave me alone even for a moment.

One afternoon, she asked Sami to take her to the doctor; she was feeling so ill, both physically and emotionally, that she was about to faint. Needless to say, my mother wanted me to go to the doctor's with them and make sure he understood her symptoms.

"No!" said Sami with malice. "She won't go with us. I will take you! She will stay here, she is grounded."

My mother gave her all to convince him that she needed me with her more than ever, but to no avail. Sami was adamant and unyielding as always. I prompted her to go anyway, because I was concerned for her health, while I stayed behind, once again enduring my objectification and degradation.

I waited home alone for quite a long time. When it got dark, I started to get really worried. I was alone, without a telephone and with no means to communicate with my mother. Her safety was in Sami's hands. Filled with anxiety, I was pacing up and down the house. Three more hours passed until he finally brought her home.

"What happened?" I asked my mother.

"I'll tell you later," she whispered so that Sami wouldn't hear. "I kept thinking about you, being all alone here for so long," she continued, while Sami, unconcerned, retreated to the bedroom—he had an early flight the next morning.

When we were certain that he was out of earshot my mother started to relate to me everything that had happened.

"Sami gave me such a hard time! I could not fully explain my symptoms to the doctor just by sign language and when Sami spoke to the doctor I don't know what he told him, but then the doctor asked me some questions to which I couldn't give any answers. The doctor was unable to make a diagnosis. I am guessing he did not want you to come with us because he feared you might tell the doctor what he has been doing to you. Then, as we were coming out of the hospital, he started to talk about you so loudly that a Saudi man approached us from the other end of the street to inquire what the matter was. Sami told him off and the man left frightened. I told him we should hurry back because you shouldn't be left alone for so long, but Sami took his time. He was deliberately loitering like he did not care at all about you. Finally, after a lot of pressure from my part, he drove us back home."

At the end of the day, neither my mother nor the doctor had determined what was wrong with her. Sami left the next morning and he was going to be away for two days, so I asked Mohammed to take us back to the hospital to see and speak with the doctor myself. Seeing as there was a health issue at hand, Mohammed did not deny my request. He kindly took us to the hospital and I spoke with the doctor.

"I was quite astonished myself," the doctor said. "Your husband was telling me other things than what you are telling me now and I was unable to pose the questions I needed to pose to the patient. Clearly, something was wrong. In fact, I asked your husband to have your mother take a cardiogram and then they left."

After filling me in as to their visit of the previous day, the doctor proceeded to re-examine my mother. His diagnosis was arrhythmia and tachycardia due to excessive stress. How could she possibly not suffer from stress, risking her health, in such a setting! There were not enough words to describe what was really going on in our home on a daily basis. One had to be extremely resilient to withstand it. Sami behaved as though he was not aware of what he was doing—not guilty by reason of insanity; and yet, he was "of sound mind" and fully aware of his actions.

Mohammed was a gentleman. He waited for us to take us back home and he kept our visit to the doctor to himself like he had promised. He was a lifesaver! I was beginning to trust him and my mother was warming up to him, too. I didn't know the reasons why he was being so nice and helpful to us, but I took advantage of it all the same. Every good Greek tragedy had its "deus ex machina"—and ours had Mohammed!

Our days and nights were agonizing. Time was a meaningless continuum. We'd only wake up to face another horrid day. Enaam had cut off all contact with us; she wouldn't even speak with my mother to keep up appearances—admittedly, she wasn't very fond of her.

Upon coming home from a trip with a layover in Riyadh, Sami handed to me a parcel with a glow of joy on his face.

"Here, these are from my mother," he said.

"What are these?" I asked but my question was left unanswered.

I opened the parcel and took out two photos of me, one golden ring and a couple of clothing items.

"What does this all mean, Sami? Why is your mother returning my gifts to her? And if it has come to this, why is she not returning *all* of our gifts to her instead of these pieces of garbage? I wouldn't deign accept those!" I said, putting the items back into the parcel.

After that incident, the situation deteriorated further. A few days later and after another brawl, he simply and plainly said to me: "I divorce you." He thought that would intimidate me, bring me to my knees to kiss his feet and be subjugated to him for life. Instead I talked back.

"Well, there's your first good deed in a while!" I said stanchly. "But you will have to compensate me for all the misery and suffering you have caused me as well as for giving up my work."

I moved my stuff to my mother's room and settled there to see what would happen next.

Over the next three or four day we simply avoided each other, refraining from any contact. We were living under the same roof but there was a clear rift between us. According to the Koran, the married couple was allowed to think things over for three months before irrevocably ending their marriage contract at the end of that period. The Koran also contained a special passage regarding women with child who were divorced by their husbands, which stipulated that the child should be born first and then the couple should decide about their future life together. Of course, no one told me about all this at the time, so I simply relied on my instincts.

I began to pack my clothes and personal possessions into a suitcase. I had cleaned out almost half of my closet. I locked my suitcase with a pass code so that he wouldn't be able to open it and possibly destroy everything. I had already lost enough to that man's frenzied fits! The war was now out in the open and there was nothing to stop these people from their disastrous work. But my mother and I were also determined and made sure to show it. Justice was on our side and we weren't there to beg or endure all the sufferings in the world, cut out from any communication with the rest of the world, simply because that man had home court advantage in Saudi Arabia, where I was considered his possession and my mother was in a disadvantage because she was a woman in an Arabic country.

Our silent treatment got him worried. Before long he caved and took me back as his wife. At the time I didn't know exactly how all that worked, how he'd temporarily divorced me only to reinstate me without my knowledge or consent; but on the fourth day after our "divorce" I was his wife again, apparently for his benefit. It is a terrible thing when people take advantage of your ignorance to further their own self-serving purposes.

My pregnancy was coming along in that disturbed atmosphere and I was an emotional wreck. I kept thinking how I had absolutely no reason to be there anymore and wondering what it was had made such a mess out of my life, making it dreary and insipid. Feeling so desperate, I couldn't look forward to my baby's coming with the proper tenderness and affection. My poor baby, who was probably already suffering my ordeal as an embryo.

Once the separation interval was over, Sami resumed his contemptuous behavior towards me. That man kept me starving even during my pregnancy, showing absolutely no respect for the sanctity of motherhood and, at the same time, depriving me of any joy in my life. The only person he cared about and took good care of was himself; everything revolved around him, I was indifferent. He would gorge himself on royal Moroccan prawns right in front of me, without offering me any, and the mere sight of him made my stomach churn. No sign of human emotion, no compassion, not even the slightest concern for his unborn child that was growing in my loins. It was pure beastly inhumanity!

"I don't need a Filipino maid," he told me one day. "I have you to serve me in every way," he continued emphasizing every word to belittle me.

But I was unaffected by his words and left them unanswered; any conversation with that man had become a bore and a waste of time. Anything that came out of his mouth was meant to disparage me, to put me in my place, the one he thought I ought to have, as he could not imagine his wife being an equal, intelligent partner with a personality of her own. The only woman in his pantheon was his mother, who had in turn disparaged her own husband, using him as a token spouse. She'd use him at will, taking him out of her cupboard any time he could serve her purposes. Such was the role of Abu Sami, a pip-squeak of a man, although Sami had attempted to present him to me as a bugbear in the beginning. He had collected Enaam from Lebanon some fifty years ago, at a time when it took them thirty-three days to get from Mecca to Riyadh on the back of a camel. He had made her a queen at the golden age of oil, he had loaded her with jewels and brought her maids from Sri Lanka and the Philippines, whom she gravely mistreated taking out her prior poverty's grudge upon them, until she eventually sandbagged her own husband.

The local custom was that the mistress of the house would have her acolytes and maids; but I, being an "inferior" foreigner, was not afforded such privileges and comforts. I was there to be both mistress and maid myself, because my master-husband thought that was the proper way to break my spirits and keep me in check.

Deep down inside him, I believe he was secretly admiring me for everything that I was and everything I was capable of, but his admiration would manifest in the form of hatred, jealousy and anything else a dark soul can produce. Whenever he'd see me read something, he'd throw away my books; and in our place there was not a single piece of paper or pen for me to write something if I wanted to. He had thrown everything out, so I had to memorize anything I wanted to remember.

Still, in front of his extended family, especially his cousin Ahmed, he would pretend he was happily married. Ahmed lived in Jeddah with his wife Reda, who was an "import" from Syria. Ahmed had "bought" her cheap to serve his own purposes—such as, for example, having a few children. Reda was always locked inside the house, having absolutely no authority or power of her own, while he would spend his time philandering or having casual affair either while travelling abroad or with women from the famous compound. There was a mortal jealousy between Sami and Ahmed, which was not obvious to the outside observer. On the surface, Sami and Ahmed had the best of relations.

In response to an invitation, Sami took us one afternoon to the house of his cousin Ahmed's brother. The man of the house was seated like a pasha between two women who were his wives. I felt frustrated and repulsed by that image. I had never witnessed anything like it with my own eyes; I had only heard about the practice of polygamy. The younger wife was literally all over him, while the older one was sitting aside, looking resigned, tolerating everything unable to react. She was sitting down on the floor, legs crossed, fully covered from head to toe, looking prematurely older than she was probably owing to the kind of life she was leading. She was only twenty-five years old!

"When will you be taking on another wife, Sami?" I was stunned to hear her ask him in front of me. Sami laughed, visibly satisfied with that question; nevertheless, flattered as he was, he responded that one was good enough for him! Then he turned and looked me tenderly in the eye, his gaze radiating warmth for a change... *God, why couldn't he be like that all the time?*

The poor girl was apparently trying to find solace in sharing her predicament with others. She went on to recount to my mother and me how the three of them all lived together, along with their children. In fact, they lived in London, because the husband worked at the Saudi Consulate. And even though they lived in Europe, their behavior appeared completely unaffected. As naturally as can be, she would tell us how the two wives took turns in bed with the same man: he would spend one night with the one wife and the next with the other. *Jesus!* I thought to myself. *Is all this really happening?*

There was obviously a lot of jealousy between them; especially the second wife demonstrated such an erratic behavior that was telling of her meanness and resentment. She was also resentful towards me; her insecurity was palpable. Surely she was afraid she might soon be displaced herself, replaced by a newer wife. Everything was possible; and perhaps that was why the men kept their wives out of sight. One wrong move and they might lose their wife forever. What a strange world that was!

Ahmed was very nice, almost too nice, to me. He looked overeager. His intense gaze and sideways glances towards me made me feel suspicious.

Sami had painted Ahmed in quite a bad light—as if he was any better himself! He had described him to me as an opportunist and an untrustworthy person, while Reda was a victim who had conceded to living in Saudi Arabia, possibly because her life back home would be even worse, so she'd halfheartedly adopt Ahmed's beliefs and lifestyle. But Reda was not the only one to accept that way of life; that kind of acceptance was generally considered an expression of love and devotion, because women believed their unconditional obedience was rendering them more desirable. That was all they knew, so that was what they lived by. They had never experienced anything else in their lives that might stimulate a different line of thinking inside their heads.

Our visit to Sami's cousins was disheartening. That depressing image was typical of the daily married life in that country and I had begun to realize it more and more day by day. The sight of the two women with a common husband had made a dire impression on me. It kept going through my mind and I started to connect that with something Mohammed had told me when I had first arrived at Sami's.

"You know," Mohammed had said to me one day, "Sami told me that he had a great time on his trip to Germany. He visited various 'establishments' recommended to him by the hotel with beautiful creatures in them—"

"That's enough, Mohammed," I said. "Say no more."

I had felt betrayed from the very first day. Sami was no different than his fellow countrymen.

When I mentioned something about it to Sami, he not only failed to own up to it, but he even turned the whole thing against me, blaming me as if it was my fault…

It was under such circumstances that I kept living and breathing under the roof of our home at Knuz Al Elm Street, a "home" that was getting more and more haunted and haunting with every passing day. The repeated abuses and beatings were on his daily order of business, taking place even in front of my mother's stunned, sad eyes.

One night he left around midnight and my mother and I could finally breathe free from our jailer. I fell asleep next to my mother seeking her protection and affection, wretched from my life in a world of demons and nightmares that were mercilessly hounding me even in my sleep. At three in the morning I felt a jolt and woke up with a start! It was him, tugging on my legs so that I would get up. I heard his voice brutally ordering me to go make him tea. I got up quietly to not wake up my mother and make a big issue of it in the middle of the night. Indignant but silent, I succumbed to one more torture. I knew what he was after: he wanted to disrupt my sleep, make me yield to his domineering intentions and toy with me like a cat does with a mouse.

Monotony, confinement and abuse were driving me insane. I desperately yearned for deliverance. One day, I even tried to escape through the window, but it was too high. I felt forlorn. I could not find a way out of that horror I was living on a daily basis, unintentionally dragging my mother along through it. She, on the other hand, was doing everything she could to stand by me, encourage me and fight by my side to the final battle. The only question: what would I do if my mother wasn't there to have my back?

Sami had completely gone off the handle, especially since the announcement of my pregnancy. His twisted mind led him to contrive ways to avert our child's coming to the world. One evening he volunteered to take us out on a car ride about town. I rode shotgun and my mother sat in the back seat. At some point as we were riding along the paved road in the middle of the desert, I saw him driving without looking to the front; he had turned his head to the left and we were seconds away from crashing into the curb of a huge roundabout. I screamed with horror and, at the very last moment, the fatal crash was averted. I was so shocked that God only knows how I didn't miscarry. But his plan was out in the open: he wanted to make me lose the baby.

That was yet another premeditated criminal attempt of his beyond anyone's imagination. His obsession to harm me was so blinding he had overlooked the fact that he was putting himself in harm's way too.

My mother and I were shaken to the core by that episode. The next day, my hitherto restrained mother in view of his cruelty thus far, tried to have a talk with him;

but he just howled back at her, screaming that he didn't want either me or the baby that would be born in a few months' time.

"Fine!" my mother said. "If you don't want them, I will be taking the child!"

"Let us pack our things," my mother said to me a little later. "Enough is enough."

CHAPTER SEVEN

SAMI IN MADRID – BACKSTAGE IN JEDDAH

He left us alone for quite some time so that we could finish up what we'd started. After we had packed several of my valuables and clothes, we took a break to rest.

Sami walked into the room, his traditional white thobe flapping about due to his feisty gait.

"Are you done?" he asked us in a thundering voice and, before waiting for an answer, he picked up the heavy bag packed with crystals and flung it to the other side of the room. Everything broke to shards in a fraction of a second! Then he started to pound on my Samsonite suitcase with a hammer and, finally, he turned towards my mother with his arm stretched out in an aggressive way.

"Go ahead, hit me!" my mother said courageously and decisively. "Bring it on!"

Sami immediately recoiled, bowed to his knees and kissed her toes. He was trying to atone! He was asking for instant forgiveness by that obsequious act; he knew the consequences would be dire, so he thought an act of contrition would be the best antidote. Screaming and yelling once again, he turned towards me, warning me that all this was against me. At that crucial moment, he was attempting to renounce his own responsibilities. He ordered us to put everything back where it was, because "he wanted his home to be in good order."

And while the theatre of the absurd persisted in our home, my brothers back in Athens had stopped hearing from us because of all the obstacles we were faced with in our lives in Jeddah. Naturally, they were alarmed, so they took the first step by contacting the Greek Embassy in Jeddah. The official Greek authorities in the country had been notified of our presence there.

Sami's trip to Madrid for eight days came as a godsend, a divine intervention, because the Good Lord would never leave us alone during those moments of utter despair. Sami had turned his back on us, leaving us alone and helpless. Enclosed in that apartment we were forced to look after ourselves. Enaam had stopped any and all contact with us, as she was realizing her plan was materializing. Abandoned to our own devices, lacking even the bare necessities, my mother and I were in a deplorable situation. Nevertheless, his being away for a while allowed us some space and calm to think more soberly and prudently, as required in such circumstances. My mother's health was deteriorating and her arrhythmias were aggravated. The time had come to do something. Sami's absence was a golden opportunity for us to take action, although we were still tightly monitored by his inner circle who recorded our every move.

On the first afternoon after he left, my first order of business was to take care of my mother. So I suggested that I take her to the doctor.

"How will we get there?" she asked me, troubled.

"You'll see," I said.

We got ready—I put on my Saudi outfit while my mother dressed European style—and stepped out of the house. Abdulrahman, the guard, was standing by the entrance.

"Where are you going?" he asked me quizzically, apparently acting under Sami's instructions.

"To the hospital," I said in Arabic to silence him and preclude any further conversation.

I didn't know where the hospital was but I would try to get there anyway. It was daytime and we had plenty of time.

After we walked alone for quite some time on the deserted streets of Salamah (our neighborhood in Jeddah) we reached a clearing. In front of us was an intersection with some traffic. I instantly made up my mind and lifted my hand to hitchhike a passing car. It was a very risky decision, but I had no other choice. Hitchhiking was, of course, forbidden, especially to women.

A Saudi man in a Buick slammed to a stop, perplexed by my signal. I explained to him in Arabic that we needed to get to the hospital and he let us inside the car.

"Get in," he said appearing very willing to help us.

Seeing that we were evidently not local, he was curious to find out what the matter was. The explanation that my mother was ill and might need to be hospitalized was a lifesaver; the pertinent laws of the country were very tough. The strange driver dropped us off at the hospital he knew—the Erfan Hospital—and even promised to come pick us up and take us back home.

There we met with Dr Erfan, a psychiatrist and apparently the owner of the establishment, and I thought it might be a good idea to solicit his opinion on our situation. I told the doctor in detail about everything I had endured since I had arrived in Saudi Arabia, as well as how particularly concerned I was now that I was carrying the child of the man who was making me suffer so much. I made it clear that I was very confused as to what I should do and I pleaded with him to hear his opinion. After listening to me with great attention, Dr Erfan finally said:

"You will need to be hospitalized yourself so that we may use this opportunity to have a doctor approach your husband and examine him, because I don't believe he would do it voluntarily."

The proposed course of action sounded slightly exaggerated to me. Nonetheless, the good doctor appeared to be familiar with such situations in their country.

True to his word, the stranger who had driven us there was waiting to take us back when we were done. Instead of dropping us off right in front of our house, he pulled over at a side street so no one would see us—you see, the same rule of fear applied to him as well. But before we parted, he made it perfectly clear that he wanted to help us and he even invited us to his house at the beach.

"Very cautiously, I will come pick you up tomorrow from this same spot. You should come to the beach house and relax a bit."

We thanked him kindly, although we were rather alarmed. His conduct had exacerbated our fear and made us feel guilty. I found all the secrecy and cautiousness rather suspect. We never took him up on his invitation; but at least our first attempt at hitchhiking had been crowned with success!

With Sami away, it was also much easier for Mohammed to offer to help my mother in anything she might need.

"No problem," he'd say when she asked him for anything. "Just make sure you never tell Sami that I helped you." And then he'd turn to me. "You know how he is and

I'm more worried about you than about myself. Just the other day, he came over to my place and told me about that incident when he broke the door. 'I don't know what came over me,' he said, 'but it felt like it wasn't me who wanted to do those things. I am worried that something else might be going on…'"

"What do you think he meant by that?" I asked Mohammed.

"How would I know? Perhaps you should look into it. Whatever he meant, the way he has been acting surely isn't normal."

"I too would like to believe that he's not himself when he's acting like that," said I. "But I feel like, every day, my life is at stake, to be decided on the toss of a coin. I can't take it anymore!"

Sami had also called Mohammed from Madrid and explicitly instructed him not to bother with us at all, even if my mother or I needed to see a doctor. "Pay no attention to them," was what he had told him.

When we had spent two days of relative calm amidst that stressful environment, our doorbell rang unexpectedly. It was high noon on a November day, the sun shining mid-sky and a blue Mercedes was parked outside the house.

"Samia, open up! It's me, Ahmed!" I heard the voice behind the door. I would never dare open it if I were alone, because I had gradually been inducted into the isolationism and fear they had instilled in me. But since my mother was by my side I courageously opened the door.

We could hardly believe our eyes! Ahmed was standing there, loaded with supermarket bags so high up you could hardly see his face. He took the groceries to the kitchen and then went back down to the car to fetch some more.

"Hello, Mama, how are you?" he said to my mother, in half-Arabic, half-English.

Then he looked at me, still in shock from what I had just witnessed. As if he had read my mind, Ahmed said with a smirk:

"Don't you worry! I know my cousin very well; he will appreciate the gesture. Trust me!"

Working for the same company as Sami, Ahmed had seen him leave for Madrid. And now he had showed up at my house with the air of a savior who had come to rescue us. Soon thereafter he began to badmouth Sami and taunt me in the process. *Great! That was exactly what I needed with my nerves frayed already...*

"I overheard him speaking to a Tunisian hostess on the plane, making plans for their eight-day stay there and all the places they would visit," he said.

I got very upset with what I was hearing from Ahmed—although I was more upset with myself than with anyone else. I thought about who I used to be and what I had become: a miserable, insubstantial reject, a nonentity that had been depraved of all joys of life, condemned to act as a nobody. Shrewd Ahmed could tell what was going through my mind and was happy to see that he had achieved his objective.

"What am I supposed to do with all these groceries, Ahmed?" I asked.

"Given how well my cousin is looking after you, I'm sure you'll need them..." Ahmed replied sarcastically. "I'll be leaving now, but I'll be back again later on tonight, around eight, to check up on you."

He rushed away, leaving us pondering what to do with all those provisions. He had brought over so many things I could hardly store them away and we could certainly not consume them in a week's time. And if they were still around when Sami returned, that could only complicate things and bode disaster: Sami would immediately know there had been a third-party intervention because we were explicitly forbidden from going out to do shopping ourselves and, besides, Sami knew how much money he kept at home and he'd know if any of it was missing—by then I knew all the little traps he would shrewdly set for me before leaving to go on his trips, and how not to be ensnared.

After giving it a lot of thought, I figured out a way to kill two birds with one stone. I summoned Abdulrahman and gave all the groceries to him. That way, I was getting rid of them without a trace, while at the same time scoring a few points with the guard and hopefully getting on his good side.

Abdulrahman was content to get on with a pittance for a salary, but when he saw all those bags full of groceries meant for him, his face lit up as if he were standing at the gates of heaven. He couldn't believe the generosity; he was extremely grateful because nothing like that had ever happened to him before. His menial job ranked him in the lowest of classes, quite literally the class of slaves: lowest wage earners enjoying absolutely no privileges, as also attested by the place and way they were living.

Abdulrahman shared our gift with his peer from the house next door; the groceries were enough for them to share and they both welcomed the gift like manna from heaven. Ours was an unprecedented gesture, as they told us, and they both vowed to never forget it! Although not better off than them at that point, mother and I felt very happy to help them out while at the same time giving away every last thing cousin Ahmed had brought over.

At about eight in the evening, Ahmed came back to visit us as promised. My mother was happy to see him because she needed to talk to somebody about all the ugly things she had been witnessing; they were weighing down on her and she needed to get them off her chest. We knew we were sidestepping our instructions and restrictions, but we needed to blow off some steam.

We had a long talk with Ahmed about Sami, a great part of it concerning his clandestine dealings with the Tunisian hostess. Ahmed was trying to get under my skin by talking about it over and over, emphasizing Sami's mockery and betrayal. Still, I never learned the whole story because everyone was lying through their teeth!

"I am here for you," Ahmed assured me, "for anything you need. You just say the word and I'll do it." He said it so many times in order to convince me and, in the end, I must admit I was a little moved by his eagerness. And while Ahmed talked, I kept translating for my mother so that she could weigh into the conversation.

"Enaam, or rather Umm Sami, is a very powerful and very rich woman," Ahmed said by way of filling me in about Sami's family situation and making me feel powerless by comparison in the process, at the same time highlighting his role as my savior.

"I'll be staying over tonight!" Ahmed announces at about eleven at night.

The blood drained from my face when I heard him unilaterally making a decision that was quite literally putting our lives at stake. Never expecting such a proposition, his announcement caught us off guard.

While Ahmed went down to his car to fetch some proper clothes—apparently he had everything planned out well in advance—my mother and I held a brief family council as to how we should deal with the situation. I was caught between a rock and a hard place; I had no idea where this would lead us, or who or what was behind Ahmed's mystery visits, or what his true motives were behind his eagerness to help. For a moment I thought he might actually be genuinely nice—evidently I was overlooking the fact that such kindness was quite uncommon there, especially when it came to dealings between people of different gender. But I was not used to thinking and acting in accordance with their world view, and my natural reflexes and instincts would often be in conflict with theirs. Could it be that Ahmed was attempting to set me up, acting upon a secret arrangement he had made with Sami? Or was he perhaps acting in pursuit of some ulterior motive of his own, regardless if that meant putting my life in danger? Could it be that I was an apple of discord that Sami's cousin was claiming for his own? Whichever way one chose to see it, the situation was brimming with dangers!

Employing a great deal of diplomacy, caution and sangfroid, we were forced to accept what Ahmed had suggested like a done deal and let him spend the night in the living room. My mother and I withdrew to the bedrooms and I locked up all in-between doors, cutting off any possible contact. I was afraid of the possible shock of waking up in the middle of the night to see him standing in front of me, so I made sure that could not happen. I didn't want to take any chances given those men's strange beliefs and desires about the opposite sex.

The next morning, pale and misty due to the hot weather, found all three of us waking up in the same house. I dressed very conservatively, snubbing any wishful thinking he might have. But as I was brushing my hair, Ahmed came close to me, took a seat on the floor next to me, made himself comfortable and cozy, and proceeded stare at me as if I were an object of pleasure.

"So, where do you want me to take you?" he said. "Would you like to fly out to Riyadh and meet with Prince-Minister so-and-so? You can tell him everything. I know people in high places and can give you guidance."

"How shall I get there? Where shall I stay? How will I get around Riyadh? What if someone sees me?" I reeled off all these questions at once about the difficult mission he was urging me to undertake.

"I will put you up at the house of one of my sisters," he said. "Sami isn't close to them, they don't get along."

I gave his proposition a lot of thought and, in the end, I responded:

"I'm sorry, Ahmed, I cannot do it. I would love to meet with the Minister, but it is too risky for me. I'm afraid for my life."

If anyone realized my mother and I were traveling without my husband's explicit permission, accompanied by his cousin at that, we'd be lost causes. I would be subject to severe repercussions stipulated for such cases by the Islamic law. Nobody would take mercy on me; quite the contrary. They would all call for my head on a plate because "that's just how these unfaithful foreign women are!" Out of love and respect for my life, and despite all the sufferings I was going through, I thought it wise to turn Ahmed down on his proposition—God knows what his true intent was anyway.

"As you wish," he answered me mildly seeing his effort fall through. But then he resumed his offer to be of assistance saying, "I could take you to the Greek Embassy!"

Now that was a proposition with a nice ring to it. Taking all necessary precautions, we stepped out of the house a short while before noon. Luckily, Mohammed was probably out so we didn't run into him; it was best he didn't see us, because he might be keeping tabs on me and reporting back to Sami—everyone played a part in that unbelievable mesh of backstage conspiracies! It was as if everyone saw the perfect scapegoat in me, taking out all their grudge about possible family conflicts, discriminations or any other bone to pick between our two different cultures and religions on me.

We reached our destination, the Greek Embassy, which was located on a small street, close to Sands Hotel. We asked to meet with the Ambassador and indeed I met with him and recounted to him my entire experience in Saudi Arabia up to that point. He told me that, in addition to calls he had received from my brothers in Athens, keenly inquiring about my wellbeing, he had also received an anonymous call from a Saudi man in Riyadh, possibly a member of Sami's extended family, who was asking for my protection, arguably out of intrafamilial rivalry.

"Unfortunately, I am not allowed to help you escape because you are a Saudi's wife and, thus, subject to Sharia Law," said the Ambassador. "He has exclusive jurisdiction over you and he is the only one who can permit you exit the country."

I was utterly dispirited by the discouraging answers I was given, once again realizing how trapped I really was.

"Still, you should keep us informed," instructed me the Embassy staff, who were unable to do anything more for me. They too had to operate in harmony with the tough regime of the country. Nevertheless, I let them know that I didn't have a phone that I could use whenever I wanted and they took that under serious consideration.

We left the quasi-Greek territory of the Embassy rather satisfied, since we had at least made a first contact and there were now several people of authority who at least knew we existed.

Ahmed was waiting to take us back home and, when we got there in the early afternoon, he triumphantly announced that he'd be back to pick us up in the evening and left.

He was being very persistent and his overeagerness to help had me thinking there was something in it for him. Apparently, the latent rivalry or bad blood that existed between him and Sami had found a fertile ground and opportune timing to manifest. I was an asset that could be exploited and the window of opportunity was wide open.

Even beyond Ahmed, the whole "family" atmosphere was one of conspiracy, intrigue and scheming where everyone appeared to want to make the most of the situation for his or her personal gain. My presence there posed a fortuitous occasion to be exploited and capitalized on to settle old differences or grudges. Hard as it was to believe, I don't think there was even one member in that family that would do something for me out of the goodness of his or her heart. Being a powerless foreigner, I was ideally poised to be used at will; and the fact that I had a family of my own, albeit some fifteen hundred miles away, didn't seem to concern them at all.

The general atmosphere called for worry as to what was going to become of my mother and me. I was very frightened! And it seemed that there was only one path for me to follow, a one-way street that I had to keep going down slowly and cautiously, even now that Sami was away. I knew for sure that there were minions of his all around serving as his eyes and ears.

As promised, sprightly Ahmed came back in the evening, acting as if he owned the place. My mother and I had prepared ourselves to go out, as he had instructed us when dropping us off earlier on.

"Where are you taking us?" I asked him once in the car.

"Don't worry, you'll see," he replied and then turned to my mother: "Are you alright, Mama?" he asked her while driving into areas I had never seen before.

At a certain moment he thought was the right time, and while he continued to drive the car, he handed over to me a small jewelry box.

"Open it up," he said. "It's for you. It's your wedding gift, I owed it to you!"

Dumbfounded, I opened the box to see inside a gold watch, much nicer than any present Sami had ever given me.

"Do you like it?" Ahmed asked me.

"Thank you so much," I answered with a smile. I was truly astonished.

"You're welcome," he said, looking satisfied and with an air of superiority about him.

After a few minutes he pulled over and turned off the car. The area was completely unknown to me. We walked for a while until we entered a courtyard surrounded by old buildings. It was the first time I saw traditional architecture in Jeddah—I was used to being among ultramodern structures all the time—so I assumed that must be part of the old town.

"Where are we?" I asked him.

"At a lady friend's place," he said.

A lady friend's? That was weird! I was quite confused, feeling all the more perplexed about everything in my mind. I was living my life in Jeddah under the constant fear and terror of segregation, and now Ahmed was overturning everything I had been instructed by that very environment!

He knocked on a door, which was opened by a middle-aged woman of Arabic origin, although from some other country in the Middle East, who was well groomed and dressed more European-style, her hair pulled back in a bun. The woman greeted us casually, Ahmed kissed her hello—quite the unusual gesture in Saudi Arabia—and then introduced us, before picking up a conversation with her in Arabic, throughout which he would not stop looking at me and saying my name. It seemed as though they were discussing some sort of arrangement, and the woman kept looking at me too, smiling approvingly as if satisfied with what she was seeing. When they seemed to have reached an agreement, we left.

As our tour of underground Jeddah continued, Ahmed kept quiet about the identity and capacity of that dubious woman we had just met. There didn't appear to be any man present in her house that would "justify" her staying in Saudi Arabia, and I had heard stories about women from other Arabic countries who had stayed in Saudi Arabia after a divorce from a Saudi man, taking up the oldest profession in the world—which happened to be quite lucrative—or, even worse, working as madams and procuring women to sheikhs and emirs of the greater Gulf region in return for a considerable commission. That woman's entire appearance and demeanor attested to such a shady role.

Ahmed pulled the car over again, stopping in front of another such shifty place, where another woman, similar to the previous one, opened the door to have a similar conversation with Ahmed—apparently negotiating about me, taking advantage of the fact that my Arabic was not nearly good enough for me to understand what they were saying—and then we left again.

"They're friends of mine," Ahmed said finally to cover his back. But in my mind there was no doubt he was acting as an intermediary or pimp—quite a suitable line of work for him—looking to sell me out to some harem or make me disappear forever in some obscure, oriental bazaar. On the surface, he behaved as if he had suddenly taken to caring for me so deeply, as if his emotional world had been shattered by the way his cousin Sami was treating me. But in actuality I knew such people wouldn't lend a helping hand to anyone unless there was something in it for them. Human solidarity meant absolutely nothing; there always had to be an ulterior motive to their actions of pseudo-kindness.

Ahmed eventually dropped us off back at home and left after promising to be back to visit with us soon. My mother and I went over everything we had witnessed during our evening escapade around Jeddah and we both drew the same conclusion: Ahmed was taking advantage of Sami's absence and my shaken emotional state because of all my sufferings to try to funnel me into some oriental bazaar, where I would be acquired by some portly, pervert Arab to keep him company during his endless nights, until he would have had enough of me and wish to replace me with a newer model.

Chills ran down my spine and my hair stood on end at the thought that I might have fallen prey to some unscrupulous man who'd see me as an object to be exploited instead of as a human being. Not a day goes by that I don't praise the Lord that my mother was there, beside me, my guardian angel who protected me with all her strength from all the vultures lurking to gorge on me simply because I was a woman.

The next day Ahmed came back to pick up some personal items he had left behind. In keeping with the dirty plan he had set in motion inside his head, he asked me unhesitatingly:

"How far along are you, Samia?"

"I'm in my fourth month," I said, quite puzzled.

"You know what? I could take you to London to get rid of it. Over there they perform abortions even during the second trimester."

"What makes you think I'd ever do such a thing?!" I said to him in revulsion and rage. His insolence was unbelievable! I started to seriously resent him as I was realizing, once again, that these men are all the same: with no remorse or inhibition. Their strict religious rules applied only to the women of their own kind and they were most probably abiding by them out of fear rather than out of respect.

Ahmed took a seat, looking rather ill at ease. He had run out of "brilliant" suggestions and was now staring at me with trepidation. Apparently he had started to fear what might happen if I told Sami of Ahmed's shady role and about everything that had happened during his absence. There was no doubt in my mind that he was terrified of such a possibility; nevertheless, I had no intention to meddle with their intrafamilial problems. I just wanted to find a way out of the unexpected evil that had befallen me.

Albeit concerned and pensive, Ahmed eventually left, presumable putting an end to one more round of my adventures there. Having seen so much of the ugly side of life in such a short period of time, I couldn't help wondering what fate had in store for me next… Whatever it was, I was prepared to face it. I no longer expected anything good to happen anyway. The wretched souls, the meanness and pettiness of the people I had encountered lately had made me wary of everything that comprised my surroundings in that country. My only hope was to get away…

In striving to achieve my salvation, I felt that I should brief the airline where Sami worked. I was looking for a lifeline and, seeing as all other paths appeared to lead to dead ends, I thought the company could act like a judge of sorts, somehow contributing to my vindication. That was what I was hoping for. I was a former employee of Saudia myself and, even after quitting my job in the unprecedented way that I had been forced to do so, I believed my good reputation had been left intact. I knew the company people in the pertinent posts and I believed that they would take my case under serious consideration. Besides, the recent violence and abuse I had been suffering by Sami didn't leave me with that many other options.

 I had to make up my mind. My life that was at stake so I had to take action. In line with the rules of both morality and law, I would give my ultimate fight to protect God's two precious gifts to me: my life and the life of the child I was expecting. I could no longer live—or rather keep dying a slow death—as the neglected wife that had no right to life's joys and nothing more to expect other than continuous humiliations, which would eventually crush me to the ground and break my humanity into pieces. For reasons only he knew, Sami was preparing to bring another wife into our home. Unwilling to accept our child, Sami was even desecrating the sanctity of parenthood. I had to act now that he was away. I had to do everything I could to defend and protect myself and the child I was carrying.

 On the day following my visit to the Greek Embassy, I decided to take action. Despite my isolation at the house of

Knuz Al Elm Street, I had spotted during one of our walks in the immediate surrounding area a small convenience store, which served the urgent needs of the neighborhood for food and other supplies. *That is where I should go,* I thought to myself and let my mother in on my plan. I dressed appropriately, keeping only my face uncovered, and stepped out of the house very cautiously, evading the guard's attention. I hadn't taken my mother along with me, in order to avoid drawing attention to us. Moving swiftly, I soon reached the convenience store.

The Saudi grocer was surprised to see a foreign woman at his doorstep, standing there alone, dressed in the local traditional way. Arguably he knew everybody in that neighborhood and had probably heard about the "imported" wife living in Sami's house. Unafraid, I spoke to him using the little Arabic that I knew.

"Hello." I said. "Can I please use your phone to make a local call because mine is out of order?"

"Of course!" he said, gawping at me as if I came from another planet. "Where are you from? Is anything wrong?" he began his grilling, curious to know everything about me.

Of course, I was reluctant to divulge any information because I did not know him and could not trust him. As far as I knew, he might even call the police on me in order to protect himself and their phallocratic rules.

"I live nearby," I said curtly and started to dial the number of Saudia. I wanted to get in contact with one of Sami's managers.

My call was answered. I spoke calmly and in English, trying to keep a straight face, so that the curious Saudi checking me out would not know from my expressions or tone of voice what I was talking about. I told my interlocutor that I would like to meet with a company manager to discuss a serious issue concerning me and one of their captains. I refrained from saying more over the phone for fear of my request being rejected and the content of my call being relayed to the wrong ears. I wanted to feel safe and certain that nothing would happen to me first, and then I would ask for their help.

"Who are you?" asked the voice at the other end of the line.

"I cannot tell you my name, but I am kindly asking for your protection because my life is in danger," I said in a trembling voice. "Please, do something for me!"

"Who is your husband?" my interlocutor kept pressing me for answers.

"I need to meet you in person," I kept imploring over the phone.

"Alright then, stop by our offices," he eventually responded.

"I'm afraid I cannot do that," I said. "If I am recognized by people who know both my husband and me, the next time you will hear of me will probably be through the newspapers."

As politely as I could, I explained to the man on the phone that Saudia offices were a dangerous place for me due to my marriage. People knew both me and Sami and he would be notified of my visit there in no time. And then all hell would break loose! And I would be at the mercy of "my husband" and the law. I asked him nicely if he could meet me outside company premises, perhaps somewhere at the International Mall.

"Fine," he said. "Let's meet tomorrow morning, at eleven, at the International Mall," I was thrilled to hear him agree to that bold step I was about to take.

"You will recognize me by a lady dressed European-style that will be standing next to me," I told him. "She is my mother."

I thanked him kindly and hung up the phone, quite satisfied from that first contact.

The Saudi grocer, who had been watching every movement of my lips, resumed his efforts to figure out who I was.

"How much for the phone call?" I asked him.

"Nothing at all," he said.

I thanked him kindly and left, as swiftly and unnoticeably as I had come. As far as I had seen, no one took notice of me on the street.

As soon as I came back home, I updated my mother on the phone as well as the importance of my next day's appointment.

"But how will we get there?" she asked me reasonably.

"Good question," I said while giving it some thought. "We'll ask Mohammed to take us there."

I had opted not to call Saudia from Mohammed's phone because I didn't want him to know what I was up to. I couldn't know how he would react to that or if he would report it back to Sami. As much as I had come to trust him, he was still a childhood friend of Sami's who shared the same principles and beliefs. It was high time for me to juggle the situation masterfully myself. Just as they were always keen to know everything but wouldn't reveal anything about their intentions, I would now do some secret-keeping myself, keeping my cards close to my chest. By then I had been taught my lesson many a time. I knew exactly what it meant to open up your heart to someone only to have them trample upon it by betraying you.

Not hesitating for a moment, my mother and I went across the hall and knocked on Mohammed's door. He opened the door and welcomed us with a smile.

"Come in!" he said.

We cautiously entered.

"Please, have a seat!" Mohammed offered.

"We didn't mean to disturb you," my mother said by way of prologue and then I picked up the baton.

"You know, Mohammed, we need to do some shopping at the International Mall. Could you perhaps give us a ride there at eleven tomorrow morning?"

Mohammed didn't even give it a second thought. Of course, he couldn't have known my true intentions, so he accepted immediately. Thus, we had secured our transportation, which was a huge problem for me in Jeddah. Sami had me trapped from all sides, leaving me there with no phone and no car and driver—as women were not allowed to drive themselves.

As we anxiously waited for the day to pass, I thought of Asadour, an Armenian man who lived with his wife across the street from us. Asadour was our decorator. He had done some work at our home so he had gotten to know all of us, including Enaam, of whom he had gathered a negative impression. "She barged in and scolded me fiercely for not being done yet," Asadour had told us once about her.

"Would you like us to pay a visit to Asadour and his wife?" I suggested to my mother in an attempt to alleviate the dullness in which we were forced to live.

It was quite dark when we opened the yard gate to walk across the street. Our neighbors welcomed us with kindness and much more gregariously than the locals. They had migrated from Syria to strike it rich in the land of the black gold.

Asadour told us several stories involving Saudis breaching their agreements.

"I once worked for a grand sheikh who had hired me to decorate his entire house, a job worth several thousand dollars. When I finished the work, he wouldn't pay me. He said he was dissatisfied with something in one of the bathrooms and had me redo everything from scratch."

Everything about these people was unbelievable! They were so eroded by money. Still, that was the dominant mentality and nobody could get through to them. I recalled there was a Lebanese man who would come by our place from time to time, asking Sami to pay him for some work he had done and Sami wouldn't—apparently Asadour was not the only one who suffered from that common practice…

Time went by fast at the Armenian's home. It was almost eleven at night when we said our good-byes and left. It was dead quiet out in the neighborhood and my mother and I crossed the street quickly, like two shadows in the middle of the night, looking left and right for fear of anyone seeing us. That omnipresent feeling of fear had worn me down emotionally. I was so tired of being constantly scared, both inside and outside my home.

When we reached the front door of my apartment, I suddenly realized I had forgotten to take my keys with me. My mother and I panicked. It was late and we were locked outside the house all alone. What could we do at this late hour? How would we get in?

Something clicked in my mind and I thought of Abdulrahman, the guard. I headed to his cabin and called on him with a stifled voice. Abdulrahman came out immediately.

"Abdulrahman," I said to him in a pleading voice, "we were at the doctor's but now we cannot get back into the house. I forgot the keys."

Our apartment was on the second floor. Abdulrahman ran up there to check the door and then came running back down.

"I cannot do it on my own," he said. "I'll need to call the guard from the house next door for help."

And so he did. He woke up his friend and the two of them together tried to find a solution. As my mother and I waited, secretly and silently, making sure no one saw us, I saw one of them climb up the building, clawing from wall to wall like a feline, until he reached the second floor, got into our apartment through a window and opened the door for us.

We were so relieved! And we thanked God that Sami was not there! I had been so out of it lately, with everything that was going on inside my head, and I was so unused to holding the keys to our home myself that something like that was bound to happen sooner or later. The mere thought of what would have ensued if Sami were in Jeddah and would show up any minute during that episode gave me the chills. I could imagine the havoc that would wreak if he came home to catch us out in the streets, the two of us alone, so late at night, locked out of the house! His trip to Madrid was proving to be a godsend! It had been proposed to him by his superiors and he couldn't have said no even if he wanted to.

We thanked the two guards by giving them a generous tip. They both looked at it like they couldn't believe their eyes, because they were completely unaccustomed to such gestures.

"Thank you, Sister," they both exclaimed and left, as we finally entered our lodging.

All night I kept tossing and turning, anxious about the meeting I had set up with Saudia's manager the next day.

As promised, Mohammed showed up punctually and took us to the International Mall, even offering to wait for us at the car and give us a ride back. That seemed like a fabulous idea to me; this way, he wouldn't follow us into the mall, but we would also have a ride back.

Being cautious, I had put on my abaya and chador, which provided the best cover for my covert action, the success of which was all but guaranteed. Everything was done in utter secrecy, in sync with the general atmosphere, the local way of thinking and their lifestyle. I had been forced to completely identify with all that, blend into their mentality of mystery and intrigue, in order to be able to survive. Forthrightness and transparency were unheard of in a culture that imposed such strict discriminations between the two genders.

When my mother and I had waited for about half an hour and no one had showed up, I began to lose hope. Full of anxiety and devoid of expectations, we waited a little longer. Still, no one showed up.

Utterly disappointed, we decided to head back home. Once again, my hopes had fallen through and I felt betrayed. Apparently the man on the phone had not taken my claim to heart, perhaps because I was a woman and I meant nothing to him. Still, I refused to lose my nerve. That incident reinforced my resilience and will to succeed. Their utter disregard for my efforts filled me with renewed energy and persistence to stay the course on my way to deliverance!

As soon as we got back, I thought I'd pay another visit to the convenience store around the corner—I still wanted to keep Mohammed out of this.

The Saudi grocer was surprised to see me enter his store for a second time. And this time he had company.

"Hello," I said. "Can I please use the phone to make a local call again?"

"Are you Mr. Sami's madam?" he immediately threw his newly acquired piece of information in my face to catch me by surprise. His little store doubling as a hub for neighborhood intel, he had managed to gather information on me in no time.

"Yes," I responded fearlessly, although on the inside I felt certain that he would try to get a hold of Sami and report back to him. I decided to ignore the prying glances and the murmur among the bystanders. I could not understand what they were saying, but their feelings were pretty obvious. They wouldn't even try to keep up appearances.

I dialed Saudia's telephone number and asked to speak with the same person I had spoken to the previous day and was supposed to meet at the International Mall.

"It is I who had contacted you yesterday with regard to a serious matter concerning my husband, who works for your company," I said. "I showed up at our appointment but you didn't even though you had assured me you would," I made sure to emphasize.

"Indeed. Company regulations wouldn't allow it," he said. "If you have anything to report, you must come by our offices."

I paused for a moment, took a deep breath to ponder on my dilemma and then said:

"I would love to come by myself, but you will need to protect me. I'm sure you can understand the difficult position I am in, how dangerous this would be for me, how delicate a balance this is. No one else inside the company should see me; I can't afford to be the object of rumors. If you can cover me, I'd be happy to come over."

"Of course, I can do that," he said. "Come by tomorrow morning, at eleven o'clock, to the eastern wing of the building. There is a hidden side door there and one of us will be there to escort you in."

So we agreed on a new meeting time and place, under a veil of secrecy.

My only concern at that moment was how I should dress for tomorrow's meeting. If I showed up in traditional Saudi women's attire, on one hand, I would draw the attention of all men and women around as no local woman had access to that area—it was reserved for the airline crews only. On the other hand, if I dressed in regular European style, I would be immediately recognizable; most of the crew members knew me since my days with the company, and they would be surprised to see me and eager to talk to me, either to ask me where I'd been all this time or to ask me what I was doing there without Sami. I hoped that sideway entrance was secret enough to spare us all that commotion.

Absorbed in my thoughts, I had failed to realize that the Saudi men in the store had come closer during my phone call, presumably in an attempt to figure out who I was calling and for what reason. As soon as I hung up the phone, I saw them trying to pierce through the veil of mystery surrounding my presence there. They wanted to find out what was going on in order to rat me out to Sami. I eluded them and rushed back home, never to return to that convenience store.

I reported the developments back to my mother who had been watching me discreetly from the veranda while I was talking on the store's phone. I told her about the new arrangement I had made and she consented that this was the best course of action in spite of the risks involved.

Now that my plan was back on track, I had to think about how to approach Mohammed. I needed him now more than ever before to take us to the Saudia crew scheduling building, which was located literally in the middle of the desert. Amidst a vast expanse of sand, the Saudia building sprang up like a desert mushroom, its premises directly connected to the airport ramps. That was where we were supposed to meet the following day and Mohammed was the only "driving force" that could get me there—I don't know where we would have ended up if it weren't for his generous offer to drive us around. But how should I ask him for this favor? Our destination would probably give away my intentions, in which case I wasn't so sure he would accept to do it. Still, I braced myself and decided to open up to Mohammed, in the hopes that he would help me. It was a bold decision, but my mother's presence there gave me the strength to do many bold things that I wouldn't have dared do otherwise, perhaps remaining a doomed powerless woman for the rest of my life.

That same afternoon my mother and I knocked on Mohammed's door to invite him to have a talk. He was particularly respectful of my mother and made sure to show it. We chose to stay at his apartment instead of ours; I felt safer there, as Sami's shadow was haunting me even when he was away.

"Mohammed," I started my introduction, "I'm sure you know by now all that I have suffered by Sami over the past several months. And, no doubt, I'm sure you know many more things about him than I do. In addition, I'm sure you've noticed the behavior of his mother, the shady role she has been playing and the way she has treated me."

"Tell Mohammed," I was interrupted by my mother, who was now into her second month with me in Jeddah under such dire circumstances, "about our financial contribution to the whole wedding ceremony. Tell him how much it cost us, both in money and in emotional turmoil."

Mohammed appeared stunned. "I would see him come back from Athens every month, carrying with him huge parcels and luggage," he said, "but both he and his mother would say it was Sami that was spending a great deal of money to furnish the house."

"It was all mine!" I assured him.

"For real?" said Mohammed in disbelief. "But I thought… Well, they have so much money so I thought…"

"Now you can appreciate the ploy they had cooked up for me? This is why I am asking for your help," I said to him. "I am to meet with members of Saudia management tomorrow morning, at eleven, at the airline's operational headquarters by the airport. I have spoken with them over the phone and they'll be expecting me, so that we might perhaps come up with a solution to my problem."

"Where exactly shall I be taking you?" Mohammed asked with an expression of relief.

"The eastern wing. Someone will meet us at the side entrance."

"I will not come in myself," said Mohammed to clarify that he wouldn't get more involved than absolutely necessary. "I will drop you off and leave right away. I'd be willing to wait for you but it might be too risky. I hope you know you are playing with fire, so be careful!" he warned me.

"That's perfect," I said. "I'm sure we'll figure out a way to get back from there. And if you call this playing with fire, what would you call my staying in that horrible situation? I cannot take it anymore; I have to get out of this quagmire."

Even in a gingerly fashion, Mohammed was nevertheless being supportive of my plan, which he might also be seeing as his indirect way of getting back at Sami for past acrimonies. Perhaps he could only resort to such roundabout ways because of his Palestinian descent, which rendered him "inferior" to the true Saudis; he was, after all, a man with no country, bearing a Jordanian passport. Thanks to me, he was now in a position to perhaps settle old scores. That was one trait of the Arabic culture that seemed to hold true across borders: they would rarely express their true thoughts straightforwardly. Instead, they would passive-aggressively pretend and wait for the opportune moment to release the piled up tension and act out on their resentment or intolerance. And I was there to bear the brunt of it all, be everyone's punching bag and patsy, a tool to be used at will, in a give-and-take of conspiracies and counter-conspiracies.

Everything was set for tomorrow, the big day. I wouldn't change my decision to reach out to company management for anything. My sense was telling me it was "every man for himself;" there was no room for emotionality. I had done nothing wrong, my conscience was crystal clear. I was the unfortunate victim of the strange mentality of a man who had brought me over to his country and showed me off as a trophy in the beginning, only to dump me a short while later like a piece of trash.

The whole night I was overwhelmed by a feeling of sweet satisfaction and anticipation in light of the imminent events of the following day.

Early the next morning, my mother gave me her last bits of advice and we started prepping each other mentally. When I was wrapped in my veil of mystery, dictated by my capacity as a Saudi's wife, and we were almost ready to step out, we heard the doorbell ring. We assumed it was Mohammed who was picking us up to go down to his car, but when I opened the door I was shocked to see Abdul Aziz and his wife standing on my doorstep.

"We came to pick you up to go for some shopping at the mall," Sami's friend said.

"I'm sorry, but we can't," said I. "We are on our way to the airport. My brother is visiting from Athens!" I said readily and naturally, not hesitating even for a second.

At the sound of that, Abdul Aziz went pale; apparently he realized that Sami's toying with me was coming to an end. Without even bothering to ask how we'd be getting to the airport, as would be expected of him, he simply took Fauziah—whose makeup was showcasing all colors of the spectrum, the sweltering heat notwithstanding—and left with a thunderstruck expression on his face and his wings clipped. Surely he must have had many questions on his mind, but he dared not ask them as he had no right to; still, he would certainly make sure to teach me a lesson by ratting me out. I was quite certain that the shopping trip was a pretense and that his visit there was most probably the upshot of Sami's calling him up and instructing him to spy on us. No one would go out walking or shopping at this time of day, with the sun shining its blinding light and the temperature at its peak. He must have thought me quite naïve if he expected me to believe him; instead, I jumped the gun and put one over on him!

After I got rid of them I heaved a sigh of relief and, when I made certain they were gone, I let Mohammed know we were ready to go. He went down to his car and waited for us. The great moment was nearing; the airport was not that far from where we lived.

We flew down the city's main avenue, the Medina Road, and reached our destination right on time. As Mohammed was parking the car outside the Saudia building, my heart was pounding in anticipation, the vast desert sprawling before our eyes.

The great adventure was just beginning!

A middle-aged man in a snow-white thobe was indeed waiting for us at the side entrance. He approached us very discreetly and, after verifying our identities, he asked my mother and me to follow him. We said good-bye to Mohammed whose mission was over and set out to do what my self-preservation instinct was telling me was the right thing.

Keeping our presence there away from prying eyes, we walked in a big circle to get to another secret entrance. We entered the vast space of the crew scheduling room and walked right across to reach the offices of the second floor.

Although I was covered in black head to toe and my mother was beside me, we were not spared some curious glances as we clearly did not "belong" there. Awkwardly coughing a dry cough and keeping my eyes lowered to the ground under my chador, I waded through those final steps, the "home stretch" that seemed never-ending. Until, finally, we were there!

Three or four Saudi company managers were gathered in a room, anxiously waiting to find out who I was, who my husband was, and what was going on. After we shook hands, they folded their hands and waited in anticipation. Jittery and nervous, my mother showed them her medication by way of an introduction. I took a deep breath of relief and began to recount everything I had experienced since I had relocated to Saudi Arabia. When they heard Sami's name their eyes popped and their jaws dropped.

"But he seems like such a nice person. There is nothing anyone can say against him!" Captain Said said.

"And he is exceptionally good at his job," added Mr. Ghazi, the manager responsible for the TriStar aircraft.

As the discussion moved on, they started to change their minds. I told them I was pregnant and that he had intensified his tortures now in order to end my pregnancy, and I told them everything I had sustained since the beginning of our marriage. I made sure to underscore that the reason I was standing before them was because my life was in danger and I was in urgent need for support as I had no one else to turn to. The gentlemen kept glancing at my mother with compassion and exchanging looks among them, trying to figure out how they could help us. After a while, Captain Ghazi spoke up in high dudgeon.

"If he isn't capable to command his own home, how can he command an airplane?" he exclaimed. "Why don't you check yourself into a hospital so that, when he comes to visit you, he can be subtly approached by a specialist?"

"I have already tried that," said I. "Dr Erfan had suggested that exact same thing. Only Sami is too smart to fall for that. He is sharp-witted and fully aware of his actions."

"Have you talked to his family?" the third manager asked me.

"Yes! But they are in on it, especially his mother!" I made sure to underline that woman's shady involvement.

"We can help you inasmuch as the company in concerned. You have our unreserved sympathy and support in whatever you might need," they all said almost in unison.

"Please, never reveal to him that we met here because he will kill me if he finds out!" I beseeched them.

"Rest assured!" they said. "Captain Marahalani will escort you back to your home."

It seemed I had won them over, my mother's presence there having played perhaps a determinant role. We thanked them for their time and assurances and left quite content that, finally, we were not alone. People of a certain authority were now informed of my plight and had sympathy for it. That was certainly something compared to the nothing I had going for me before.

Captain Marahalani took us home indeed. Before dropping us off, he once again assured us that we could rest assured now.

My round of moving about relatively freely was coming to an end. A week of dramatic developments had gone by and Sami was expected back any minute. My mother and I were saddened by his imminent return, which foreshadowed only more trouble. Everybody had disappeared and there was a false calm in the air. Nothing revealed the secret meetings that had taken place. On the surface everything appeared to be exactly as he had left it!

My mother and I were expected to be ready to welcome back the "big boss" in an atmosphere of warmth and joy. I had to muster a great deal of strength and effort in order to persuade myself to act contrary to my true emotions.

The moment of truth had come. After eight days away, Sami walked into our home in a silent, sulky mood. Our presence there was obviously quite a nuisance. He tried to hide it but he couldn't. His first thought was to contact his mother—who had lost our tracks in the meantime. So, he stepped out only to return after a while, livid with anger. Still, he seemed reluctant to talk about it even though his long face was so red he looked like he was going to blow up.

"What's the matter?" I asked in an attempt to approach him and find out what was going on.

"My mother is very mad at me," he said crossly.

"For what reason?" I asked him calmly, although I knew the answer would probably have something to do with my mother and me.

In yet one more attempt to bully us, Sami, as usual, laid the blame on my mother and me for having disturbed the beast. They were desperately looking for something to accuse us of, but they came out empty.

The next day, Sami was notified by his company to report to his managers, without being given any more details about the meeting's agenda. The storm was averted. Saudia was too precious to be ignored. Sami recoiled and set aside his fits of fury for the time being; he had more important things concerning his career to worry about now. "Saudia is my life," he would often tell me, exalting his job while ignoring my devastation, which he had so easily and readily brought about. As if I were the child of a lesser God!

Focusing all his attention on his company's inquiry, he left my mother and me alone for some time. One day in late November, he invited his closest friends and colleagues over to our place around noon in order to discuss with them the issue at hand. I saw them talking privately, huddled together in one corner of our spacious living room. I took a quick glimpse without being noticed. The ball had been set rolling. My mother and I exchanged a triumphant glance. The countdown had begun…

It never crossed Sami's mind to share with us what his trouble at work was; when it came to issues that concerned him he knew how to keep silent. A procedure was to be followed according to company regulations. I felt certain they would never disclose my involvement; instead, they would employ certain techniques to approach him in a way that would allow them to investigate those traits of his personality that had taken such a severe toll on me, almost annihilating my true self.

All of a sudden, the once rigid, almighty Sami began to think things over and act in a more humane way. Inside of me, I was feeling immense satisfaction; the company had played its part decisively and brilliantly and I was feeling perfectly protected…

I never found out the final outcome of that disciplinary inquiry launched against him at work, but, as far as I was concerned, it was enough that he felt his professional standing threatened.

During that time, Sami began to tighten the noose around us. Every time he'd go away on a trip, he would immediately call up Mohammed to explicitly instruct him to ignore us and do us no favors. Meanwhile, Mohammed had found out from my mother many truths concerning the past and present backstage actions of Sami's family, but he refrained from talking back to Sami. He was trying to find conciliatory solutions even when every last hope was fading away… Still, I couldn't shake the feeling that deep down Mohammed was gloating over Sami's troubles; on some level he had been jealous of his childhood friend and wouldn't mind having an imported trophy wife himself. In fact, back when I had first met him he had asked me if I had a sister for him to marry—and he had meant it too! If I just showed him a picture and he liked it, he'd be willing to tie the knot!

The closer I got to these people, the crazier I found their beliefs. Both men and women entertained some utterly absurd notions. One day when my mother and I were at the house of a nice lady from Medina, a woman I had just met turned to me and said:

"If it is a girl, Samia, I will marry her to my son!"

Apparently, she was being quite serious, as it wasn't strange in that culture to have the parents arrange the future bride or groom for their child as early as the age of two!

"We live in Kuwait and my husband is very rich," she went on, bragging. "Okay, Samia?"

She was actually hoping to shake hands on it! I was appalled to hear my unborn child being objectified if it were a girl even before it came into this world! Such notions were shocking to me, even at the level of "negotiation." Theirs was a world that was the absolute opposite of mine!

Then, that woman's sister brought us her newborn baby for us to see. The sight was rather hideous: the baby had the outline of her eyes dyed with henna.

"Why have you painted the baby's eyes?" my mother and I asked her in the nicest way possible to avoid offending her. "Is that some sort of local tradition?"

"No, we just do it to make her look beautiful!" she responded proudly.

Similarly, when I used to work on domestic flights back in the day, I had seen several older passengers with their beards and eye contours dyed with henna. It was impossible for me to grasp their concept of beauty. In spite of all the wealth and state-of-the-art technology, that world was deeply rooted in the past. It was like a parallel universe running its course in spite of evolution. Our two worlds coexisted but never met...

The well-meaning group of women kept asking me about my married life, thinking that I was ineffably happy with Sami. They were exalting me by saying I was a sought after bride and that his whole family should be taking very good care of me. When they heard that Enaam was of Lebanese descent, their reaction was rather unexpected.

"Poor girl, we understand," they said.

Up until then I didn't know about the differentiations among Arabs depending on their place of origin or that the Lebanese didn't enjoy a good reputation in Saudi Arabia. Besides, the only thing that mattered to me was the fact that I had suffered, and was still suffering, terribly.

One of those otherwise enchanting Arabic afternoons, tainted only by the absurdity in some people's minds, found me sitting quietly by myself. My mother had taken to sewing something in another room, killing time and avoiding possible confrontations. We each kept to ourselves in our effort to preserve the delicate order and quiet of things. We were living in a fragile glass world, in danger of being shattered to pieces by the slightest move at any given moment.

Sami came close to me and sat down beside me, despite our shaken relation and lack of contact. We were simply coexisting; that was how I felt. Nevertheless, I was the woman and he was the man and he was entitled to use me as he wished...

That particular time he was in the mood for taunting me. Knowledgeable of his nature, I chose not to react to avoid aggravating the situation. I preferred to be silent and ignore him. So, without thinking twice about it, Sami sat down on my belly, a scornful smile on his face. Again without saying a word, I merely pulled myself away from under him, stunned by that unprecedented behavior. He kept on jumping up and down on my belly and I kept on pulling further and further away. Eventually, I couldn't take it anymore. I started to scream at the top of my lungs but he kept at it. He was laughing and trampling on my belly, reveling in his monstrosity. I kept crawling away from him, from one end of the room to the other, and he kept coming back to me like a cruel, vindictive yo-yo. In the end I snapped and shouted with all the strength that I had left:

"Help, Mother! He is stepping on my belly!" and my voice resounded throughout the apartment.

My mother jumped up in a state of panic and rushed over to see and avert my torture.

"What are you doing to her?" she yelled at him furiously.

"Nothing!" he exclaimed, reluctant to admit the truth like the coward he was. He was now sitting at a distance from me as if nothing had happened.

Solid as a rock, my mother stayed beside me to protect me.

I was four months pregnant and he was once again trying to make me have a miscarriage, seeing as his previous attempts had failed: he had left me without food and he had tried to cause a car accident after inviting my mother and me out for a ride—which proved to be a death ride… Only Divine Providence had helped me stay safe and alive and I was thankful for it! My faith was growing stronger and stronger in light of the war waged against me by evil itself, even now that I was expecting. I could feel with all my senses how difficult the situation was for me, so much so that only God could intervene to save me. Once again, I didn't cave, I didn't lose my nerve. I mustered all my courage and convinced myself I had to make it all the way to the end, which was not far off anymore... *I will make it, I will make it, I will make it...* That was my only thought, my personal bet with myself.

Sami did not cave either. He was firm in his obsessions, obstinate and selfish and wouldn't budge an inch. He was bent on seeing through the mandate issued to him by his sick mind. I was sure he had done it all deliberately and in a premeditated fashion, even though his response to my mother was that it was just a silly joke on his part. So, he just stepped back temporarily to distance himself and muddy the waters.

Amidst all the madness surrounding us, my mother had shifted her entire focus and energy in doing house chores, trying to keep her mind distracted with trivial tasks. It hurt her too much to constantly think about where we were and to whom I was married, so she was blowing some steam off by quietly keeping occupied, while at the same time serving as my vigilant guardian angel. She did not trust Sami one bit; his every move appeared suspicious to her. Keeping a discreet distance, she would nevertheless keep an eye and ear on everything Sami was up to that concerned me. She was well aware of his insidious intentions towards me.

After stressing and toiling away for many hours at a time my mother would rest, and deservedly so. On one such instance, when the entire apartment was tidied up to a tee, Sami told her after inspecting everything:

"It's a good thing I have you two to do all the work around the house so I don't need to hire any help. Especially you"—he turned to me—"are good for everything!"

Once again, he was trying to degrade and belittle us. I was very upset at this derision coming from the man who used to exalt me in the beginning of our relationship only to trample all over me and humiliate me now. Apparently, such were the teachings he had received, even though in his family it was rather Enaam who was at the helm, having displaced her husband in many respects.

Sami had said his scorn in Arabic, so I turned to explain it to my mother.

"Do you know what he said?" I told her, to release some of my anger. "He said he thinks of us as maids."

"Don't pay any attention to him," my mother responded calmly. "It's probably his complexes talking. He only wishes the women of their kind knew and did one iota of what we know and do." That was my mother's wise way of putting an end to an episode before it broke out.

Meanwhile, Sami had gotten himself ready to go out.

"I'm out of here," he said. "I'm invited at a friend's place for lunch." And with that he was out the door, completely unconcerned that we would be left alone with nothing to eat—leaving us to starve was one of his favorite tactics since the beginning of my pregnancy.

I had never regretted my visit to the company and was still optimistic that a way would be found for me to be liberated from my oppressor. Still, I knew that the wounds he had caused me would never heal, the damage to my soul would last forever. Unwary, I had been put through hell by that man. Every passing day was another eon of tortures. I wanted out. I belonged in the world of civilized humans…

My mother and I had endless discussions about what my life would have been like if I had not followed him to Saudi Arabia. Seeing what it had come to, my mother had a hard time understanding how that man had managed to ensnare me.

"How you could ever make the decision to come over here after living in Paris is beyond me!" she'd say over and over, to release her chagrin. "That you'd give up France and your job for that man!" she kept mulling it over in her head, unable to come to terms with it.

Truth be told, there was no rational explanation for it. What reason could explain a passionate love one chooses to follow even if it leads nowhere? The intense sensuality of the oriental lusciousness and ceremonial mystique were enough to win my heart and mind and make me daydream of a life in a paradise on earth since the time I was working as an air hostess. It all seemed like a wonderful world that made you soar up high, but, if not cautious, you could come crashing down and fall deep into the mire of the netherworld—which was exactly where I had ended up. Back then I was inexperienced, innocent and unaware of the deep divide separating our two worlds; or rather, I thought I could bridge that gap when I was captivated by the seductive Sami, who ambushed me somewhere in London like fair game.

Now trapped in that house, I was looking for solutions that would take me to the secret way out. The fairy tale of love had turned into a true tale of witches and dragons, a cruel reality I was experiencing with all my senses, struck by the terror and awe in the light of the magnitude of the evil that had befallen me. I was going through the most difficult times of my life, suffering unprecedented trials—but I would never be subdued!

Such were my thoughts as I was hearing my mother's questions and seeing the sorrow on her face, a sorrow that had been caused by my emotional nature that had led me to be trapped in a place, the mere thought of which would stir only discomfort and irritation inside us now. We were two worlds, worlds apart, that had come together for one brief moment, sharing absolutely no common ground, doomed to become two worlds colliding. The chemistry of romantic love was no panacea; apparently, it ran skin-deep and, no sooner was the surface scratched than everything transformed into a disaster. Now there I was, mustering all my remaining emotional reserves and waiting for the next moves to reveal themselves.

Later on that night, when Sami came back from the feast at his friend Saleh's house, he stirred up a hornet's nest once again. I had already turned in and Sami barged into the room, stood over my bed and started to pull my legs apart as if trying to tear apart a burlap sack. I saw him standing over me in a state of frenzy, in a position that allowed him to completely overpower me, tugging on both my legs with all of his strength.

I started to scream at the top of my lungs, as did my mother, who was shocked at the sight of his heinous act.

"Help!" I kept screaming desperately.

"Help! Leave her alone!" my mother kept screaming too—but there was no one there to hear us in the middle of the night…

"If you don't let go of her right now, I will run out to the streets and shout for help so everyone can hear!" she said as she got up and moved towards the door.

Sami let go of me abruptly, giving up on his procrustean-bed-type torture and averting the worst, not so much for me as for himself, in case my mother acted on her threat—his selfishness and self-preservation instinct had once again kicked in, saving him from punishment and me from further torment.

The storm had passed! But those images of horror would be forever etched in my memory, as a constant reminder of the man who had so rabidly tried to hurt me and my baby, attempting to deprive both of us of the sacred gift of life. He was still hell-bent on making me miscarry and would come at me like a menacing demon every chance he got. Perhaps he was abiding by the doctrine that "the unborn is not a living person" and didn't consider harming "it" a sin. Over the past few months, I would be possessed by fear even before I would actually see him before me; I could sense his ominous presence even as he approached. There were times when I felt the blood freeze in my veins by his negative aura and I'd turn into a breathless, brittle pillar of salt. One morning when he heard me impulsively heave a deep sigh as soon as I saw him, he suddenly fell to the floor, wriggling and squirming as if possessed by demons. Faced with that sight that was dangerously bordering on the abnormal, I took to my heels and fled the scene. Something outlandishly strange was going on in that place. And perhaps that was the reason why Sami kept up his relentless pursuit against me.

The bad dream I had had three days ago was coming true! "Mama" Enaam had visited me in my sleep, in the form of an angel of evil, to presage my future. Dressed in a pink dress of mine, her hair jet black and her eyebrows arched in an unnatural way, she was standing next to me, in my house, triumphantly pointing at my bed split in half, a big, gruesome crack gaping open in the middle... The dream had shocked me but I was reluctant to make too much of some vision from the sphere of the subconscious—yet it was proving to be a prophetic one! All omens pointed to the fact that I had to brace myself for another Calvary ahead. That woman was haunting me everywhere...

The first actions I had taken while Sami was away in Madrid had mapped out the course of my future actions, pinpointing the people and authorities I could turn to. Despondent after the latest events, which proved that nothing would hold Sami back from his frantic quest to make me miscarry, I thought I might take my chances again with the small convenience store around the corner to place a call to the Greek Embassy. Sami was out of the house but he would be back any minute, so I had to hurry.

Without wasting any time, I covered myself up and ran towards the exit, but before I could make it out of the house, I ran into Sami at the entrance hallway of our building. There was no way I could avoid him; I got very scared. He grabbed me by the neck and pinned me to the wall.

"Where are you off to?" he yelled at me, his eyes peering into mine.

"I was about to ask Abdulrahman if he could buy me some salt," I muttered, gasping for air.

He gave me a shove and had me follow him back to our apartment. For once, my endeavor had failed, but it was a risk I had to take—such risks were all part of the lack-of-freedom "game" we were playing. Everything was part of his plan to make us feel like pariahs. But perhaps he had bought my excuse; there were no stores for foodstuffs in the immediate area and sending Abdulrahman made sense…

After a while, Sami left again. Things were quiet for a short while, but that was the calm before the storm. I could feel it. Any day, any minute, the tempest would flare up and wipe out every last remaining wreckage of me. Nothing at all was getting any better. My mother and I were fodder in the lion's den. All the consecutive episodes of violence and torture forced me to become quite inventive. I had to run for my life and the life of my unborn child.

Keeping the spark of hope alive deep inside me, I had to be constantly vigilant to identify any small window of opportunity. I kept my eyes and ears open, my mind racing all the time. I couldn't, I *wouldn't* accept being enslaved, being an object instead of a woman. My physical freedom might have been confined, but no one could confine my freedom of thought.

One day when I was riding in the car with Sami, he had driven down Knuz Al Elm street and then taken a left turn, where I spotted a small supermarket. It was hard to miss as it was literally in the middle of nowhere. And now I thought I might pay it a visit; it was worth a try.

As soon as Sami left on his next assignment, leaving us plenty of time alone, I seized the opportunity and suggested to my mother that we go to that supermarket, just to get out of that place, but also to get some groceries and have something to eat around the house. It was late in the afternoon when we once again ventured to go out, moving like two hounded shadows. As we walked past the barber's shop he sure enough came out of his store to spy on us, but we rushed to turn around the corner and headed to the supermarket.

"Hello," I greeted the store clerk in Arabic. He was young and, judging by the way he was dressed, he was probably not a Saudi, which put me at ease. Still, he gave us a curious look. My foreign accent and our overall appearance gave away the fact that we weren't Arab. I got some bananas and, when we reached the checkout counter, we were faced with a barrage of questions in his attempt to find out as much as possible about us.

He told us he was Egyptian—my guess was right—and that he was working there as an employee. After he satisfied his curiosity about the reason why two European women were at a store on the edge of the desert, he offered to help us with anything we might need. As our conversation unfolded and my distress became more and more obvious, one thing led to another and, before long, I found myself divulging my problem to that man.

"You must be under some spell!" he proclaimed with certitude. "Let me look into it for a few days. I know someone who is knowledgeable of these things. I will try to get in touch with him and I will let you know," the lovely Egyptian said to me.

"Alright, we'll be coming back here when we get the chance," I said as we left the supermarket in a climate of secrecy.

The Egyptian man was astounded by my story and was truly willing to help. Egyptians were indeed different from the Saudis and neither thought very highly of the other. Quite the opposite, in fact: they hated each other! I had made sure to tell the young man how scared I was and how dangerous it was for me to go out, which, of course, he had no trouble believing as he was quite aware himself of their unimaginable customs and traditions.

"They are very strange people," he said, "and they can harm you for no good reason at all. I am scared for my life myself," he went on, emphasizing how hard it was for all non-locals there. Before we left the store, he added:

"As soon as I hear back from that acquaintance of mine, I will come by your house to let you know. I will pretend to be delivering some groceries. Just make sure you are there, otherwise I will have no way to deliver my message to you."

I gave him my address and we left. I got my hopes up that the Egyptian might prove somehow useful to us and that I was at last beginning to gain the trust of even a few people within that hostile environment.

It was Tuesday afternoon and the sun had just begun to set after another day like all other days. Sami had left since Sunday on a three-day flight assignment, bound to come back on Wednesday night.

My mother and I were startled by the doorbell ringing. I opened the door and saw the Egyptian man from the other day. He was carrying two boxes of milk and Coca Cola.

"Here's your order, Madam," he said in character as he took a step further into the apartment in an obvious state of panic and fear. Then he signaled me to close all curtains.

"Danger never sleeps," he said. "Around here, everyone sees and hears everything, even though everyone is locked inside their houses," he added, the boxes still in his hands. "I came to tell you that I got in touch with the man I had told you about. He is willing to meet with you. Just let me know when you'll be available." His eyes kept darting glances left and right, giving away his trepidation. He was afraid of his own shadow.

"Okay," I said, taken aback by his suggestion. "We will let you know."

"All right, Madam. I shall return them then," he said a little louder, back in character, before he disappeared in a fraction of second.

He had found us! I would have never thought that he would act so fast and indeed put up that act to come over and let us know. Fear was in the air all over that place and in all manifestations of life! Nonetheless, that meeting he spoke of was never meant to take place; once again, reality had other plans...

Some fifteen minutes after the Egyptian left, my mother and I had taken a seat on the sofa, feeling content at the glimpse of hope that we might be seeing some light at the end of the tunnel after all. My mother was mending one of my brand new clothes, which Sami had torn during one of his rabid fits, and I was immersed in reading. It was so quiet one would hardly guess there were any people in the house.

Suddenly we heard a thunderous thump on the door. We were scared to death and, before we could even think of what that might be, we saw Sami standing before us. He had kicked the door in to spring up on us, as if he were starring in some crime thriller and he was trying to catch us "in the act," doing whatever his sick imagination had concocted. He was expecting to catch me dead to rights on something that would give him grounds to terrorize me with threats of calling the police on me!

Feeling mortified and exposed by the picture before him—my mother and I harmlessly busying ourselves on the sofa—he fell onto the floor feigning a sudden stomach ache! He had no excuse or explanation for his surprise arrival so he had to deflect our attention. When his "stomach ache" subsided after a couple of minutes, my mother confronted him, asking him to explain why he had barged in like that and what he had been expecting to accomplish by expediting his return without notifying us. Screaming and yelling as usual, Sami simply changed the subject. Of course he had machinated the whole thing to somehow catch us at fault and be in a position to hurt us; but his plan had fallen through.

I felt that it was the right moment for us to speed up our actions because Sami had started to lose ground. He was getting nervous, possibly at the thought of my mother's discussions with Mohammed might point us in the right direction as to where to turn to and what to do. His guilty conscience was eating at him, especially after the last tortures he had put me through right in front of my mother's eyes. At the same time, his secret discussions with Enaam were leading him along a sure path to disaster. Their obsession against me wouldn't let them think straight; motivated solely by their wild instinct to annihilate me, they were getting ready to escalate the confrontation. The rift had grown vast and they weren't even able to keep up appearances anymore. They would employ any means to eradicate me.

Abu Sami was away on a month-long vacation alone—it wouldn't be a vacation otherwise—in Cairo, so Enaam had the perfect opportunity to expedite and coordinate her plans with Sami. As proven on many occasions before, Abu Sami was just a stooge of Enaam's—although I had always wondered how she had managed to turn that colossus of a man into her lackey.

It was the beginning of December and Abu Sami was expected back any time now. My mother and I were still pulling through, each passing minute a haunting eon of a living nightmare, hounding me in all manifestations of my life as a constant reminder of how tortuous and torturous my life had become. Still, I would not give up trying to hold on, especially now that the latest developments had started to indicate that my hopes and efforts might bear fruit after all.

One afternoon of that December—a December that was nothing like the wintery Decembers we are used to in the West—Sami pompously announced to us that his father was expected to arrive any minute from Cairo.

"My father is coming!" he said pompously in the hopes to inspire fear in us and then he left to go to the airport.

Abu Sami's arrival at our place came to stir the waters even more. My mother and I retired to our rooms, ignoring Sami's indirect attempt to intimidate us. Dispassionately, as was suitable for the occasion, but also firmly determined, we waited to find out what "good" would come of his father's not-so-innocent arrival.

When I heard the door open and close, I knew it was them. His spirits raised by his father's arrival, Sami came directly towards us in the back rooms and said:

"My father is here!"

The tension palpable in the air, my mother and I went into the living room to greet Abu Sami while his son put on a histrionic show, yelling and screaming to affirm how miserable he was. His behavior was petty and profane as he tried to convince his father that I was a good-for-nothing wife. He would hurl nonstop insults my way, all the while trying to ridicule and downgrade me to a nonperson of foreign origin. I felt unprotected and exposed to people who did not deserve my attention, and in the heat of the moment I could not help the urge to defend myself. I was being put on the spot and his father was acting like a rhadamanthine adjudicator who had come to judge me without taking into consideration the extenuating circumstances of his son's heinous acts. At some point I'd had enough of that theatre of the absurd, so I went into the kitchen and began to cook something for us to eat, moving about like an automaton since my heart wasn't in it at all. I simply had to get away from that scene!

"Samia!" suddenly I heard Abu Sami's voice calling me and rushed back into the living room to see what was wrong.

I saw my mother in a very bad shape. Her health had been compromised by everything she was witnessing there on a daily basis and she was now trying to make Abu Sami understand how bad she felt in that moment and all the time she had been in Jeddah. She told him she was sick, and she meant it. She was in urgent need of hospitalization, her strength and energy were completely depleted.

Abu Sami signaled his son to take my mother to the hospital, as was the right thing to do, but Sami refused even his own father, demonstrating once again how cruel and inhuman he really was. His priority was to pick up his brother Waleed from the airport—he was the reinforcement coming in from Riyadh. The reserves had been conscripted to join in from wherever they were into that cowardly war waged against two women. The domestic forces were on standby. Waleed was a milder character who acted as an envoy of Enaam and Sami, acting on their commands and executing his orders in loyal obedience to them.

Meanwhile, my mother's health was deteriorating. She was asking to see a doctor but Sami was obstinately refusing to give her any help and would not allow me to take her to the doctor either. The situation was out of control. There were tears and screams and groans, the apogee of our tortures, in front of an audience who watched on relishing our drama. Scenes of torture and misery, that have been etched indelibly onto our minds and will haunt us forever as a reminder of the eternal fight between good and evil: some worlds are meant to create and some are meant to destroy.

When the situation had escalated to a peak, Sami's coarse voice broke out in hatred and anger:

"*She* will NOT come to the doctor with us!" The "she" was me and he wanted to take my mother to the doctor unaccompanied by me, like he had done before in the recent past. Sami was foaming at the mouth as he struggled to determine our fate.

My mother was begging his father, crying and telling him again and again how much she needed me near her. Abu Sami was convinced of that self-evident fact and was trying to make his son embrace his opinion.

"Fine!" Sami eventually gave in. "But she will wear what I'll choose for her."

And with that, he went into my wardrobe and fetched my wedding dress, a maxi gown made of white muslin gossamer. The situation had shifted genres from the theatre of the absurd to the theatre of the grotesque.

The urgent state of my mother's health left me no room to engage in argumentations with that madman who was still toying around with me even at that eleventh hour. So I just put on the gown, covered myself up like a Saudi woman and let Sami and his father drive us to the nearest hospital.

By the time we reached New Jeddah Clinic Hospital it was dark out as it had already been several hours since my mother first asked to be taken to a doctor. She was obviously about to lose consciousness so the paramedics rushed to take her into the emergency room. Standing by her side, I could tell she was losing touch with her surroundings. My heart and soul were aching terribly to see her like that and my blood was boiling in anger. Uninhibited, I stayed by her side, while Sami and his father had distanced themselves in some corner, keeping their guilty faces out of sight in light of the imminent tragedy. The insolent villain had turned into a weakling shrunk in fear and venom.

"What is your relationship to the lady?" the doctor asked me.

"She is my mother," I said in a voice colored by a blend of anger, anxiety and oppression.

"What is wrong with her?" he asked me.

As I had started to brief the doctor about the recent events, Sami approached to about ten feet from my mother's bed. He stood on his tiptoes and looked at her as if she were virulent, his arms crossed before his chest and his one hand pensively holding his chin, as if he were an uninvolved observer.

"*There* is the culprit and instigator of her condition!" I said to the doctor pointing at Sami in a sudden outburst of all my anger and exasperation. Seeing him was the drop that spilled the cup. I couldn't hold myself back anymore.

Sami put on a solemn expression and walked away.

"Your mother needs to be checked into the hospital," the doctor said.

Abu Sami, who had been nervously pacing up and down the hospital corridors, approached the doctor and was informed of the need for her hospitalization.

My mother gradually regained consciousness and, when she realized I was standing by her, she implored me in a whispering voice: "Don't leave me!"

"Of course I won't leave you!" I said to her as reassuringly as I could.

I felt like I was losing the ground under my feet and I would now have to face all those who had it in for me all alone. Neither Sami nor his father made the humane gesture to even go near my mother, who was lying down on a hospital bed, a stranger among strangers. I was the only one standing by her side, albeit shyly and warily. I comforted her with my words, even though I was at a loss for anything hopeful to say, while my heart and mind were slowly sinking into an abyss of dark, bleak thoughts.

One more problem I had to deal with was going back home with them to pick up some clothes that my mother might need during her stay at the hospital.

"You'll come with me," Abu Sami said reassuringly, "and get whatever you need."

He knew I had my inhibitions because of Sami so he encouraged me to take the first step.

I promised my mother that I would be back with her very soon. She looked at me with misty eyes, her face contorted with concern for my fate.

"Don't be afraid!" I said to her as I stroked her hair.

I followed the two men from a distance. When we got to the car it was nine o'clock in the evening.

I didn't say a word throughout the ride home; feeling all alone in my miserable world, I was trying to replenish some of my inner strength. Still, I couldn't shake that eerie feeling that I didn't belong anywhere, that I was merely a shadow going by unnoticed.

When we got back, I wanted to run up to the apartment but was forced to slow myself down to keep up with their pace. One heavy step after another, I got up to the place where that man had kept me a prisoner for so many months. Waleed was there with two other men that I didn't know and they had all taken their seats as if in a roundtable where they were to discuss my future.

I walked to the back of the house, my only concern being to pick up the necessary change of clothes for my mother and pack them inside a leather bag, where I had recently also stashed away all my jewelry, hurriedly emptying all the boxes in anticipation of speedy developments. Moving fast, before Sami had a chance to suspect anything, I crammed the clothes inside the bag and held it in my hand.

Then I heard his father's voice calling me to join them in the living room. Five men sitting in a circle were in session deciding upon my future.

"What exactly do you want?" his father asked me in a coarse voice.

"I want to leave!" I said resolutely. "You will compensate me for the damages and emotional suffering inflicted upon my life by your son, including the loss of my work and all the damage he caused to all the objects I had carefully selected and bought from around the world. You will grant me all the privileges afforded to your brides, which were not afforded to me, and you will compensate me for the emotional distress I have suffered," I went on and on in a tirade of mixed Arabic and English. "Oh, and let's not forget the beatings…"

Before I got to finish that last sentence, his father jumped in.

"A woman has to sustain a beating; it says so in the Koran," Abu Sami said as if proud of his son's feats.

"And all of the above was executed with your wife's approval, because these two—"

I was interrupted mid-sentence again, only this time it was a strong whip to my face that cut my phrase short. In order to silence me immediately, Sami had dared hit me with his *igal*, the black cord holding his headdress in place, in front of all those people!

I yelled and cried, pleading for help, but no help came. Mortified I retired to the back rooms in search for mercy and release from the beasts that had surrounded me. I was going crazy thinking of my mother being alone and sick at the hospital while I was in that deplorable situation at home. In that apex of human drama I felt like I was losing my mind!

Sami followed me into my room. Once again, he started to taunt me and torture me. The leather bag clenched to my chest, all I could think and wish for was that he wouldn't take it away from me. That bag contained my small fortune comprised of the very few possessions I could salvage!

Exploiting the general commotion, Sami wouldn't let me go; he wanted to crush me first as a human being. That was his intention: to fully debase me. He wanted to treat me like rubbish, to make me feel like I was nothing.

"Somebody, please, help! Get me out of here!" I screamed; and his father responded.

"Sami!" he roared on his way to the room, while I stood up and ran to the door.

"I want to get back to my mother! She is waiting for me and you are keeping me here. I want to go!" I demanded sternly.

The task of driving me to the hospital was assigned to Waleed. Finally, I was out of there! I had managed to leave, relatively unscathed, taking my memories with me.

It was eleven o'clock at night. Two hours had passed since I had left the hospital and my mother was lying helpless in a bed, all alone, with no documents or money. She burst out crying when she saw me.

"I didn't know if you'd be back," she said, her eyes radiating her terror. "The longer I waited the more I worried; and no one around here knew what to do."

The hospital staff had kept asking, "Are you going to stay here?" "Where do you live?" "Who are you?" "Do you have any money?" My mother was unable to give them any answers; all she knew was Sami's name and that he was a pilot with Saudia.

"What happened to you?" the doctor asked me when he saw the marks on my face.

"He hit me," I said crying.

They had all figured out plenty, but no one dared talk...

They took us to a first class room equipped with a couch where I was to spend one whole week. Never letting my mother out of my sight, I stayed close to her all the time—besides, there was nowhere else for me to go.

That third-floor hospital room would serve as my basis of operations. From there I could finally use the phone undisturbed, lay out my plans and put them in motion. The news about our case had already spread like wildfire around the hospital and we had become the center of an ephemeral interest.

Sami and his father stayed completely out of the picture. Not a single phone call, not one visit! As I was later informed by Mohammed, Sami had even moved to a different place, in fear of being located by the police, a body of law enforcement with considerable power in the country.

My mother sustained a comprehensive round of medical tests, while I had available to me the space and time to act. My rebellion had begun!

The first person I contacted was the gynecologist who had diagnosed my pregnancy the one and only time I had been to see him with Sami. He worked at that same hospital, so one afternoon I went to his office to get checked after all the tortures I had sustained in the meantime.

The doctor was revolted to hear about all my sufferings and that I was currently staying at the hospital together with my mother. He performed an ultrasound to check on the baby's state. After all the violence I had suffered I was extremely worried about the baby's wellbeing, my horror exacerbated by something Sami had told me during one of our altercations and kept ringing between my ears: "Even if you give birth to just a head, that baby is mine and I will take it!" Apart from attesting to his selfishness, possessiveness and lunacy, that gruesome statement was also an indirect admission of his violent acts against me. After all the hardship, suffering and malnutrition I had sustained, thanks to which I kept losing instead of gaining weight, I was not very optimistic about the status of the fetus.

Luckily, the doctor informed me that my pregnancy was progressing well as he optimistically showed me the image of the baby on the monitor. That was a wonderful feeling! At last, one piece of good news, a breath of life amidst the storm that had broken full force.

Then I went on to contact the Greek Embassy. My one and only visit there had caused them great concern and they were eager to hear from me. Thus, I filled them in about the latest events and, on that same afternoon, I received a visit by the Second Secretary of the Embassy at the hospital. Everyone was surprised at the fast pace of developments. The Embassy assured us of their undivided sympathy and support for me and my mother.

Over the next few days, I placed a call with Saudia and spoke with the same people I had met during that clandestine meeting when Sami was away in Madrid. I recounted to them our current situation and they urged me to call the police. That, however, was not an easy decision to make; everybody was feeding me advice that was based on their own perspective of things, but acting on their advice might prove to be irresponsible, or even perilous, in my case. No one could give me the full picture with candor.

At some point, Waleed started timidly coming by to see which way the wind was blowing. In other words, he was once again assigned with spying on us. Whatever he heard, saw or noticed, he would report back to "headquarters" after each one of his short visits.

Often he would say to me something like, "Is there anything that you need me to get for you?"

Once I did ask him to get me a particular pack of cookies, which I was craving probably because of hormonal changes attributed to my pregnancy.

"My brother wouldn't let me," he told me unashamed the next time he showed up empty-handed.

I had no money myself to buy anything and none of them had given me even any petty cash to pay for minor items I might need. As a result, I would suppress my cravings, convincing myself to think of something else in order to forget. It was really hard but I managed…

While at the hospital I had plenty of time to reach out to several people in the way I deemed best, after having been deprived of all social contact for so long. One of the people I decided to get in touch with was George, a well-respected Greek man who had been working with an Arabic company for several years. He had treated me impeccably while I was working with Saudia and both my mother and I thought very highly of him. Of course, he had lost track of me when I left the airline and had no idea of my whereabouts thereafter. So, I called him up and, thankfully, he came by.

He was astounded to find out that I was still in Saudi Arabia, so I recounted to him the latest events of my life. I also explained the reasons why my mother and I were at the hospital for so many days. I trusted him immensely and, seeing as I was in a difficult situation, I kindly asked him if he could keep my leather bag safe for me.

After hearing my story, George immediately offered to help.

"I will take the bag with me and give it back to you in Athens," he reassured me.

"Great!" I consented unreservedly without hesitating even for a moment. I don't know exactly why, but I trusted that man as if he were my father.

Exhaustion, confusion and panic wouldn't let me think clearly. I was looking for a shoulder to lean and a safe place to stash away my possessions so that Sami couldn't get a hold of them. The hospital was not the safest of places and having these items with me made me feel insecure. George was the ideal person to provide protection in that respect.

"I will be back tomorrow to see you," he said before he left, "after giving you a call first."

Days passed without so much as a word from George. I had no idea where he lived and, even if I did, there was no way for me to get there. I placed several calls looking for him at the company where he worked, but the "well-respected" Mister George was nowhere to be found! I got so angry at myself for having trusted him so blindly and acting so thoughtlessly! That man had taken advantage of my position of weakness and had struck me a death blow. One misfortune after the other, blow by blow, it seemed as if everyone was chipping in to finish me off.

Amidst my daze and confusion, I thought of Ahmed, Sami's cousin. I called him on the phone and filled him in on everything that had recently happened in my life, including George's disappearance along with my jewelry.

"You must be crazy!" Ahmed yelled at me furiously. "Give me that man's name and telephone number," he said and hung up the phone.

Ahmed worked his miracle! Within only a few hours, George showed up at the hospital. Clearly upset, he handed me the bag, its contents intact, and left without saying much by way of explanation.

Sharia law was very strict and the punishment it stipulated for theft extremely harsh: amputation of the thief's hand. If the case ever got to the police, the involvement of Ahmed, a Saudi, and the mention of Sami's family would put George in a very difficult position. I thanked Ahmed very much for helping me out at that crucial moment. Nevertheless, I had once again been betrayed and disillusioned about a person whom I had hitherto considered trustworthy and honest...

Another incident was over, leaving inside me the marks of yet another traumatic experience. Apparently I could trust no one. I came to be afraid of my own shadow. No one around me appeared to have preserved their moral and emotional integrity; everyone seemed to have been corrupted by the overall mentality of that place. Such were the thoughts going through my mind after my latest incredible experience. Through those hardest moments of my life I was realizing that, when the going gets tough, the masks come off of even so-called "friends" who sometimes join in to kick you when you're down if they think they might benefit from it. I felt utterly disappointed in all respects.

At the same time, though, the sadism and lack of respect for a pregnant woman, as expressed among other things by Waleed's refusal to get me even the smallest delicacy I had craved, reinforced my persistence and resolve. So, one day I called the police from my mother's room at the hospital. I spoke to them in the little Arabic that I knew, explaining to them that I was calling from the New Jeddah Clinic Hospital, that I was a battered wife and my mother had been mistreated as well.

"What room number are you in?" the police officer on the phone asked me from the other end of the line. I told him our room number and, after he verified it with the hospital, he hung up the phone.

After quite some time, two savage-looking police officers—for some reason all members of that profession looked savage in that country—came into the room.

After darting a glare my way, they reluctantly gave me a phone number to call and turned around to leave. Right at that moment, Waleed was entering the room. His face turned red when he saw the police officers. They exchanged a few words and then all three of them left.

Of course I had tried to speak to the police and convince them to listen, but to no avail. I was a woman, and a foreign one at that, hence inconsequential. Once again, mine was "a voice crying out in the desert."

When my mother and I were alone again, I dialed the number the police officers had left with me. Once again I explained to whoever picked up the phone who I was and what was happening to me.

"You need to come over," said the voice on the phone and hung up on me before I could say another word.

Either I was losing my mind or they didn't want to understand! How could I get there when I had to stay at the hospital? Where was "there"? Where was the police station? Who would accompany me there? It appeared as though these people were living blissfully in their men's world, having no idea, and no interest in finding out, what it meant to be a foreign woman there!

No matter how exasperated and put out I was, there was no one around who could empathize. It seemed I couldn't strike a chord with anyone. I was left to my own devices which were proving miserably inadequate in that "magical" land, where being born anything other than a man was tantamount to being doomed to inexistence.

I had put up a good fight, tried really hard to make my story heard, to make sure someone would remember something of me. And on our last day there, the day my mother would be released from the hospital, Abu Sami showed up to pay the bill and pick us up to take us—where else?—back to the house of joy, the inferno of Knuz Al Elm Street…

When we got home our feelings of sadness and melancholy were exacerbated by the profane image we were faced with as soon we entered my mother's room. Sami was gone—apparently, he had "temporarily" moved out of the house, as per his family's instructions—but had made sure to leave his mark behind: he had taken all my mother's clothes out of the closets and her suitcase and had tossed them around all over the floor, some torn and some badly stained. I guess that was his "enviable" way of welcoming her back home and showing her how much he loved her!

While we were away at the hospital, Sami had broken my mother's suitcase open. Furious at the sight of it, my mother called Abu Sami to see the spectacle with his own eyes. Her letters, photos and personal notes were all missing!

"Look!" she said to Sami's father in the few words of Arabic she had learned in the meantime. "Look what your son did! I had more personal things and I cannot find them! I will talk to the police!" she said terribly annoyed.

Abu Sami froze. Her last word reverberated in his ears; he was fully aware of the stipulations of Arabic law. Acting at lightning speed, he got hold of Sami who was quick to show up at our place.

They said something amongst themselves and then Sami bent over to kiss my mother's feet in a gesture as a sign of penance. Naturally he wished to avoid the legal repercussions so he tried to pour oil on troubled waters, leading a remarkably calm discussion with my mother. He knew very well how to humble himself when his self-interests were at stake and was willing to put on whatever act was necessary to come out of a difficult situation unscathed, unblemished and immaculate. His behavior was disgusting!

His father stayed with us for three or four days while Sami was staying somewhere else. My mother and I were very guarded in the presence of Abu Sami; we didn't know exactly why he was staying with us while his son was absent, so we handled the situation with extreme caution. He didn't appear to be respectful of us; many times he'd enter our room unannounced, putting us in a difficult situation as we would try to cover ourselves, startled. He, too, was one of the Islamists that Enaam was using to convey her messages of fear to me, especially now that Abu Sami had returned from Cairo recuperated and revamped—new teeth, dyed hair and beard.

On the evening of the day before Abu Sami left to return to Riyadh, Waleed affably offered to take me to a shopping mall, after ensuring his father's permission to do so. My mother would stay at home and Abu Sami was receiving a friend of his, named Halil.

Even in my absence, the wheels of my fate kept on turning. The two men decided between themselves that I was to be ousted as "unsuitable for Sami."

"She has to go," Halil kept saying. "Sami has had enough! Off with her!"

They had failed to take into account that my mother was there and was picking up on the vibes of their conversation. As soon as I came back, she asked me about the meaning of certain words she had kept in mind.

"Who said that?" I asked her in astonishment.

"Halil and Abu Sami," she assured me.

Exasperated, I waited for the opportune moment to unleash my anger—a moment that came shortly thereafter, when the doorbell rang and another man, named Mohammed, walked in. Without wasting any time, I called at him from the kitchen.

"Mr. Mohammed, I would like to speak with you," I said.

Unwarily, Mr. Mohammed came close to me and then I went on speaking in a loud voice.

"Please, tell Mr. Halil that he may kick out his own wife if he'd like to and that, as long as I'm here, I don't want him stepping foot in this house ever again!"

I saw Abu Sami and Halil walking to the door without a word and the latter leaving. Abu Sami didn't dare say anything even after Halil had left.

I was fed up with their backstage games and the way they were relentlessly undermining me. I was sick and tired of maneuvering around in that morose environment that had nothing to offer me except sorrow, frustration and erosion.

On the day that Abu Sami was to leave for Riyadh, he called Sami back to the house, allegedly in an effort to reconcile the situation, at least for the time being. Alas, the die had been cast a long time ago…

"I will be back in ten days," Abu Sami told me with a sinister expression on his face that was meant to scare me.

My mother and I bid him farewell with a blank expression. Waleed stayed with us in Jeddah to keep an eye on us while Sami would be away on a flight assignment. Enaam was out of the foreground but pulling the strings from backstage, using all three of them to carry out her intrigues while she pretended to stay out of it.

While my mother and I were away at the hospital, they had rummaged the entire apartment, leaving no stone unturned. All my personal belongings had been violated. I had no idea exactly who had done this or to what end until my question was partly answered when I discovered several "magical" curios they had assiduously planted among my cosmetics. I looked at them curiously and then threw them away with repugnance. The more they saw me rebounding from every attempt to knock me over the more they kept resorting to absolutely anything. Undaunted they continued their pursuit.

A short while after Abu Sami had left, Sami, Waleed, my mother and I were all invited to dinner by Abdul Aziz. Gathered at his place were several men, whom we couldn't see—they were sitting separately from the women—but from what I overheard it seemed the main topic of their discussion were my mother and I.

Shortly before the evening was over, Abdul Aziz told my mother that she was to spend the night there while I would go back home with Sami. Their plan was to keep her away from me and arrange her trip back to Greece behind her back and without her consent, while I would have to carry my pregnancy to term under Sami's roof and rules. Despite the immense pressure exercised on my mother by Abdul Aziz, their plan fell through, because my mother was onto them.

"NO!" she said decisively. "I'm neither staying nor going anywhere without my daughter!" Her answer was definitive, leaving no room for negotiations. As a result, all four of us left to go home.

On the ride back, Waleed was riding shotgun while my mother and I were riding in the back seat. Sami was driving like a frenzied madman, glaring at my mother and me through the rearview mirror. Driving down the empty Jeddah highway, he was swerving the car in consecutive zigzags from the left curb to the right and back, like a raging bull run amok, as if he was trying to fling us off the side doors.

"Talk to him!" my mother yelled at his brother who was silently condoning his behavior.

"What do you want?" Sami's growled to her furiously while continuing his frenzied race through the night.

Shrunk to my seat I waited for the horror ride to end. Like a fundamentalist persecutor of Christians, Sami was "fighting the good fight." But by the grace of God we made it home in one piece.

Sami dropped us and left again—thank goodness!

We were obviously past the point of no return. There was no reason for us to keep on living together. Why wouldn't he just let us go? Was he hoping to take his revenge on us first at all cost? Clearly, his intentions were not innocent at all. Nothing indicated that he had repented any of his action, in spite of his theatrical acts of contrition before my mother to be absolved of his gross mistakes.

The conversation he had the following day with his brother, while I was also present, revealed his intentions as well as my standing. Using code language and Arabic words he thought I wouldn't understand, Sami said to his brother, "It's done; she's rubbish." I kept my cool at that moment, but a short while later I asked them what that sentence meant, pretending that I had heard it someplace else. Unsuspecting, they corroborated my guess. The decisions had been made by everyone and all there was left to do was put their plan into action: the plan for my termination.

Thus, once everything had been settled between the two brothers, Waleed also left to go back to Riyadh. Their plan was on.

All those involved in their backdoor scheming started to visit us quite often. Abdul Aziz's visit one early afternoon was accompanied by great turmoil. Eager to seize any opportunity to finish me off, Sami began to insult me and call me names in front of his friend and even threatened to hurl a heavy item against me.

I ran to the bathroom but before I could lock myself in, Sami followed me and locked the door behind us. He was beating me and I was screaming while my mother was yelling and trying to open the door. Naturally she also called out to Abdul Aziz to help, but to no avail. He just stood there, uninvolved, and watched on.

After a while, he set me free and the two men took off. I was alive! Yet, once again, it had become painfully clear that I could not count on anyone there to sympathize with me and help me; I was a "foreign body" and treated like one. "These foreigners don't understand anything," you'd often hear them say, their heads swelled with arrogance. The way they saw it, they were God's elect, and despite their innumerable vices and flaws, they firmly believed in the supremacy of the Saudis over any outsider.

The rest of our days there indicated that the end—whatever that might be—was near. The air was charged with so much tension it was suffocating. Clear messages were coming from all directions, including from our own intuition, that the time was nearing when the final act would be played out. My mother and I were worn out by being constantly surrounded by intrigue, conspiracy and scheming, but we had to abide until the very end.

Other than the calendar, nothing was even hinting at the fact that it was December. Somewhere very far from where we were, Christmas was nearing to warm peoples' hearts. In that other world we were in, we were rather looking forward to our resurrection.

The weather was balmy. The extreme summer heat was over, as was that horrid incessant hum produced by the air conditioners. It was a typical Jeddah winter. The genial sun ran its brief trajectory to quickly set in the horizon amidst an aquarelle of deep purple hues, just like I remembered it from my first days in Saudi Arabia, back when everything around me was magical and fascinating, as if straight out of the fairy tale of *One Thousand and One Nights*, back when I could still open my wings wide and soar wherever my heart and soul desired. Alas, this wasn't the world that used to make me so happy anymore. Now, lonely and sad and unable to fly, I was patiently waiting for my fate to catch up with me. Sitting at the veranda of our home at Knuz Al Elm Street, I had learned to gaze at the twilight, searching for a beacon that could brighten up my life. Sami's Jeddah had sunk me into deep darkness and I was struggling to find my way back to the world of light from which I had once come.

I yearned to be romantic again, revive the values and joys of life that I had once been offered so generously, but fate had forced me to give up... I needed to feel like a human being again.

Still, my trials had also made me stronger on some level. My religious feelings kept growing stronger and stronger; the search for the divine was comforting and God appeared to be giving me some solutions. Someone was looking after everything, myself included...

The door suddenly opened to interrupt my reverie. My meditation was cut short and I was abruptly transposed back to the banal.

It was Sami with Ali, a friend and colleague of his. They impudently walked into the room of my mother and me, defying their own traditions, and took a seat. In fact, Ali sat immodestly in the rocking chair opposite me, his thobe slightly pulled up, and began to rock back and forth cheekily. Neither of them cared the least bit about us; I was considered a closed case, so neither of them showed any respect towards me or my mother.

"I had told you so many times, Sami: you shouldn't have married a foreign woman; once a foreigner always a foreigner," Ali would say in a brassy tone trying to provoke us.

But talking back or engaging in a conversation with these people was of no use. They were determined to hold on to their blinders and I was extremely tired of their provocations and rude offences. Earlier that afternoon I had been once again subjected to one of Sami's usual tortures. As I was coming out of the bathroom after taking a shower and drying my hair, he looked at me and started to make fun of me. And in order to ridicule me even more, he poured a bottle of shampoo on top of my freshly washed hair. Then came a second bottle, and a third, and a fourth, and a fifth— five bottles of shampoo were spilled all over my hair and body! I could barely take a breath. One bottle succeeded the other until I was covered by a thick, syrupy layer of shampoo. Sami rejoiced at the sight of my torture. My mother and I were screaming for help but no one came to our aid. In the end, my mother threatened to call the police to make him stop. But it was already too late. The chemicals of all that quantity of shampoo staying on me for a prolonged period of time had taken their toll on my face and breast.

It was three in the morning when Ali left. My body felt so heavy I was dragging my feet across the floor. I was worn out by physical and emotional strain and, when I dozed off, I fell into an unusually deep sleep. By my side was my mother, my guardian angel.

CHAPTER EIGHT

THE GETAWAY

Early in the morning, a shadow on the wall rushed by trying to go unnoticed. It was Sami. My mother had seen him from the corner of her eye. He was holding a briefcase possibly containing all the documents pertaining to me and arguably he was trying to scare us again, pretending he was on his way to do something with them. My mother didn't see much more than that nor did she react. She was so tired she went right back to sleep.

At about eleven in the morning an eerie silence reigned in the apartment. I felt my mother's hand awaken me gently.

"Wake up, he's gone," she said to me softly.

I sat up on my bed, my heart racing. My mother cringed. Her eyes popped wide open in astonishment as she looked at me clearly upset.

"What happened to you?" she muttered. "Look what he did to your face! Your skin is discolored, your breast is red."

She felt my forehead; I was running a fever. I didn't know exactly what the matter with me was, but I could feel the skin on my face very tight, like a piece of stretched out cellophane…

Seriously alarmed, my mother went into panic mode.

"Get up and get dressed," my mother said without giving it a second thought. "We're getting out of here right this instant!"

"No!" I said frightened. "What if he catches us? Don't you remember that time when he caught me by the main entrance and grabbed me by the neck and pinned me to the wall?"

"Let's go!" my mother insisted. "I will not let you die in here. I'd rather sacrifice myself!"

The big moment had come. The great escape was underway!

My mother's last words shook me to the core, tearing down all my inhibitions. Armed with renewed strength and courage I got dressed, put on my black abaya, covered my hair, grabbed the bag containing my few valuables and we both headed to the door.

The first obstacle we had to overcome was not to bump into Sami between our door and front entrance to the building. If we did, we'd be dead. Scared to the bone, we went down the staircase and crossed the hallway to the front door. We had made it!

Our anxiety had peaked. We were out on the pavement, completely exposed from all sides. There was no place to hide and Sami would probably be back any minute. I took a quick glance up and down the street and I saw a big American-made car approach. Without giving it a second thought I raised my hand and hitchhiked. The man at the wheel slammed on the brakes. He was not a Saudi as I could tell by his clothes.

"Greek Embassy!" I said to him hastily in Arabic.

The man's eyes popped wide open in surprise and his reaction was to speed away without saying a word. Naturally, he was afraid to act upon our request.

The time was counting down. I was so anxious and scared I felt like crying.

"Let's go to the supermarket," I suddenly said to my mother quietly. I had remembered the young Egyptian who worked there.

We walked very quickly disregarding all rules and dangers and, after walking amidst the desert for some time, brimming with fear and agony, fearing for our lives, we reached the store.

We rushed in with a feeling of temporary relief. We had made it!

The Egyptian looked at us in astonishment.

"What is the matter?" he asked.

"You have to hide us," I said to him panting. "We ran away, we escaped!"

Flustered, the young man tried to come up with an immediate solution. It was almost noon and there was no one else in the store.

"Go over there…" he said with a nod of his head.

We rushed to the spot he had indicated and he hid us behind a bunch of shelves loaded with cans. We stooped to make sure we were out of sight. When he made sure no one could see us, he spoke in a quiet voice.

"You will stay here until I close the store."

"He has hurt me so much," I tried to explain to him as much as I could. "He intends to do something terrible to me, and very soon. I couldn't stay with him any longer."

"I will close the store at two," said the Egyptian. "I have to find a friend of mine who has a car so he can drive you to the Embassy."

"The Embassy doesn't know," I said. "We need to notify them before they leave their office."

"But I don't have a telephone," the Egyptian noted.

"Please, you need to help us," I insisted. "Can you please find a telephone to notify them on our behalf so they wait for us?"

And with that, he closed the store and left to go find a telephone while we stayed in hiding at the store to make sure no one would see us.

After making the phone call, the man rushed to find a friend of his with a car.

It was almost two in the afternoon when a van pulled over outside the supermarket. The young Egyptian came into the store and cautiously signaled us to come out. The vehicle's side door slid open and my mother and I crawled onto the floor of the van.

Huddled together in the back of the van, my mother and I finally breathed once we reached the Greek Embassy, near Sands Hotel. The Consulate clerk was waiting for us. The road to freedom had just started to appear before us. We were almost past all Cyanean Rocks of our odyssey, only a breath away from salvation. When we saw the Embassy staff also waiting for us our spirits were positively raised.

"Why did you fall out of touch?" a staff member asked us. "You went 'missing in action,' so we sent someone over to drive by the house and check up on you, but there was no sign of life in the apartment."

"I think I remember!" I said excitedly. "I remember someone driving by and honking the horn…"

"So, what do we do now?" the diplomat said. "We need to find a way for you to leave, but this will take some time."

"Well, I am never going back to that house!" was my final declaration.

My mother and I recounted everything that had transpired since we had last contacted them, especially the very last episode that had prompted our escape from Sami's apartment. Besides, the Embassy staff could see for themselves how my face was discolored.

After all of us deliberated on the situation for some time, we decided that the best course of action at the moment was that I be hospitalized.

The night had already fallen by the time we got ushered to the hospital, the same one in which my mother had been hospitalized a week before.

We were escorted there by three people from the Embassy, but when we got there it was impossible for me to be checked in!

I saw the doctors and showed them the bruises and scars and burns from the shampoo, but their stance regarding my hospitalization was negative. They wouldn't allow me to be admitted in spite of my critical condition. They were Saudis and the law wouldn't allow them to admit me without my husband's consent.

We were running out of time and I was going out of my mind. I felt lost, I needed help badly. We had literally no place to go to.

Desperate, I sat down on a parapet while my mother negotiated the matter with the Greek diplomats. Sami was not my primary concern at that moment, but I just finally needed to see a ray of light at the end of that tunnel!

"Mr. Katsoulis," I told the Consulate clerk, "we need to get hold of my attending gynecologist who knows me and my situation very well."

I looked and looked and, finally, I found my physician. He was my last hope. I literally begged him to help me because I was at a point where there was no turning back. I really needed to be put up at the hospital.

Touched by my drama, the Egyptian gynecologist examined me, ascertained my multiple bruises and severe skin irritation and, in the end, took it upon himself to bend the rules and approve my admission to the hospital.

My mother and I were greatly relieved. It was eleven at night when I was taken to my room. Everyone else was gone except my mother, who stayed by my side.

I immediately called Saudia as I had no money and no passport on me and needed to be covered by the company's insurance. Before long, Saudia sent over Feyzal, a competent employee, to bring me the insurance paperwork and offer his assistance.

"You shouldn't be in this room," the small-built man said. "You are covered for a first-class private room," he added, smiling to make me feel better.

The surroundings were very familiar to my mother and me. Ten days ago we were at the room across the hall, going through the drama of my mother's health. The doctors could hardly believe their eyes seeing us again in converse roles: me being the patient and my mother sitting by my side, strong as a rock.

It was late. Almost twelve hours had gone by since we had escaped from the apartment and had now found refuge at the hospital. The past few months flashed before my eyes for a moment—if someone had told me years ago that fate would be playing such cruel games on me, I could have never believed it. Just like I could have never believed it when I was deciding to put my faith in that man who was to become my husband and found my hopes and dreams on his phony words and promises... I had been so naïve...

Just as I was dozing off, two men suddenly appeared in our room. One of them was Waleed who had been summoned by Sami to return from Riyadh immediately following my disappearance. The other one was Mr. Mohammed, Abu Sami's friend, whom they used as a negotiator. I had no idea how they had found me.

They both looked at me with scared, inquiring eyes. I was in no mood to negotiate anything and I didn't need their pity or mercy. I looked back at them, my face devoid of any expression. I was already past the point of no return. The only thing I wanted was to be salvaged as soon as possible from the nightmare I had been living over the past several months.

"Sami is ready and willing to give you whatever you want, satisfy you in whichever way you see fit," Mohammed said disingenuously, in an apparent attempt to gauge my intentions.

No answer ever came out of my mouth. I was done playing their game. They lingered there for a short while, but it was in vain. In the end, they left empty-handed.

The next day was a day of checkups. Several non-Saudi physicians who examined me wouldn't hide their compassion and sympathy; they had fully understood my problem. Besides, they appeared to be quite familiar with cases of battered women—perhaps a side-effect of the prevailing male-dominated mentality.

"Acute dermatitis caused by chemicals," was the dermatologist's diagnosis. At the same time, I was expecting the results from gynecological lab tests checking on the baby's condition. I was almost five months pregnant. A marriage and a pregnancy that were destined to mark me for life… Never in my wildest dreams could I have ever made up a plot such as the one weaved for me by fate itself. And never would I have imagined that I would prove strong enough to make it through!

Certainly not out of the goodness of his heart, Waleed started to pay me frequent visits again, most probably acting upon the orders of his brother, in the hopes of finding out what my plans and thoughts were. On my second day at the hospital, Waleed told me that Sami would be going to Karachi where he would lay over for two days. When he left, I cross-checked that piece of information by calling up the head of crew scheduling at Saudia, who confirmed it was true. And then I had an idea…

I summoned my gynecologist, who had been extremely humane and nice to me, and asked him for permission to go out for a few hours the next morning.

"Of course I will sign you out," he said. "But what is it for?"

"I would like to collect my things from my home," I said in all honesty. "He has abused me and deceived me in all other respects; I want to at least take back what is mine."

"Alright," the doctor said in agreement.

The Consulate clerk paid me regular visits at the hospital. I shared my daring idea with him. In addition to my clothes, I wanted to take back everything that I had brought with me with love and care from Athens. These items were precious to me, but if they stayed in Sami's hands they would surely end up destroyed or dumped since they were of no importance to him—as was I.

The clerk and the Consulate consented to my plan. Thankfully, I had the key to the house with me. It was Wednesday morning and I had already spent three days at the hospital. Everything had been arranged: I had the doctor's permission, my mother was ready to accompany me and two large Consulate cars manned with Consulate staff were waiting for us outside the hospital. Operation "blitz-raid" was set in motion.

Sami was flying to Karachi, completely unsuspecting of my plan. The two Consulate cars proceeding in a convoy, we eventually reached Knuz Al Elm. I felt my stomach in knots as soon as I saw the street, the house, the surroundings. The Consulate cars pulled over in front of the building and I hurried upstairs. I unlocked the door; Waleed wasn't there. I had been followed upstairs by three Consulate staff and the four of us were now hastily collecting the items that belonged to me. I emptied the closets, packing eight suitcases with clothes, which were loaded onto the first car to head back to the Consulate. Abdulrahman had remembered my kindness and generosity to him, so he was now returning the favor, recruiting the guard from the house next door to help carry down to the second car the valuable chandeliers and curtains that I had bought in Paris.

The apartment was being stripped bare. This was an unheard-of thing to happen in Saudi Arabia, especially by a woman. But I was not about to leave stripped of both my dignity and my belongings. At least one part of that unfairness had to be settled. I had to at least put up that last fight that would partly vindicate me, restore one small part of my self-respect, and assert my having being there as a human being instead of as a mere object to be exploited and mistreated at will.

Finally, I could at least deprive him of the pleasure of having violated and usurped every last bit of me, everything I was and everything I owned. At least that small part of my possessions that I could take back with me would be spared from his destructive rage. He could not brag to his people how he had utterly outwitted and ripped off an infidel. It was payback time. I was no longer the weakling he could knock about whenever he felt like it. My revolution was in progress; my oppressed instincts had awakened.

When we were almost done packing and getting ready to depart, Abdulrahman looked really sad to see me go and kindly asked me for a keepsake.

"Here, take this to remember me by," I said smiling, handing over to him a small memento that I picked out of my belongings.

Moments before we took off, Waleed showed up. And when he realized what was going on he turned blood-red in the face.

"Is there anything you'd like to say?" I said to him boldly. "I am simply collecting my things."

Without saying a word, Waleed turned around and left.

When everything was over and done, we went back to the Consulate. My things were quite bulky, so the staff gathered everything together and stored it safely in a designated room.

Then, my mother and I went back to the hospital so that I could complete my treatment. It was matter of a couple more days, three tops.

As soon as the hospital staff found out that our mission had been crowned with success, they congratulated us wholeheartedly. The plan was completed; there was nothing to stop me anymore.

When Waleed came back to visit with me at the hospital, probably to protest on behalf of his brother, he was instead approached by a Consulate clerk and recruited to help out with my getaway! The clerk obliged Waleed to follow him back to the Consulate, where the latter reluctantly helped pack all my things into thirty-two suitcases and boxes!

Meanwhile, Sami had returned from his trip and, in his refusal to admit defeat, he demanded the hospital director to throw me out!

"You have to leave," said the little man serving as the head of the hospital coming to see me personally.

"I am not going anywhere!" was my response. "I have not completed my treatment, so how dare you order me to go? Are you prepared to take full responsibility for my life and wellbeing?"

The poor man was struck dumb. Unable to assume such risk and liability, he turned around and left. Meanwhile, I not only needed to be fully treated, but I also needed to take with me the diagnoses and hospital documentation to be prepared for any eventuality...

Time kept counting down—only one day and a few hours to go until the great departure. The Greek Consul had taken care of everything, including our tickets and bill of lading for my belongings, all bought and paid for with checks issued by none other than good old Waleed—his brother had made sure to make himself scarce and was nowhere to be found.

It was Friday, December 31, nine o' clock in the morning of New Year's Eve. Only a few hours left before we'd ring in the new year; a brilliant new year that was promising to bring along with it my freedom and salvation and, above all, the coming of my child.

The airplane was already flying over Arabic soil, bound for Athens...

Good-bye, Saudi Arabia. Good-bye forever, my deceitful dream...

I was leaving the nightmares behind me once and for all.

I had to pinch myself to make sure it was not a lie. I had made it! I had escaped!

Peaceful for the first time in years, I leaned on my beloved mother's shoulder.

Her self-sacrifice and magnanimity had saved me.

The danger had not been completely averted. My story with Sami was far from over. But I was now free from his prison. And back in my home country, a new great chapter of my life was about to begin, as growing in my loins was the child that was his baby too…

Printed in Great Britain
by Amazon